Humanizing Collectivist Critical Pedagogy

Humanizing Collectivist Critical Pedagogy

Teaching the Humanities in Community College and Beyond

Edited by
Sujung Kim, Leigh Garrison-Fletcher, and Kaysi Holman

New York - Berlin - Bruxelles - Chennai - Lausanne - Oxford

Library of Congress Cataloging-in-Publication Data

Names: Holman, Kaysi L., editor. | Kim, Sujung, editor. |
Garrison-Fletcher, Leigh, editor.
Title: Humanizing collectivist critical pedagogy : teaching the Humanities in
community college and beyond / edited by Kaysi L. Holman, Sujung Kim,
Leigh Garrison-Fletcher.
Description: First edition. | New York : Peter Lang, [2024] |
Includes bibliographical references.
Identifiers: LCCN 2023055796 (print) | LCCN 2023055797 (ebook) |
ISBN 9781636675916 (paperback : alk. paper) |
ISBN 9781636675930 (epub)
Subjects: LCSH: Community colleges—United States. | Humanities—Study and
teaching (Higher)—United States. | Critical pedagogy.
Classification: LCC LB2328.15.U6 H86 2024 (print) |
LCC LB2328.15.U6 (ebook) |
DDC 378.1/5430973—dc23/eng/20240122
LC record available at https://lccn.loc.gov/2023055796
LC ebook record available at https://lccn.loc.gov/2023055797
DOI 10.3726/b21497

Bibliographic information published by the Deutsche Nationalbibliothek.
The German National Library lists this publication in the German
National Bibliography; detailed bibliographic data is available
on the Internet at http://dnb.d-nb.de.

Cover design by Peter Lang Group AG

ISBN 9781636675916 (paperback)
ISBN 9781636675923 (ebook)
ISBN 9781636675930 (epub)
DOI 10.3726/b21497

© 2024 Peter Lang Group AG, Lausanne
Published by Peter Lang Publishing Inc., New York, USA
info@peterlang.com - www.peterlang.com

All rights reserved.
All parts of this publication are protected by copyright.
Any utilization outside the strict limits of the copyright law, without the permission of
the publisher, is forbidden and liable to prosecution.
This applies in particular to reproductions, translations, microfilming, and storage and
processing in electronic retrieval systems.

This publication has been peer reviewed.

Dedication

To our students, past, present, and future.
To all the instructors out there trying to change their piece of the world.
To all the staff, administrators, and advocates fighting for change in higher education.

Table of Contents

List of Illustrations	ix
List of Abbreviations	xi
Acknowledgments	xiii
1. Introducing Humanizing Collectivist Critical Pedagogy SUJUNG KIM, KAYSI HOLMAN, AND LEIGH GARRISON-FLETCHER	1
2. Critical Pedagogy of Humanities in Neoliberal Times SUJUNG KIM	27
3. Interdisciplinary Questions that Inform Our Pedagogy: The Who, What, Why, and How that Guide Us KAYSI HOLMAN	43
4. A Toolkit for Questioning Everything: Collaborative Deep Reading for Critical Thinking DAVIDE GIUSEPPE COLASANTO	67
5. Teaching Linguistics to Promote Social Justice: Ending Exclusionary Language Practices OLIVER SAGE AND LEIGH GARRISON-FLETCHER	79
6. Visualizing Identity, Fandom, and Representation MICHEAL ANGELO RUMORE	95
7. Subverting White Androcentrism in Psychology Curricula MIKE RIFINO	119
8. Affective Injustice and Student Dis/Engagement EDUARDO VIANNA, ARAMINTA POOLE, AND RAFAEL COSTA	143

9. Centering Humanness in Project Development and Learning Goals   163
KAYSI HOLMAN AND STEFANIE SERTICH

10. Socially Engaged Administration and the Potential for Graduate Education   193
KATINA ROGERS

Notes on Contributors   209

List of Illustrations

Figure 1.	The Professor	95
Figure 2.	Syllabus Page	98
Figure 3.	Stop & Frisk	110
Figure 4.	Terry Stop	111
Figure 5.	Serena Williams	113
Figure 6.	A Self-Made Woman	114

List of Abbreviations

ABPsi:	Association of Black Psychologists
APA:	American Psychological Association
BIPOC:	Black, Indigenous, and People of Color
BME:	Black, Asian, Minoritized, Ethnic
COVID-19:	Corona Virus Disease of 2019
CUNY:	The City University of New York
ELL101:	Introduction to Language Course at LaGuardia
ESL:	English as a Second Language
Fellow:	CUNY Humanities Alliance Fellow
FYS:	First Year Seminar
GC:	The Graduate Center
GED:	General Equivalency Diploma
GPA:	Grade Point Average
HA:	CUNY Humanities Alliance
HR:	Human Resources
LaGuardia Scholars:	LaGuardia Mellon Humanities Scholars
LaGuardia:	LaGuardia Community College
LGBTQ+:	Lesbian, Gay, Bi, Trans, Queer Community
Mellon Foundation:	Andrew W. Mellon Foundation
NYC:	New York City
Op-eds:	Opinion Editorials
PALC:	Peer Activist Learning Community
PhD:	Doctor of Philosophy
PFV:	Psychology's Feminist Voices
RefAnnBib:	Reflective Annotated Bibliography

STEM:	Science, Technology, Engineering and Mathematics
TAS:	Transformative Active Stance
U.S.:	United States of America
WEIRD:	Western, Educated, Industrial, Rich, and Democratic

Acknowledgments

We would not have pedagogically developed in this same way or come together to write this book without the CUNY Humanities Alliance. We are deeply grateful to the Andrew W. Mellon Foundation for so generously supporting the creation of the CUNY Humanities Alliance and our participation in it from 2016 to 2020. We owe as much thanks to Cathy Davidson, who in conversation with the Mellon Foundation, developed the idea of the program, as well as Katina Rogers for developing much of the grant proposal when CUNY Humanities Alliance was just a dream. Of course, that grant relationship would not have been successful without the support of the Graduate Center Foundation, in particular Helen Koh, who supported the development and implementation of the program.

We would also like to thank the Graduate Center and LaGuardia Community College leadership for helping us build a meaningful collaboration across our campuses. In particular, we would like to thank Joy Connolly and David Olan for serving as Principal Investigators; Gail Mellow for being a remarkable partner; as well as Cathy Davidson, Bret Eynon, David Olan, Katina Rogers, and Luke Waltzer for being Directors of CUNY Humanities Alliance and guiding our goals and implementation through the years. We are also grateful to Kaysi Holman who developed and ran the program, tended to all the collaborations, and oversaw its growth throughout the first iteration, from 2016 to 2021. The Futures Initiative, particularly Cathy Davidson, Katina Rogers, and Lauren Melendez, were instrumental in getting CUNY Humanities Alliance established at the GC, and being supportive collaborative partners through the years. Similarly, our program would not have been possible without the initial and ongoing partnership with the Center for Teaching and Learning at LaGuardia, particularly Howard Wach, Michelle Piso-Manoukian, Eric Hoffman, Priscilla Stadler, and Aarkieva

Smith, as well as the LaGuardia faculty who served as faculty leaders and our program liaisons throughout the years, including Demetri Kapetanakos, Jacqueline Jones, and Stefanie Sertich. The Teaching and Learning Center at the GC, particularly Luke Waltzer and CUNY Humanities Alliance Humanities Scholars Elizabeth Asop and Luis Henao Uribe, also played an important role in translating and pivoting our work to the GC more broadly. The postdoctoral researchers based in the Futures Initiative, Kitana Ananda and Sujung Kim, were also instrumental in leading our program evaluations to support the iterative process of our program, and for their intellectual contribution and pedagogical expertise.

As is referenced many times throughout this book, the CUNY Humanities Alliance was truly a community. All of the faculty mentors and graduate fellows that participated through the years contributed to our overall reflections, learning, and growth. That is especially true for those who pushed us to do better than we were normatively required to do, and helped us struggle through tough times—you know who you are. Most of our co-authors were participants in the program: Kaysi, Katina, and Sujung have been mentioned already; Leigh Garrison-Fletcher and Eduardo Vianna were both faculty mentors; Davide Giuseppe Colasanto, Mike Rifino, Micheal Rumore, and Oliver Sage were graduate fellows; Stefanie Sertich was the Codirector of the LaGuardia Mellon Humanities Scholars program; and Araminta Poole was a student participant in our sister extracurricular program, Peer Activist Learning Community, to which Rafael Costa added theoretical grounding and analysis. There were many other participants who wanted to contribute chapters, but either opted to take quicker publishing routes or had obligations that prevented them from joining in this journey. We wish more students could have co-authored with us, and we hope we did their work justice as we described the classroom communities that we built with them and the rigorous, scholarly, theoretical work they provided alongside us. Truly, our biggest debt of gratitude is owed to our undergraduate students—those who were in our classrooms, our extracurricular programs, and those who worked and volunteered in many different capacities through the years—all who were willing to engage in new and rather experimental educational spaces with us. We hope we offered you as much as we received!

There are still more folks who had a hand in our work: The LaGuardia Mellon Humanities Scholars program would not have had a showcase every year without Stefanie Sertich, Michael Alifanz, the LaGuardia theater crew, and the LaGuardia Performing Arts Center. The CUNY Humanities Alliance Conference would not have been possible without the amazing and dedicated graduate fellows, Emily Eagen and Chelsea Haines, and numerous LaGuardia

Acknowledgments

students who served as conference staff and local ambassadors for attendees. As time passed and leadership shifted, Adashima Oyo became codirector of the Futures Initiative and provided guidance and leadership to the CUNY Humanities Alliance, and Kashema Hutchinson and Lauren Melendez served as Co-Directors, with Chinyere Okafor as a Futures Initiative Fellow, in our undergraduate leadership space, eventually renamed CUNY Peer Leaders as it expanded beyond LaGuardia. We also relied on a lot of infrastructure at both campuses: the IT crew, HR professionals, and financial administrators who supported our program over the many years; Security staff, who kept us safe, especially when there were very real threats, and unlocked many doors; the catering and janitorial staff who work tirelessly, without nearly enough thanks, to keep us well fed and our environment clean. Thank you for all of the time, energy, sweat, and (hopefully more smiles than) tears that went into making the CUNY Humanities Alliance come alive!

Finally, thank you to our families, friends, communities, and supporters, who have kept each of us going during this intense program and long book-writing process, who encouraged us through the process, and made sure we had food, sleep, and other human things.

Each of you made a difference; each of you shares a part of this book with us!

Introducing Humanizing Collectivist Critical Pedagogy

Sujung Kim, Kaysi Holman, and Leigh Garrison-Fletcher

> Despite the contemporary focus on multiculturalism in our society, particularly in education, there is not nearly enough practical discussion of ways classroom settings can be transformed so that the learning experience is inclusive. If the effort to respect and honor the social reality and experiences of groups in this society who are nonwhite is to be reflected in a pedagogical process, then as teachers—on all levels, from elementary to university settings—we must acknowledge that our styles of teaching may need to change. Let's face it: most of us were taught in classrooms where styles of teachings reflected the notion of a single norm of thought and experience, which we were encouraged to believe was universal. This has been just as true for nonwhite teachers as for white teachers. Most of us learned to teach emulating this model. As a consequence, many teachers are disturbed by the political implications of a multicultural education because they fear losing control in a classroom where there is no one way to approach a subject—only multiple ways and multiple references. (hooks, 1994, pp. 35–36)

These words were written 30 years ago. What progress have we made as educators toward this goal? We must meet this public outcry for anti-racist practices throughout academia and change the way we teach to meet the needs of *all* of our students (not just the white, middle-class, native English-speaking, straight, neurotypical, American men), to rise to the challenge of embracing antiracism (in its many intersectionalities). But unlearning these norms of teaching and learning—in fact, the only form of teaching and learning some of us have experienced—and restructuring our teaching requires more than just good will. It requires knowledge and imagination of new teaching methods, either from workshops or from books like this, and also remunerated time to innovate. Unfortunately, there is a dearth of investment in pedagogical professional development, time and resources for higher education pedagogy. As teachers, we have dozens if not hundreds of students every semester. We barely have time to update the syllabus for new required textbooks and to grade the assignments required by our departments (not to mention all the non-teaching work we're expected to do). We may want to change our syllabus. We may even be bored stiff continually teaching the same things over and over to a litany of new students each semester. But how can we move forward?

Institutions can and should be doing a lot to support transformations of syllabi and teaching methods. Teaching and learning centers are a start, but course releases, other remuneration, and intentional, interdisciplinary learning communities are also needed to provide teachers the desperately needed time to transform their teaching. We need to reinvest in education, at all levels, as a public good, being mindful of the equity imbalance currently structured into academia, for institutions to make these overdue changes. Even without additional funding, a cultural shift that values teaching (more equally with research) within academia can shift the way that pedagogical development is supported in the institutions. This change in academia is both fundamentally related to the argument of our book, and also not our direct focus.

The need for shifts in institutional culture does not mean that each of us, as teachers, are not responsible for this change as well. We are still the ones faced with students every day. Colleges across the nation are faced with a burgeoning awareness of diverse cultures and norms and the need to serve and include students from a wide spectrum of backgrounds (Grawe, 2021). Our book is grounded in community college teaching, where, for decades, we have been serving diverse students and have been striving to meet their needs (Jacobs & Worth, 2019). Open admissions in community colleges further contributes to this diversity—every student is welcome into community colleges. Now, four-year colleges across the nation are looking increasingly like community colleges in student composition (Grawe, 2021; Smith, 2020). In four-year colleges, when we are paying attention to national origin, ethnicity, gender identities, sexual orientation, ability, and neurodivergence, the classrooms are much more diverse than they may first appear (Grawe, 2021). These students have deep questions related to the meaning of life, the value of higher education, individualized institutional cultures, as well as the issues that affect their daily lives such as racism, sexism, poverty, gentrification, ableism, mental health, multilingualism, their and their families' precarious employment conditions, and transnational migration.

Whatever changes we have made as teachers thus far, we need to do better! Especially when the country is encountering increasing awareness of tensions over racial disparity and racialized violence, restructuring teaching and learning to better support social justice—in particular within the humanities—is an essential part of our path forward as a society. Higher education and the humanities are still steeped in teaching methods for a homogenous white, upper-middle-class student life experience (hooks, 1994; Matsuda, 2006; Nussbaum, 2010). Non-white, working-class, and/or migrant students often feel alienated and experience systematic violence by both the classical canons of texts and by classical teaching practices where they are expected to regurgitate knowledge that is exclusionary of their experience or perspective (Apple, 1995; Benjamin, 2022; Darder, 2015, 2017; Freire 1970; hooks, 1994; Sawyer & Rifino, 2020; Zembylas, 2022). Teachers, from the classroom to curriculum design to articulation agreements, are the ones empowered to promote social justice in this arena of education. Implementing critical pedagogy is an initial step in doing this. There are some phenomenal texts on critical pedagogy, but let's face it: most of the classics, and even some of the new books about pedagogical praxis, have limited contemporary practical examples of pedagogical methods you can take directly into a classroom. Authors, in general, write either critical pedagogy theory or practical teaching practice—in isolation of the other.

This book provides concrete examples for faculty to start employing what we call a humanizing collectivist critical pedagogy—an approach to teaching that centers students in all their humanness in a community endeavor to learn, strengthen agency, and lead change in society—in their classrooms, reversing practices and assumptions of traditional teaching methods. These practical tools for a humanizing collectivist critical pedagogy were developed by contributors of this book, through deep analysis of critical pedagogy texts and iteration in some of the nation's most diverse classrooms. To engage with today's students, we developed methods that are student-centered, representative, and multilingual, go beyond classrooms, and encourage students' agency. The methods are grounded in the specific context of each discipline and classroom that we taught in, yet are easily modifiable to other classroom compositions. We hope that you will apply these methods for the context in which you teach and the students in each of your courses. This book offers practical pedagogical tools for you to modify for use in your classrooms, as well as deeper questions to guide you in restructuring your own pedagogy in a way that is unique to you as an instructor.

Whether you are just starting out in your professional career or reflecting on your teaching after many years, we hope our methods will challenge you to think through how teaching can address and include *all* the students in the class. This book details the experiences and reflections of full-time community college faculty, graduate student instructors, and staff, all of whom were part of a community focused on rethinking pedagogy in the humanities in a program called the CUNY Humanities Alliance. The chapters show how we responded to specific challenges of diverse classrooms and the practices we adopted in and out of the classroom to transform the learning experience for our students. We want to offer practical methods based in critical pedagogy for other instructors to modify and use in their teaching to respond to the needs of the new majority of students. All the chapters detail, in one form or another, innovative teaching methods grounded in deep interdisciplinary analysis of critical pedagogy that speaks to much of the division in our country today based on race, gender, citizenship status, class, sexual orientation, ability, and mental and emotional well-being.

The Positionality of the Contributors

Contributors to this volume are past participants of the first iteration of the CUNY Humanities Alliance program, from 2016 to 2020, which was generously supported by the Andrew W. Mellon Foundation. In its first iteration, CUNY Humanities Alliance created a partnership between the Graduate Center and LaGuardia Community College, both part of The City University of New York (CUNY) school system, the largest public urban university in the U.S., located in New York City (NYC), providing us a naturally diverse, multicultural setting with globalized and urban classrooms. The students of LaGuardia Community College (LaGuardia), specifically, represent roughly 100 native languages, which means that each student comes with their own culture, history, language background, and citizenship status, at a minimum (LaGuardia Community College, Office of Institutional Research and Assessment, 2020).

The CUNY Humanities Alliance (to our knowledge) is the first program in the country to formally connect practitioner-professors in the community college classroom with doctoral students at an elite urban public university. Structurally, this program attempts to address the lack of contemporary, engaged pedagogical training for PhD students, especially within community college contexts. By writing collectively, as graduate student instructors, full-time community college faculty, and staff from various disciplines, we present a breadth of practical experience and theoretical grounding uncommon in single-author pedagogical texts.

The CUNY Humanities Alliance sought to connect graduate education, community college teaching, and the values of the humanities by (1) supporting graduate students, as active instructors and future faculty, in developing and practicing the newest, most innovative teaching methods in community college humanities classes; (2) inviting expert community college faculty to mentor and collaborate with graduate student instructors in an exceptional and highly experimental space that allowed for redesign and iteration of pedagogical practices; and (3) working closely with community college students in order to better understand the new majority of students and how to engage them in the humanities. The program created intentional interdisciplinary cohorts across both graduate student instructors and full-time community college faculty, who also brought their other professional experience (outside of academia), as artists, union leaders, multilingual authors, political activists, and transnational citizens, into discussions. This continuity of conversation over the course of years allowed graduate fellows and faculty alike the opportunity to iterate class syllabi and activities, and get continual feedback and reflection from the rest of the group, as well as their students.

We all brought something different to the table: graduate students who inhabit a dual role as both students and instructors, and often see directly the ways that contemporary higher education classrooms do not address the needs of contemporary students. Full-time community college faculty steeped in long-term disciplinary-based teaching brought a depth of experience using critical pedagogy along with scholarly rigor, and navigating department requirements, articulation agreements, and other administrative obstacles. Academic professionals, trained in community organizing principles and facilitation practices, bring methodologies otherwise excluded from higher education, and offer an important bridge for advocacy and public engagement. As an interdisciplinary group of teachers and practitioners in the humanities at a graduate school and a community college, we reflected together on the ways in which core components of the humanities—critical thinking, group engagement, communication skills, emotional intelligence, flexibility and integrity—are embedded in students' lives in different ways than they have been for past generations, and are also increasingly valuable for students' future education and career pathways.

The CUNY Humanities Alliance was created out of a recognition of the change necessary to respond to more diverse students in higher education and their cultural, social, and political contexts. While our work is based in community colleges, all institutions of higher education need to change to respond to these new majority students (Davidson, 2017). Community colleges, which are inclusive of 100 percent of applicants, have been working toward restructuring learning to suit the needs and aspirations of *all* students for decades (Jacobs & Worth, 2019). As four-year colleges begin accepting more of this new majority into their student cohorts, they must also change their educational structure to be inclusive of all students.

The CUNY Humanities Alliance program has been extremely fortunate to be able to remunerate all of our graduate student instructors with full fellowships, to provide course releases for all community college faculty involved in the program, and to have staff dedicated to making these collaborative learning spaces possible. We understand that most colleges will not have the financial support to provide this level of remuneration or time to commit to intentional learning communities, professional development, experimentation, and classroom innovation. That is partially what motivated us to write this book; we want to share practices we developed through many iterations, in the form of easy, adaptable activities and lesson plans to modify and implement in other classroom contexts. Taken together, we hope this serves as a model of a humanizing collectivist critical pedagogy that attends to the varied identities, aspirations, goals, responsibilities, obligations, and emotions that people carry.

The New Majority: Changing Student Demographics

The higher education landscape has been changing for decades; now due to the COVID-19 pandemic and with the Black Lives Matter social movement, we are experiencing even more shifts (Brock & Diwa, 2021; Congressional Research Center, 2021; Grawe, 2021; Hatch, 2022; June, 2022; National Student Clearinghouse Research Center, 2022; Smith, 2020). Two decades in, it is high time that we think about how best to meet the diverse needs of students in the twenty-first century. Colleges in the U.S. now serve student bodies that are more diverse than ever before on indexes ranging from race and ethnicity, to immigration status, language background, age, religion, gender, sexual orientation, physical ability, and mental and emotional health (Jacobs & Worth, 2019; Smith, 2020). It is widely agreed that these students, sometimes called the "new majority" students, are crucial to America's future—economically, socially, and politically (Davidson, 2017). These students do or will soon form the engaged citizenry that is needed to face crucial challenges, from economic innovation to anti-racist policy making, from climate change to transnational migration. They are the very agents who will play a critical role in designing and materializing equitable futures based on their new imagination of desirable societies.

Community colleges, which have always had a high percentage of students who are first-generation college students, first- or second-generation immigrants, multicultural, multilingual, low-income, and students of color, now educate 44 percent of all undergraduate students (Community College Research Center, 2021b). According to a 2019 Pew Research Center study, the percentage of low-income and non-white students enrolled in two-year schools has increased dramatically over the past 20 years, from 13 percent low-income students in 1996 to 27 percent in 2016, and from 31 percent non-white in 1996 to 50 percent in 2016 (Fry & Cilluffo, 2019). Altogether, community colleges are now responsible for equipping roughly half of all undergraduate students to navigate their complex and ever-changing realities. These students, in or recently graduated from community colleges, *are* the new majority of students in higher education.

The history and practices of higher education presume that we are teaching a homogenous group of white, (self-defined) middle-class, education-pipeline students, making our default teaching practices eurocentric, white, masculine, and English-only (Best Colleges, 2021; hooks, 1994; Matsuda, 2006). The maintenance of this system relies on a rigid reaction to different ideologies, beliefs, ideas, values, and systemic structures (Darder, 2015, 2017; Freire, 1970; hooks, 1994; Jacobs & Worth, 2019; Love, 2019; Woldeyes & Offord, 2018). Even when we are teaching in institutional or regional environments that seem to be more homogenous in social and economic composition, if we look closely at all the intersectionalities of identity, we find incredible diversity (Fry & Cilluffo, 2019; Smith, 2020). It is our duty as educators to prepare students not just for academic success—which also needs to be redefined because of its basis in white, masculine, wealthy, citizen-based, straight, normative culture—but also the new multicultural and multilingual world in which they are immersed. When students bring their own experience into the classroom, which contradicts white, male theorists sometimes from hundreds of years ago, they are often countered offhandedly in an intention to teach the student. Because these defaults are so entrenched within education, unless we are actively reimagining our pedagogy, we are not responding to the diversity of the students in the classroom, or the multicultural nature of the world we live in. If we hope to expand or to revisit the existing knowledge base and theories within higher education, the incorporation of multicultural perspectives is necessary.

Each student has their own identity; their own ambitions, family pressure to succeed in particular ways, responsibilities and needs as a person. When we, as instructors, insist that we have the most valuable information in the classroom, and that all of these incredible and multifaceted people should sit and listen to us, we ignore the talent and expertise in the classroom (Darder, 2015, 2017; Freire, 1970; hooks, 1994; Woldeyes & Offord, 2018). Often, these failures are simply due to faculty being overworked. Sometimes, these are due to an internalization of old teaching and learning norms. Sometimes, the failures are blatant misunderstandings (due to uninterrogated privilege) of what students are seeking when they come to college, and what their lives demand. Students, even, may have been disciplined to be passive learners and alienated in their classes, and therefore not have any desire for more equal and democratic class dynamics (Friere, 1970; Giroux, 2005; Kim, 2018; Love, 2019; Mitchell, 2006; Sawyer & Rifino, 2020).

With the current neoliberal values that make profit-making the essence of democracy (Chen & Buell, 2018; Giroux, 2005, p. 8; Kim, 2017, 2021; Eagleton, April 16, 2015), students' economic and career outcomes often take precedence over an institution's commitment to democratic values. Ayers (2011) investigated the mission statements of 421 community colleges and found that over 64 percent of the community colleges included economic development as their core mission—not merely the financial and social mobility of the student, but the contribution of students to the broader workforce thanks to degree completion at the institution. American Academy of Arts & Sciences (2013) points out that economic anxiety is the primary reason people pursue higher education, and as a consequence, the perceived value of higher education is often focused on short-term payoffs rather than a broader consideration of the contribution of higher education to students and to society (Dougherty, 2023). This set of values makes it harder for public institutions to address students' and local communities' diverse needs and goals, and focus on elements related to community college students' qualities of life beyond their time as students (Kim, 2017). The current state of higher education can be deeply alienating, and often overlooks the embodied realities of students, including hunger and housing insecurity (see Laterman, 2019; Sawyer & Rifino, 2020).In this educational landscape, questions about "what is living well and what it means to live a humane life" are overlooked and suppressed by higher education administrators, faculty and sometimes even students themselves (Kim, 2019). In our observation and interviews with the LaGuardia students, we found that students who have diverse working and living experiences want to contextualize their experiences in a more structured manner and to situate their experiences in a more comprehensive way, in micro- and macro-psychological, social, cultural and political-economic contexts. Only by fostering students' awareness of their own positionality and the larger societal forces at work can faculty and education institutions hope to promote positive change in the students' lives and uphold colleges' social responsibility as public educational institutions with acute awareness of moral commitments. We must rethink our academic environments, curricula, and missions to reflect a more holistic view of student success, focusing particularly on the new majority of students. This is essential in order to promote social justice and equip the next generation with the ability to adapt and live fulfilling lives.

Redefining Educational Success

For these new majority students, we cannot define educational success merely by economic markers: grade point average (GPA), retention rates, graduation rates, and employment rates. In the words of one of our community college students, "The 3.9 GPA that I have, as an international student who is forbidden from having a job, cannot be compared to the 3.4 GPA that another student got while working two jobs and supporting their family." Likewise, it is impossible to compare the employment placement of a four-year college student who transferred from community college, and who is a first-generation college student and second-generation immigrant, to the employment placement of a student at the same four-year college who went to college straight from private boarding school and will take a job in their parents' fortune-500 company. Those who base success of education on comparisons of GPA, retention and graduation rates, and employment are ignoring the social, economic, political, and cultural structures that create and justify inequality in our society. This system of inequality further reifies the privilege inborn to white, upper-middle-class, American, straight, able-bodied, neurotypical men rather than recognizing the hard work, improvement, and expertise of multilingual, multicultural, BIPOC (Black, Indigenous, and People of Color), queer, international, migrant, neurodivergent, disabled, and low-income people (despite the structural disadvantages they face).

Instead, we argue that "student success" should be redefined to include students' development of: an understanding of their own positionality; an understanding that their individual social, economic and psychological status are part of macro social structures; tools and techniques to navigate and dismantle structural barriers to equity; practice in critical thinking; confidence in their cultural and linguistic experience; collectivist notions of empathy, group-responsibility, and solidarity; academic engagement and agency; an expanded vision of academic and career possibilities; and the ability to earn a living wage, given the realities they face.

Often in the humanities we make the claim that our disciplines are important because they help students to master essential lifelong learning skills—critical thinking, creativity, writing, historical perspective, ethics, emotional intelligence, aesthetic appreciation, and cultural understanding as well as research skills, communication, collaboration, project management, and digital literacy (Davidson, 2017; Nussbaum, 2010). And, each of those skills is steeped in structured racism, classism, sexism, and ableism that needs to be understood, challenged and dismantled. Without questioning "meta-cognition" (the way we teach students how to learn, not just what to learn), we cannot have an equitable critical pedagogy.

The humanities, in particular, offers faculty an opportunity to center the question of "what it means to be human," in a way that is inclusive to *all* identities, not just privileged ones, and that reflexively challenges what, how and why we are teaching. The humanities further emphasize the significance of the "development of long-term qualities of mind," that is, "inquisitiveness, perceptiveness, the ability to put a received idea to a new purpose, and the ability to share and build ideas with a diverse world of others" (American Academy of Arts & Sciences, 2013). In essence, this sort of structural pedagogical change within the humanities has the opportunity to foreground the larger restructuring needed in higher education post-pandemic, and in response to the national cries for anti-racist and anti-nationalist policies.

In this book, we understand students and instructors as "empowered agents" to (1) challenge the hegemonic knowledge that alienates students and instructors in terms of race, class, culture, gender, ethnicity, language, ability, and nationality, (2) recognize the significance of updating and advancing critical knowledge, which is built on especially vulnerable communities' historical experiences, and the importance of constructing systematic understanding of the macro- and micro- mechanisms and their interrelationships and impact on students' everyday lives, and (3) build learning communities where they establish solidarity based on intellectual, emotional and spiritual support toward humanity, democratization, and social justice. This is especially significant for diverse community college students, who are often subject to capitalist discourse that views them only as future laborers to support economic development (Community College Research Center, 2021a; Dyke et al., 2018; Darder, 2015; Dweck, 2006; Kim, 2017; Levin, 2001, 2002; Yeager & Dweck, 2012). The program illustrates the impact on faculty and students' lives when faculty and graduate student teachers reclaim their own agency through implementing humanizing collectivist critical pedagogy in their classrooms, which in turn recover the students' identities, critical agency, and wholeness within their educational world.

Humanizing Collectivist Critical Pedagogy

There are many different approaches to and definitions of critical pedagogy; we believe the main purpose of critical pedagogy is to engage students in thinking critically, promoting the importance of asking questions, understanding the role of power and status in society and education, and envisioning more desirable and equitable futures (Darder, 2015, 2017; Freire, 1970; Giroux, 2005; hooks, 1994; Smith & Seal, 2021). In this process, students are acknowledged as activists and knowledge producers and encouraged to become scholarly researchers. Doing critical pedagogy means "engaging learners in real-world activities that are connected to or have relevance for them and their communities" (Gordon, 2012, p. 481). As Jesse Stommel (2014) affirms, "critical pedagogy is concerned less with knowing and more with a voracious not-knowing. It is an on-going and recursive process of discovery." Rivera (1999) suggests students benefit academically when their courses are taught through the lens of critical pedagogy. Humanizing collectivist critical pedagogy moves beyond traditional definitions of critical pedagogy to be more comprehensive in supporting students' engagement and empowerment. Humanizing collectivist critical pedagogy creates a learning space *with* students, as whole embodied people with their own critical agency; values mutual-agency which is formed and strengthened through the collaboration between instructors and students and also among students; and creates space for students to play a collaborative leading role in restructuring higher education to dismantle oppressive structures that they are currently subjugated to.

Why Humanizing?

In order to achieve a humanizing transformation in our classrooms, first and foremost, students have to be regarded as whole embodied people with their own critical agency (Emdin, 2016; hooks, 2003; Thomson, 2017). That fact has to permeate the way students are treated and interacted with every level of the institution—from their applications through their graduation. This may seem like quite a simple matter. We all understand students are people. We have gotten diversity offices and wellness centers and we are training our faculty in gender pronouns. And, it is still not enough. Students bring with them everything they are and everything they experience into the institution and into the classrooms: their home, work, interests, educational aspirations, career goals, bodies, minds, mental and physical abilities, gender, sexual orientation, race, ethnicities, nationalities, languages, politics, religion, economic status, and curiosity. If this list makes you feel overwhelmed, that feeling merely demonstrates the immense gap between our current educational system and what it needs to be. It shows the deficits in our teaching, not in our students. If we do not engage the students as they are, and everything they bring with them (which includes some tremendous skills and expertise), then we are not only missing an amazing opportunity, but we are truly failing them as teachers.

Why Collectivist?

The humanizing collectivist critical pedagogy presented in this book values mutual-agency (solidarity) which is formed and strengthened through the collaboration between instructors and students and also among students. S.B. Kim (J.S. Chŏn, S.H. Pak., & S.J. Pak., June 22, 2016) explains that freedom itself is social rather than individual. In contrast to neoliberal ethos that emphasizes self-development and self-management, and defines an individual as an isolated and atomized agent, mutual-agency demolishes an explicit distinction between self and others. S.B. Kim (J.S. Chŏn, S.H. Pak., & S.J. Pak, June 22, 2016) points out that while isolated individuals become skeptical about their capability to act as empowered agents, mutual-agency encourages individuals to share others' suffering together, which is the very foundation of their formation and acquisition of critical knowledge. Students embedded in individualized education systems are more likely to feel isolated, anxious, bored, alienated, depressed, excluded, or overwhelmed when the content or teaching methods are dramatically different from their life experiences (Sawyer & Rifino, 2020). Instead of recognizing this difference as an informative moment of resistance, students' emotional responses are often medicalized and treated as individual pathologies (Venianaki et al., 2021). These students will not be empowered to make changes or speak up if the material is antithetical to their experience and taught in a teacher-centered way, where students are only responsible for their individual learning, rather than a community contribution to learning (Kim, 2017).

The exclusion of students' experiences, by definition, should not be happening in a collectivist education system, where students would know the various experiences of everyone in the room, and have space held for them to challenge the content or concepts championed by the professor or other students. Students learn more deeply, and more permanently, through asking questions, through collaboration, and through active engagement that draws on the full range of their knowledge and experience, both cognitive and affective (Darder, 2015, 2017; Davidson, 2017; hooks, 1994; Stetsenko, 2008, 2017). This kind of authentic community serves not only students, but also instructors—especially adjuncts, who can feel isolated in their professional identities depending on their relationships with peers and their departments (Kim, 2021).

Why Critical?

In addition to our discussion of critical pedagogy above, humanizing collectivist critical pedagogy also challenges contemporary definitions of "students" and creates space for students to play a collaborative leading role in restructuring higher education to dismantle oppressive structures that they are currently subjugated to. Our pedagogical practice supports students' identities, not as designated by oppressive power groups, but rather as created in the ways that students themselves want to be (Kim, 2017, 2021; also see Apple, 1995; Giroux 2011; Hall, 2003). We employ Kim's (2017) notion of *bystander's consciousness and politics* that enable students to utilize their double visions as both insiders, acutely aware of the oppressive reality they experience, and as outsiders, as they analyze the structured mechanisms of oppression through their higher education experience. With this bystander's consciousness, students are uniquely positioned to create a new pathway for future society (Kim, 2017).

This book provides some models of humanizing collectivist critical pedagogy that attends to the varied identities, aspirations, goals, responsibilities, obligations, and emotions that each person carries with them. The authors' experiences illustrate the impact of this pedagogy on faculty and students' lives when faculty activate their agency through implementing these pedagogical practices in classrooms, which in turn supports students' identities, critical agency, and humanity within their educational world.

Our Practice in the Humanities

Regardless of students' majors, we recognize humanities classes as crucial transformative spheres (see Davidson, 2017) where diverse groups of students improve their critical consciousness and build new politics toward critical, humane democracy and social justice (Friere, 1970; hooks, 1994). There is an important opportunity to revise and advance critical pedagogy within community college and four-year college classrooms, and to respond to students' local and global academic, social, cultural, political, and economic exigencies. This is true in all disciplines, but perhaps nowhere more so than in the humanities. Many college students are learning to navigate complex cultural and sociopolitical contexts, form and re-form their own identities relative to their immediate circumstances as well as the broader world around them, and empower themselves as the very agents, "who[se] acts brings about change, and whose achievements can be judged in terms of her own values and objectives" (Sen, 1999, p. 19). While students may enter college in order to pursue a specific line of certification or career preparation, nearly all will take a humanities course as part of their general education requirements—and a large number will pursue humanities fields as a major.

It can be life-changing to have a professor who sees the ways that literature, music, visual and performing arts, and other cultural creations can shed new light on students' experiences. In the edited book entitled *Race, Equity, and the Learning Environment: The Global Relevance of Critical and Inclusive Pedagogies in Higher Education*, Andrews and Castillo (2016) state:

> These humanizing pedagogies and practices foster inclusion in the classroom and can lead to transformative learning experiences that heighten students' critical consciousness and understanding of the negative systemic effects of bias and discrimination in the lives of historically marginalized people across the globe. (p. 113)

Building on Andrews and Castillo's discussions (2016), we approach humanizing pedagogy as critical educational philosophies and class practices that are characterized by promoting students' critical consciousness and their agency. This includes advocating their intrinsic dignity and their full participation in decision-making (AAAS, 2013) and supporting them as "well-informed" educated citizens, who "participate in their-own governance and engage in the world" (AAAS, 2013, p. 18). These students have the power to lead the design of desirable societies and futures. The notion of 'critical' here indicates being anti-hegemonic against the neoliberal policies and cultural politics that facilitate the alienation of students from their learning and humanity (Darder & Griffiths, 2016; Giroux, 2011). Finding new and meaningful ways to embed humanities teaching in the commitments and concerns of students has the potential to spark a vibrant renewal of civic engagement, community involvement, and professional satisfaction.

Beyond the Classroom

This pedagogical transformation within higher education starts in the classroom, but it cannot end there. Humanizing collectivist critical pedagogy could be present in every level of education, every way that students engage in higher education: from the classrooms to extracurricular activities, from academic administration to student clubs, from educating the next generation of instructors to conducting evaluation and assessment, from community college to graduate education. Pedagogical change happening in classrooms can be magnified with strong pedagogical professional training, extracurricular programs, and administrative support.

To promote a culture that values inclusive teaching in academia, we must support ongoing professional development for college instructors and also a change in doctoral education to prepare future pedagogues. Too often doctoral education is focused solely on training new PhDs for research, but not teaching (Casetti et al., February 2021; Gaff et al., 2003; Kim, 2021). Even when graduate students enter a graduate program with a love of and aspiration to focus on teaching, this prioritization of teaching is often denigrated to the point that the aspiration is forgotten. The devaluation of teaching within higher education presupposes that if you are a good researcher, you are by nature, a good teacher (Gaff et al., 2003; Ofgang, 2021; Robinson & Hope, 2013). We all know, and have experienced, the failures of that supposition. If we hope to change the future of education, to support educational success of the new majority of undergraduate students, college instructors, some of whom are currently graduate students, must value and see the importance of sound pedagogy, and need to be trained in teaching practice as a core part of their professional development.

In classrooms, there are so many restrictions on what must be taught and how it's taught. Most extracurricular programs, whether they are created by students, administrators, or grant-based programs, do not have those sorts of limitations. They are an area where radical pedagogical change can happen, where students' positionality and aspirations can be connected with the work they're actively engaged in. While not everyone can participate in extracurricular programs (though, we can make it easier by offering credit or remuneration for participation), those who do participate are allowed to imagine their future trajectories outside the limitations of forced curricula. It is often the explicit purpose of administration-led leadership or professional development programs to prepare college students for the world more broadly. However, without grounding students in their own positionality within a macro system of economic, political, social privilege, and hierarchies, we attempt to ignore the systematic barriers that the new majority will face, and instead proffer the rags-to-riches mythology. By transforming administration-led programs, and supporting student-led programs, we can more quickly reframe student success in terms of positionality and students' lived reality.

Developing and modeling engaged, scholarly administrative practices—ones that are deeply connected with and reflective of the scholarly goals of the program—is critical to develop an environment where humanizing collectivist critical pedagogy can take root. Humanizing teaching methods, continuing professional development for instructors, and transformative extracurricular programs require thoughtful and engaged academic leadership and administration. Administrative engagement determines institutional collaborations, longer-term strategies, institutional priorities, and methods of work. This applies to administrative practices throughout the university, from centers for teaching and learning to financial aid administration. It applies to the way administrators, in graduate and undergraduate settings, communicate with students, make assumptions about student behavior, and create agency and support for student voices within the institution.

The majority of this book is about teachers transforming pedagogy in our classes, but we did not want to restrict the examples of pedagogical transformation to classrooms. We introduce examples of pedagogical professional development, extracurricular programs, and academic administration. Similar to our classroom pedagogy chapters, we are hopeful these can be used as examples for others to modify and use in their institutions. Together, it is our hope that program administrators, faculty, and students can transform the way we teach and learn *for* the twenty-first century so that our students will be able to succeed in new ways, to create new worlds that will benefit all of us.

Chapter Outline

As previously mentioned, this book is a collection of pieces from CUNY Humanities Alliance participants who taught at LaGuardia Community College from 2016 to 2020. We each have different disciplinary backgrounds, theoretical grounding, pedagogical methods, and positionalities. Each of us connects with the foundational concepts of humanizing, collectivist, and critical pedagogical practices, and reexamines the way we define student success. We all do this a bit differently. We have intentionally kept individual author voices intact (rather than having everyone conform to a particular tone or style) because we apply our pedagogy, our ethos of humanness, to ourselves as well.

In ordering the chapters, we are taking readers on a journey: to begin with the broader socioeconomic and historic context of critical pedagogy of the humanities in community college; through the pedagogical questions and framework we used to develop our praxis; on to several examples of humanizing collectivist critical pedagogy in philosophy, linguistics, English, and psychology; continuing into examples of our pedagogy in extracurricular programs; and ending with a discussion of engaged scholarly administration that informs our work throughout higher education. Each piece is grounded in its own theoretical context, and is necessary to this shift in higher education that we need to lead.

Chapter 2: Critical Pedagogy of Humanities in Neoliberal Times

The first chapter of the book provides the historical landscape of neoliberal cultural politics that identifies community college students mostly as a workforce. It discusses, in a broader socioeconomic context, how the humanities can be a critical intervention point in fostering student agency. It also examines how critical pedagogy within community college contexts can be used to help students utilize their critical agency to cultivate the meaning of their lives and to navigate their further educational and career trajectories as well as to act for democratizing the institutions and societies.

Chapter 3: Interdisciplinary Questions that Inform our Pedagogy

This chapter discusses the pedagogical professional development that we used in the CUNY Humanities Alliance to further develop and iterate our pedagogical praxis. It provides our recipe for an interdisciplinary learning community that was a major piece of our work together. The chapter then details the questions that instructors can ask themselves to further reflect on their own pedagogy: Who are you teaching? What are you teaching? Why are you teaching it to these students? How are you teaching? Each segment includes questions of representation, inclusion and exclusion, connection, and engagement; it urges that faculty be specific and intentional with their choices, rather than inadvertently reproduce historical patterns in higher education that are steeped in bias.

Chapter 4: A Toolkit for Questioning Everything

Chapters 4 through 7 give practical examples of humanizing collectivist critical pedagogy in philosophy, linguistics, English, and psychology. By recognizing students' perspectives and experiences as essential sources for class knowledge, these course examples decenter many normative frameworks in higher education, and invite students to further their individual and collective agency within their historical, cultural, social, and political environments.

Chapter 4 introduces a collaborative deep reading exercise called "Primary Sources 101," created by a historian teaching an introductory philosophy course on critical thinking. The activity encourages students to become more aware of the ways in which they are already thinking critically, and challenges them to apply these skills to all of the knowledge around them, including the authority of knowledge production in colleges and elsewhere. The author details the reasoning behind the design, the learning objectives, incremental steps, and practical instructions on how to implement the exercise. The activity is student-centered, collaborative, and scaffolded to engage students and make intellectual discovery and reasoning comfortable, unpretentious, and enticing. Deep reading assignments are common in many disciplines, and this activity is easily adaptable to any situation where you want to invite students to more critically analyze the information presented.

Chapter 5: Teaching Linguistics to Promote Social Justice

Chapter 5 outlines two approaches to teaching introductory linguistics courses that aim to end exclusionary language practices while incorporating and validating the language backgrounds of students in the classroom. Linguistics is often considered a technical discipline, but language is a fundamental aspect of ourselves and our communities. The multicultural and multilingual diversity of students does not reflect the White Formal Standard American English that often is the only language welcome in the U.S. education system. Instead, the authors present lessons that invite students to appreciate and understand their own linguistic heritage and identities, including engagement with indigenous languages or languages spoken near their school setting or where they grew up, creating counternarratives against these linguistic hegemonies. Students are encouraged to express and share their experiences and ideas drawing on all their linguistic practices and resources, and build learning communities where they support one another intellectually, emotionally, and socially throughout the course.

Chapter 6: Visualizing Identity, Fandom, and Representation

Chapter 6 details the design of a literary-themed composition course that focused on popular visual culture and negotiated questions of the politics of representation. By including visual elements such as comics and illustrations, the course strives to demystify colonial and authoritative hierarchization of academic composition, and invites students to recenter their knowledge and interests alongside canonical texts. The chapter traces how students in these courses negotiated questions of representation in community-oriented ways including student responses, successes, possible revisions, and failures. The author engages the politics of representation to incorporate students' fandom and experiences into the strictures of academic rigor.

Chapter 7: Subverting White Androcentrism in Psychology Curricula

This chapter discusses the recent advances in decentering and decolonizing undergraduate psychology curricula. Drawing on Ahmed's (2006) notion of orientation, this chapter problematizes what happens when foundational courses fail to interrogate their disciplinary foundations. Specifically, the chapter describes a scaffolded research paper that aims to challenge androcentrism, Eurocentrism, and white supremacy in psychology in a First Year Seminar course. The author details a series of scaffolded assignments centered in the Psychology's Feminist Voices database that he uses to support students in completing their research papers. To conclude, this chapter emphasizes the need to promote a context-sensitive, historical, and critically engaged disciplinary introduction that is committed to a sustained critique of hegemonic psychology, while centering the multicultural perspectives, ethical questions, and social justice orientations that students bring to the classroom.

Chapter 8: Affective Injustice and Student Dis/Engagement

Chapters 8 and 9 offer extracurricular programmatic examples of humanizing collectivist critical pedagogy, extending pedagogical transformation that is typically limited to classroom activities and formal curricula. These chapters are examples of student learning communities grounded in students' own emotions, aspirations, motivations, and creativity. The hope of both of these programs is for students to learn to navigate academia on their own terms, with support from each other, and to extend their intellectual experiences outside of their coursework.

Chapter 8 follows the trajectory of one college student in a voluntary co-curricular program, the Peer Activist Learning Community (PALC). The chapter explores the emotional impact that academia has on students in terms of affective dynamics, a relational understanding of affect that counters the medicalization and problematization of students' feelings (Rifino, Matsuura & Medina, 2014; Vianna, Hougaard, & Stetsenko, 2014). Built on advances in the Vygotskian tradition, in particular the Transformative Activist Stance (Stetsenko 2008, 2016), PALC offers a solidaristic community alongside rigorous conceptual tools, so that students can interrogate and reclaim their learning journeys. Students in PALC work together to understand the affective dynamics they are immersed in, and transform their oppressive and alienating experiences in higher education into restorative practices through agentive and activist contributions to each others' educational and social journeys.

Chapter 9: Humanness in Undergraduate Projects and Learning Goals

This chapter also shares an example of humanizing collectivist critical pedagogy in an extracurricular program, where students design and implement a year-long project of their own design, which aligns their current interests, positionality, and future aspirations. Authors detail four stages of their project development process, and the pedagogical methods used to foster a transformative experience for undergraduate scholars. The scholars have complete agency in their project and how they define success for their work; the program begins with community agreements on the first day, and the group decides everything—from enrichment activities to our final exhibition structure—going forward. The facilitators show unrelenting grace by believing in students' ability to succeed with their goals, even when life circumstances present serious obstacles. The program redefines success in a way that devalues perfection, and refocuses on an iterative process where change is constant. Through this project design and implementation process, students question neoliberal pressures of previous career trajectories and the boundaries that they have assumed about their futures.

Chapter 10: Socially Engaged Administration and Graduate Education

Our final chapter expands humanizing collectivist critical pedagogy into program administration, which is a crucial but often under-examined component of higher education reform. Program administration affects work and learning that take place both in and beyond the classroom. A pedagogical approach to program administration is a natural bridge to developing thoughtful programs and preparing future faculty. Moreover, administrative roles encompass a wide range of work—from writing and public presentations to mentorship and problem solving—that draws on skills and expertise from graduate training, and could be a satisfying career for humanities scholars. This chapter focuses on engaged, scholarly administrative leadership, and discusses how the development of programs can create space and community for people traditionally underrepresented in the academy and celebrate more varied kinds of success. Administrative work is constitutive of a program's value within the institution and to the broader public, making it an important bridge position for advocacy and public engagement, and a meaningful way to prepare future faculty. How we define "success" of faculty and staff alongside the "success" of students is crucial to making systematic change that supports, rather than penalizes, the type of changes that are deeply needed in classrooms.

This book is a compilation of modifiable practices that we can offer to other faculty, instructors, and administrators who want to transform their classrooms and institutions. Mostly, this book is practical, so that instructors (and students) can take the best pedagogical practices we have formed—based on rigorous critical pedagogical theory, and honed through years of iteration and development—and modify them for use in their courses. Talking about our pedagogy, how it has developed, and why it is important, is impossible to do without simultaneously providing a theoretical grounding and research that shows our success. It is our hope that administrators, staff, faculty, and students of all levels in higher education may be able to take what we have learned, build upon it, and adapt pieces of humanizing collectivist critical pedagogy to fit their institutional environment and structures.

References

Ahmed, S. (2006). *Queer phenomenology: Orientations, objects, other.* Duke University Press.

American Academy of Arts & Sciences (AAAS). (2013). *The heart of the matter: The humanities and social sciences for a vibrant, competitive, and secure nation* (Report of the Commission on the Humanities and Social Sciences). https://www.amacad.org/news/heart-matter-humanities-and-social-sciences-vibrant-competitive-and-secure-nation

Andrews, D.J.C. & Castillo, B.M. (2016). Humanizing pedagogy for examinations of race and culture in teacher education. In F. Tuitt, C. Haynes, & S. Stewart (Eds.), *Race, equity, and the learning environment: The global relevance of critical and inclusive pedagogies in higher education.* Routledge

Apple, M. (1995). Cultural capital and official knowledge. In M. Bérubé & C. Nelson (Eds.), *Higher education under fire: Politics, economics, and the crisis of the humanities* (pp. 91–107). Routledge.

Ayers, D. (2011). Community colleges and the politics of sociospatial scale. *Higher Education, 62,* 303–314.

Benjamin, R. (2022). *Viral Justice: How we grow the world we want.* Princeton University Press.

Best Colleges. (2021). *A history of privilege in American Higher Education.* https://www.bestcolleges.com/news/analysis/2020/07/17/history-privilege-higher-education/

Brock, T., & Diwa, C. (2021). Catastrophe or catalyst? Reflections on COVID's impact on community colleges. *Journal of Postsecondary Student Success, 1*(2), 2–17.

Casetti, F., Kastan, D., Ramachandran, A., Schirmeister., Ansfield, B., Maga, M., & Razzaq, N. (2021, February). *Report of the humanities doctoral education advisory working group.* Yale University, The Humanities Doctoral Education Advisory Working Group.

Chen, G.A., & Buell, J.Y. (2018). Of models and myths: Asian (Americans) in STEM and the neoliberal racial project. *Race Ethnicity and Education, 21*(5), 607–625.

Chŏn, J.S., Pak, S.H., & Pak, S.J. (2016, June 22). "Sahoerŭl chŏnboksik'yŏon sŭlp'ŭmŭl minnŭnda": Sewŏrhobut'ŏ Sŏul Guŭiyŏk 19sal ch'ŏngnyŏnŭi chugŭmkkaji, kot'ong-gwa sŭlp'ŭme ch'ŏnch'akhan ch'ŏrhakcha Kim Sangbongege chwap'yŏrŭl mutta

["Believing in grief that has turned over a society": From Sewŏrho to the death of a 19-year old young man at Guŭi Station Seoul, Asking the coordinate to a philosopher Kim Sangbong, who is preserved in suffering and grief]. *Han'gyŏre, 21*, 1117. http://h21.hani.co.kr/arti/cover/cover_general/41936.html?_fr=mb2

Community College Research Center. (2021a, April). *Strengthening Community College workforce training*. Columbia University, Teachers College, Community College Research Center. https://ccrc.tc.columbia.edu/publications/strengthening-community-college-workforce-training.html

Community College Research Center. (2021b, July). *An introduction to Community College and their students*. Columbia University, Teachers College, Community College Research Center. https://ccrc.tc.columbia.edu/publications/introduction-community-colleges-students.html

Congressional Research Service. (2021). *The COVID-19 pandemic and institutions of higher education: Contemporary issues*. https://crsreports.congress.gov/product/pdf/R/R46666/2

Darder, A. (2015). *Culture and power in the classroom: Educational foundations for the schooling of bicultural students* (2nd ed.). Routledge.

Darder, A. (2017). *Reinventing Paulo Freire: A pedagogy of love* (2nd ed.). Routledge.

Darder, A. & Griffiths, T. (2016). Labour in the academic borderlands: Unveiling the tyranny of neoliberal policies. *Workplace*, 28, 115–129.

Davidson, C. (2017). *The new education*. Hachette Book Group.

Dougherty, K. (2023). *Choice is not always good: Reducing the role of informational inequality in producing and legitimating higher education inequality*. Columbia University, Teachers College, Community College Research Center. https://academiccommons.columbia.edu/doi/10.7916/s9ym-fh79

Dweck, C.S. (2006). *Mindset*. Random House.

Dyke, E., Meyerhoff, E., & Evol, K. (2018). Radical Imagination as Pedagogy: Cultivating Collective Study from Within, on the Edge, and Beyond Education. Transformations: The Journal of Inclusive Scholarship and Pedagogy, 28(2), 160–180. https://doi.org/10.5325/trajincschped.28.2.0160

Eagleton, T. (2015, April 16). The slow death of the university. *The Chronicle of Higher Education*. http://chronicle.com/article/The-Slow-Death-of-the/228991/

Emdin, C. (2016). *For white folks who teach in the hood—and the rest of y'all too: Reality pedagogy and urban education*. Beacon Press. Chicago / Turabian—Author Date Citation (style guide) Emdin, Christopher. 2016.

Freire, P. (1970). *Pedagogy of the oppressed*. Continuum.

Fry, R., & Cilluffo, A. (2019, May 22). *A rising share of undergraduates are from poor families, especially at less selective colleges*. Pew Research Center. https://www.pewresearch.org/social-trends/wp-content/uploads/sites/3/2019/05/Pew-Research-Center-Undergrad-report-FINAL-05.22.19.pdf

Gaff, J.G., & Pruitt-Logan, A.S., Sims, L.B., Denecke, D.D., & program participants. (2003). *Preparing future faculty in the humanities and social sciences: A guide for change*. Council of Graduate Schools, Association of American Colleges and Universities. http://www.preparing-faculty.org/PFFWeb.PFF4Manual.pdf

Giroux, H.A. (2005). The terror of neoliberalism: Rethinking the significance of cultural politics. *College Literature, 32*(1), 1–19.

Giroux, H.A. (2011). *Education and the crisis of public values: Challenging the assult on teachers, students, and public education*. Peter Lang.

Gordon, B. (2012). Critical pedagogy. In *Encyclopedia of diversity in education* (Vol. 1, pp. 479–481). Sage.

Grawe, N.D. (2021). *The agile college: How institutions successfully navigate demographic changes*. Johns Hopkins University Press.

Hall, S. (2003). The whites of their eyes: Racist ideologies and the media. In G. Dines & H.M. Jean (Eds.), *Gender, race and class in media* (pp. 18–22). Sage.

Hatch, B. (2022, June 16). Why fewer high-school graduates are going to college. *The Chronicle of Higher Education*. https://www.chronicle.com/article/why-fewer-high-school-graduates-are-going-to-college

hooks, b. (1994). *Teaching to Transgress: Education as the Practice of Freedom*. Routledge.

hooks, b. (2003). *Teaching community: A pedagogy of hope*. Routledge.

Jacobs, J., & Worth, J. (2019, March). *The evolving mission of workforce development in the Community College*. Columbia University, Teachers College, Community College Research Center. https://ccrc.tc.columbia.edu/publications/evolving-mission-workforce-development-community-college.html

June, A.W. (2022, May 26). Drop in spring-2022 enrollment is worse than expected. *The Chronicle of Higher Education*. https://www.chronicle.com/article/drop-in-spring-2022-enrollment-is-worse-than-expected

Kim, H. [EO]. (2019, July 4). *Ingandaumeul jilmunhaneun inmunhagi jungyohan iyu [The reasons why humanities that explore humanhood are important]*. https://www.youtube.com/watch?v=SJNpJfPOuA4

Kim, S. (2017). *Globalization of a U.S. community college and the politics of belonging in the time of upheaval: Remaking of race and class of Korean international community college students* [Unpublished doctoral dissertation]. University of Illinois at Urbana-Champaign.

Kim, S. (2018). Voluntarily exiled? Korean state's cultural politics of young adults' social belonging and Korean students' exile to a US community college. *Higher Education, 76*, 353–367.

Kim, S. (2021). Empowering students & creating social change through the humanities. *CUNY Humanities Alliance*. https://cunyhumanitiesalliance.org/2021/01/04/empowering-students-creating-social-change-through-the-humanities/

LaGuardia Community College, Office of Institutional Research and Assessment. (2020). *Institutional profile*. LaGuardia Community College, Office of Institutional Research and Assessment. https://www.laguardia.edu/uploadedfiles/main_site/content/ir/docs/institutional-profile-2020.pdf

Laterman, K. (2019, May 2). Tuition or dinner? Nearly half of college students surveyed in a new report are going hungry. *New York Times.* https://www.nytimes.com/2019/05/02/nyregion/hunger-college-food-insecurity.html

Levin, J. (2001). Public policy, community colleges, and the path to globalization. *Higher Education, 42,* 237–262.

Levin, J. (2002). Global culture and the community college. *Community College Journal of Research and Practice, 26,* 121–145.

Love, B. (2019). *We want to do more than survive: Abolitionist teaching and the pursuit of educational freedom.* Beacon Press.

Matsuda, P.K. (2006). The myth of linguistic homogeneity in U.S. college composition. *College English, 68*(6), 637–651. https://doi.org/10.2307/25472180

Mitchell, K. (2006). Neoliberal govermentality in the European Union: Education, training, and technologies of citizenship. *Society and Space, 24,* 389–407.

National Student Clearinghouse Research Center. (2022, May 26). *Spring 2022 current term enrollment estimates.* https://nscresearchcenter.org/current-term-enrollment-estimates/

Nussbaum, M.C. (2010). *Not for profit: Why democracy needs the humanities.* Princeton University Press.

Ofgang, E. (2021, November 12). *Why aren't professors taught to teach?* Tech & Learning. https://www.techlearning.com/news/why-arent-professors-taught-to-teach

Rifino, M., Matsuura, K., & Medina, F. (2014). The peer activist learning community: A peer perspective. In A. Blunden (Ed.), *Collaborative projects* (pp. 322–326). Brill Publishers.

Rivera, K.M. (1999). Popular and social transformation: A community-based approach to critical pedagogy. *A Journal for Teachers of English to Speakers of Other Languages, 33,* 485–500.

Robinson, T.E., & Hope, W.C. (2013, August 21). Teaching in higher education: Is there a need for training in pedagogy in graduate degree programs? *Research in Higher Education Journal.* https://files.eric.ed.gov/fulltext/EJ1064657.pdf

Sen, A. (1999). *Development as freedom.* Anchor.

Sawyer, J., & Rifino, M. (2020). Transforming educational alienation into collective agency in community colleges. In T.M. Ober, E. Che, J.E. Brodsky, C. Raffaele, & P.J. Brooks (Eds.), *How we teach now: The GSTA guide to transformative teaching* (pp. 223–237). http://teachpsych.org/ebooks/howweteachnow-transformative

Smith, D.G. (2020). *Diversity's promise for higher education: Making it work.* Johns Hopkins University Press.

Smith, A., & Seal, M. (2021). The contested terrain of critical pedagogy and teaching informal education in higher education. *Education Sciences, 11*(9), 476. https://doi.org/10.3390/educsci11090476

Stetsenko, A. (2008). From relational ontology to transformative activist stance on development and learning: Expanding Vygotsky's (CHAT) project. *Cultural studies of Science Education, 3*(2), 471–491.

Stetsenko, A. (2016). Vygotsky's theory of method and philosophy of practice: Implications for trans/formative methodology. *Educação, 39*, 32–41.

Stetsenko, A. (2017). *The transformative mind: Expanding Vygotsky's perspective on development and education.* Cambridge University Press

Stommel, J. (2014, November 17). Critical digital pedagogy: A definition. *Hybrid Pedagogy.* https://hybridpedagogy.org/critical-digital-pedagogy-definition/

Thompson, B. (2017). *Teaching with tenderness: Toward an embodied practice.* University of Illinois Press.

Venianaki, A., Timplalexi, E., & Dafermos, M. (2021). The medicalisation of learning difficulties through the prism of Bronfenbrenner's bioecological approach: The case of the remote and mountainous areas of Chania Prefecture. *Outlines. Critical Practice Studies, 22*(1), 138–180.

Vianna, E., Hougaard, N., & Stetsenko, A. (2014). The dialectics of collective and individual transformation. In A. Blunden (Ed.), *Collaborative projects* (pp. 59–87). Brill Publishers.

Woldeyes, Y.G., & Offord, B. (2018). Decolonizing human rights education: Critical pedagogy praxis in higher education. *International Education Journal: Comparative Perspectives, 17*(1), 24–36.

Yeager, D.S. & Dweck, C.S.(2012). Mindsets that promote resilience: When students believe that personal characteristics can be developed. *Educational Psychologist, 47*, 302–314.

Zembylas, M. (2022). The affective turn in educational theory. In *Oxford research encyclopedia of education.* https://oxfordre.com/education/view/10.1093/acrefore/9780190264093.001.0001/acrefore-9780190264093-e-1272

Critical Pedagogy of Humanities in Neoliberal Times

Sujung Kim

I was born and raised in a small farming village in South Korea. While preparing for my oral defense of my second qualifying exam, I received a call from my younger sister in South Korea. I was planning an ethnographic study of a Chicago community college to explore questions about the cultural politics that were embedded in institutional practices in shaping and reshaping working- and lower-middle-class Korean international students' social, class, and racial identities. In the middle of our conversation, my sister informed me that Dongju,[1] one of our cousins, had been discovered dead in his tiny room. Numerous young, poor factory workers who moved from the countryside lived in these small rooms in dilapidated buildings, called *dakjangjip* (chicken-cage units), which measure about 25 square meters. Like many of our friends and relatives, Dongju became a factory worker at Guro after he graduated from high school in our hometown. Guro, a part of Seoul, is the most representative industrial district in South Korea. I was three years older than Dongju, and we were born and raised in the same small farming village and went to the same elementary and middle schools. Dongju was not very talkative but was very kind. He always had a big smile on his face.

Reflecting on Dongju's life and death, as well as my other friends, who became factory workers or other low-wage precarious employees in South Korea, and my former co-workers at restaurants, gift shops, and a small office cleaning company in the United States, I had urgent questions about the role of education in our sociology-economic well-being. Besides the poverty that Dongju had suffered throughout his short life, like his parents and his two older brothers, it was painful to reflect on his stigmatized social identity as a child of poor parents, a low academic performer during his school years, and a factory worker suffering visible and invisible discrimination, as well as exploitation. In sustaining such unjust and violent bias and social, cultural, and economic class relationships, the ideology of meritocracy plays a critical role in blaming poor people for not being able to take advantage of upward social mobility (Ladson-Bilings, 2006; Nouwen & Vandenbroucke, 2013). Similar to the United States, the Korean state also accentuates the significance of high academic performance and postsecondary education, especially for students from poor families (Garrison et al., 2017). When this rags-to-riches, hard-working meritocracy myth is considered the most important strategy for the poor to get themselves out of poverty, it justifies and reinforces diverse forms of competition and leads people who cannot measure up to blame themselves (Garrison et al., 2017; Ladson-Bilings, 2006).

This myth of rags-to-riches meritocracy is reflected in many community colleges' missions, particularly in improving students' living conditions, where students' work skills or employability are discussed as the most crucial factors affecting students' ongoing poverty. Within this framework, community colleges are called to function as job training centers to develop students' work skills. In these dominant discourses, poverty is heavily portrayed as caused by one's personal ir/responsibilities rather than due to systemic issues.

This connection between power and personal responsibility has functioned as a dominant neoliberal ideology throughout the evolution of capitalism. Yet, the reality is often the opposite of what the myth would portray. I witness every day in Manhattan menacingly towering buildings and delivery personnel on bicycles dangerously navigating the traffic between the buildings as if they were juggling. This is explicitly captured in the film poster "Parasite" by Bergeron.

The film poster mirrors New York City's wealth built on the efforts of enumerable migrant/immigrant workers, and the reality that a significant number of native-born and migrant community college students are working in low-wage jobs. These community college students are also exploited in this inhumane mechanism. One of the community college students in the CUNY Humanities Alliance program, Juan,[2] captures this in a short film[3] about his own hopes and life as an undocumented migrant in the United States; he, as a worker-student, lamented, "Many times, we go to work and we work more than what we get paid for." In her column entitled *Reflecting Bong, Joon Ho's Movie "Parasite,"*[4] Moon Young Jo (January 15, 2020) lucidly elaborated that society acts as a parasite on the impoverished.

The reality is that a large portion of community college students come from financially precarious families but are entering community colleges with the belief that education will lead them to better lives. They are not only in associate degree programs but also enrolled in General Equivalency

Diploma (GED) programs, diverse certificate programs, and English as a Second Language (ESL) programs. For many of them, community college is their last opportunity to earn a postsecondary education or take humanities classes through which they can develop a critical consciousness about the historical, social, political, and economic mechanisms that reinforce social bipolarization and alienate people's stigmatized social identities. Researchers (Bickerstaff et al., 2020; Kim, 2021 Nussbaum, 2010) have pointed out that a significant percentage of students in associate degree programs are in the humanities, a much higher percentage than for four-year bachelor degree programs (Nussbaum, 2010, p. xiv). In this vein, community college humanities could be a critical arena to empower students, especially those from precarious social, cultural, and economic backgrounds.

As an immigrant from a working-class family, where the majority of my relatives and friends are only high school graduates and low-wage workers, I have been exploring more desirable community college education opportunities especially for underserved students, including working-class immigrants, (undocumented) migrants, first-generation college students, students of color, and LGBTQ students. In a neoliberal system that has a core ethos of entrepreneurial freedom that mobilizes individuals to act as self-responsible entrepreneurs who continuously engage in self-development to survive in neoliberal competition (Kim, 2017, 2018; Ong, 2006), it is crucial to question how community college education can empower marginalized people. Neoliberal ideology portrays one's unemployment as her failure in advancing her knowledge and skills rather than the precarious employment conditions in which even professional and high-skilled people are at risk of being laid off due to the fluctuation of the conditions of profit accumulation. I view such conditioned agency as a neoliberal subjectivity (see Kim, 2018) that facilitates students' tendency to consider that their daily lives are not related to politics, and to be reluctant to engage in political conversations in classrooms. In light of this conditioning, how can community college students become enabling agents, who can materialize a humane, democratic, and just society, where our own dignity is appreciated and secured, and through which we can lead a quality life?

With this critical question in mind, I aim to reconceptualize critical pedagogy within community college humanities. In this sense, critical pedagogy is a "moral and political practice" (Giroux, 2011, p. 5) that produces and/or disrupts authority, experience, and power supported by neoliberalism. In this chapter, I will discuss how neoliberalism affects the direction of community college education, and the significance of the humanities and the humanistic social sciences for community college students toward their empowerment and the promotion of social justice and democracy. Thus, this chapter addresses the questions related to class knowledge, power relationships, and students' social identities. While the choices we make in our classroom often feel miniscule compared to the immensity and pervacity of capitalism, pedagogy and class practices are a critical part of cultural politics. They can either function as sustaining oppressive neoliberal hegemony, or as challenging and transforming such violent social and political-economic mechanisms and practices. Even if our interventions are small, they are crucial.

First, we must examine the dominant cultural politics surrounding and influencing community colleges in the U.S. How do community colleges fit within the neoliberal system that sustains power stratification? Then, building on this analysis, I will recontextualize critical pedagogy in the humanities and humanistic social sciences so that we can, together, democratize community colleges' missions and leverage education as a public good to empower students and instructors as critical public intellectuals and agents of change.

Neoliberal Politics Instrumentalize Community College Students for Profit-Making

The way that we understand and talk about the mission of community colleges often prioritizes workforce development. While this is mostly done in a way that touts the power of community colleges to transform students' lives along a rags-to-riches mythology, the focus on education as an economic tool ultimately increases the dominant businesses' and industries' profit while strategically sustaining precarious employment conditions as part of neoliberal policies and politics (Kim, 2017). In this focus on economic mobility, the neoliberal political-economic system that we're all a part of identifies community college students primarily as a workforce, which contributes to the U.S. economic progress in the global market (Giroux, 2011; Kim, 2017; Levin, 2001, 2002). As such, in contemporary societies where the dominant neoliberal ethos prioritizes profit accumulation of the business and industry sectors, community college students are, in fact, instrumentalized as the means for profit-making.

Both the Republican and Democratic presidential administrations have highlighted the role of community colleges as producing a competitive workforce, and community college students, especially low-income and/or academically less competitive students, are seen as potential laborers who will fill the empty slots in the low- or lower-middle-sector jobs rather than as empowered citizens who can affect the ways in which the state needs to improve their dignity and quality life. For example, Trump asserted, "So we need vocational schools. Now they call them, a lot of times, community colleges" (Kreighbaum, March 23, 2018). Former President Obama (July 12, 2009) also stated,

> Our community colleges can serve as 21st-century job training centers, working with local businesses to help workers learn the skills they need to fill the jobs of the future... Now is the time to build a firmer, stronger foundation... that help us thrive and compete in a global economy.

Such neoliberal politics not only affect institutional policies, practices and curriculum design, but also operate as indirect governing mechanisms that restrict the public's imagination of community colleges as vocational centers. Such a unified public imagination mirrors the neoliberal policies enacted as a state apparatus, reinforcing the neoliberal ethos of increasing community college students' employability. This is often portrayed as a guarantee for students to make ends meet as the most significant mission of community college education, while injecting the ideology that an increase in the dominant economic forces' profits will bring improvements to vulnerable social groups' socioeconomic conditions. Yet, workers as well as researchers (Giroux, 2001, 2005; Standing, 2011) have indicated that under neoliberal conditions, the increase of dominant business and industry sectors' profits does *not* result in improvement in the vulnerable social groups' living conditions. Rather, their precarity continues to get worse. Standing (2011) noted,

> In the 1970s, a group of ideologically inspired economists captured the ears and minds of politicians. The central plank of their "neo-liberal" model was that growth and development depend on market competitiveness; everything should be done to maximize competition and competitiveness, and to allow market principle to permeate all aspects of life. (p. 1)

The idea that countries should increase labor market flexibility became an agenda for transferring risks and insecurity onto workers and their families. The result has been the creation of a global 'precarity,' consisting of many millions of workers around the world without an anchor of stability (Standing, 2011).

There are numerous stories that resonate with Standing's discussion. A laborer of Ssanyoung Auto,[5] which is headquartered in Pyeongtaek, South Korea, who had worked as a full-time employee but was laid off, reported,

> While going through the layoff, I saw the world where I've lived. It seemed like an eye-opening that I'd never known before. I learned that people will be scraping for a living more and more in this world. I felt pity for my children. (M.Y. Lee, June 30, 2018)

The laid-off worker, who developed his specialized skills in his job throughout the years, had fought for more than 10 years to return to his work, but he couldn't. He went from precarious job to precarious job and struggled to make ends meet. Under such situations, employees across the world increasingly become more vulnerable in terms of job security regardless of the level of their job skills.

Under neoliberal politics, the value of humanities and humanistic social sciences is evaluated only in terms of their impact on students' work skills. Reflecting the politicians' turn to decrease public funding for the humanities, Nussbaum (2010) asserted,

> But politicians, I said, have been increasingly calling for the defunding of the humanities. But politicians have short-term incentives, needing to win elections, which lead them to favor easily quantifiable gains (jobs and revenue) over gains less easily quantified (the quality of citizenship, the illumination to fit mind and heart). (p. xxi)

Such dominant neoliberal community college policies and politics silence the desire for community college education that supports social justice. A participant of the CUNY Humanities Alliance Conference commented that "the push toward merging (or confusing) the mission of 2-year institutions with vocational/career training institutions makes [education for social justice] a priority." Everyone in the collegiate system is trapped into this economic justification model, where programs and departments must demonstrate their economic value to students in order to be funded, and colleges must prove their economic value for students to enroll. Such a neoliberal frame problematically narrows and even distorts the missions of community colleges and the role of the humanities and humanistic social sciences. The invention of "soft skills" is a way to economically evaluate the humanities. All because students are in precarious economic situations to begin with. Moreover, neoliberal community college policies function as an ideology that justifies cultural politics that suppress the voices that advocate for community colleges as critical postsecondary institutions to respond to diverse students' and local communities' needs and empower students as democratic citizens who will advance social, political and economic justice.

Community College Education for Humanity, Justice, and Democratization

As discussed above, under profit-driven neoliberal politics, community college students, especially those from oppressed communities, are instrumentalized as the means for maximizing the dominant businesses and industries' profits. This not only reflects the ultimate dehumanization of these students at their current and/or future workplaces as disposable and replicable parts of the profit-accumulation regimes, but also undermines democracy by silencing diversified voices from decision-making positions (Darder, 2012; Giroux, 2011; Marenne, 2016; Kim, 2017). It is urgent to redirect the mission of community college education and redefine the value of the humanities to overcome neoliberal politics and conditions. Community colleges are often called the people's colleges, underscoring the role of community colleges in providing open access to students who encounter financial, social, and/or academic barriers to enter postsecondary education. I propose the meaning of 'community college as the people's college' is a counter term for the 'vocationalization of community colleges.' Thus, community colleges can be thought of as spaces that resist neoliberal propaganda while addressing students' diverse concerns and values, and enhancing their humanity. Furthermore, this new phrase would mean community colleges identify their students as democratic citizens who enhance their dignity in material aspects and social recognition, rather than viewing them as economic foot soldiers (see Kim, 2017).

Giroux (2011) pointed out that education is

> fundamental to democracy and that no democratic society can survive without a formative culture shaped by pedagogical practices capable of creating the conditions for producing citizens who are critical, self-reflective, knowledgeable, and willing to make moral judgements and act in a socially responsive way. (p. 3; also see Marenne, 2016; Nussbaum, 2010; O'Brian, 2016)

As the very agents who can reform neoliberal societies into more humane societies, students' dignity holds priority over profit-making. Moreover, community college students are in the process of making blueprints for their future ideals for a democratic public life. This denotes the shift from the economic-political power groups to the public.

However, along with the privatization of community colleges, which means missions and curricula aligned with the market logic and subordinate to their strategies, community colleges as a public sphere are at risk, where students can articulate their critical consciousness and cultivate their civic engagement (see Darder & Griffiths, 2016; Giroux, 2011, Marenne, 2016). The development of students' critical consciousness is one of the most crucial arenas that enable students to become the very agents to penetrate the social and power mechanisms that construct and reproduce their social identities as a means for profit accumulation (also see Aronowitz, 2009, cited in Giroux, 2011, p. 156; Kim 2023.

Civic engagement is a critical channel through which community college students can collaboratively voice their pursuit of social justice and more humanistic and democratic social changes. By positing new possibilities of community college education, we can disrupt the totalitarian modern citizenship project that imposes the existential value of citizens within the ideology of the profit-accumulation regime (Kim, 2017). Creating community college education for the public good includes expanding the public imagination to address what is a meaningful life, the purposes of community college education, and public cultures beyond consumerism, and to revitalize civic education, political agency and emancipatory citizenship (see Darder, 2012; Giroux, 2011; Kim, 2017). Establishing community colleges as a public sphere involves the collaborative process of making them a public space where institutional personnel and students are able to redevelop and advance the critical languages of political agency, civic engagement, and democracy.

Reconceptualizing the Role of Humanities

The notion that the humanities are in crisis indicates their vulnerability in the higher education landscape under neoliberal conditions rather than the crisis of the disciplines themselves (see Jung et al., 2000). The notion, in fact, indicates the emergence of the humanities in undergraduate education in terms of advancing students' work skills. The humanities crisis underlines the increasing tendency to devalue these skills in higher education curriculum by describing them as being comparatively less effective or related to the students' employability in comparison to science, technology, engineering and mathematics (STEM) courses. It can also be a tactic to underestimate the significance of humanities courses to students whose majors are in STEM.[3] David Rubenstein, cofounder of the Carlyle Group, remarked at the World Economic Forum that there was a tendency to overly focus on STEM at the cost of the humanities, even though "career-specific skills can be learned later" (Nussbaum, p. 2010, p. xviii). Thus, the notion of the crisis of the humanities shows how the business and industry sectors have dominant power in our valuation of the humanities within higher education.

Scholars, such as Davidson (2017), Giroux (2011), and Nussbaum (2010), contended that foundational and critical job skills such as critical thinking, reasoning skills, and new imagination are developed and advanced throughout the humanities. Moreover, regarding the rapid development in the sciences and technology, Giroux discussed (2011) how the humanities are responsible for expanding people's understanding of those areas not merely as practical knowledge and skills, but also as "sites of political and ethical intervention" in terms of a democratic present and future for all people (p. 173). H. Kim (July 4, 2019) discussed that it is impossible for the humanities themselves to be in crisis as long as human beings exist, as it is the discipline that explores and investigates ourselves as human beings. In his discussions on the significance of humanities and humanistic social sciences, H. Kim (July 4, 2019) explained,

> The place where I sense the fever of the humanities is outside (of campus) . . . . The audience at lectures invited by life-long education centers or companies are pressing. They had worked hard in their twenties, thirties, forties and up to their fifties. Then they suddenly encounter the question: "Am I living well? What does that mean to live a humane life?" Their companies don't take care of them . . . And, the period that they will live is getting shorter than the period that they have lived. In other words, they become more strongly aware of death. Then, such questions are more critical (to them). In this vein, I feel regretful about universities. The humanities include questions about what is living well and what it means to live a humane life . . . Everyone asks such questions at least once. Alas, why am I alive? What is this world? Such very foundational questions.

In his narrative, Kim highlighted the significance of pursuing the questions about the meaning of a quality life and humane life, which underlines the intrinsic value of the humanities (see also Nussbaum, 2010).

Yet, with the ascendency of neoliberal ideology that frames the value of higher education in terms of employability, students are deprived of opportunities to design and prepare for more enriched and meaningful lives. In the dominant discourses, students seem to be disciplined to believe that to live enriched lives, they should meet employers' needs. H. Kim (July 4, 2019) pointed out that higher education does not encourage students to think deeply about those questions. He explained,

> There are big differences between preparing for their future lives while pursuing questions such as "how can I live the right life?" or "how can I satisfy myself and when can I be happiest?" and just being interested in getting secured jobs at big corporations and making lots of money.

Moreover, the question about what is a good life includes "how they should live in society and face the political, technological, and existential challenges of our times" (Marenne, 2016, p. 10). The American Academy of Arts & Sciences (2013) states that the humanities are the disciplines that center on the question "what it means to be human." As such, the humanities need to also be exploring the meaning of *humanitas* (see also Nussbaum, 2010. In this vein, these questions are not limited to the students who major in the humanities, but for all students across all disciplines and areas. A respondent to the CUNY Humanities Alliance post-conference survey mentioned that the humanities can play a significant role in designing and reforming community colleges' core curriculum. Building on this comment, I propose that the humanities are critical in redirecting the focus of community colleges toward more comprehensive, humanistic and democratic blueprints.

As mentioned previously, particularly in the case of community college education, discussions on the significance of these humanizing, collectivist, and critical aspects of the humanities are not present; and, there are not sufficient examinations of the ramifications of identity development for community college students, and more broadly, on social and political mechanisms. The neoliberal conditions conceal the significance of such foundational questions in higher education curricula and subordinate the humanities to employability-centered discourses. While recognizing the value of community college education for its emancipatory possibility and democracy, the following section will revisit the concepts of agency, knowledge, and public intellectuals as a way of reconceptualizing critical pedagogy of the humanities in community college education.

Students as Agents, Knowledge Producers, and Critical Public Intellectuals

Under the dominance of oppressive politics that sustain unjust social mechanisms that enlarge social bipolarization, many scholars and activists emphasize the significance of agency (Carter & Castillo, 2016; Giroux, 2011; Sen, 1999; Tuitt, 2016). In *Development as Freedom*, Sen (1999) defined an agent as "someone who acts and brings about change, and whose achievement can be judged in terms of her own values and objectives" (p. 19). By engaging in critical pedagogy of the humanities, students are offered the political agency to overcome neoliberal governance that affects their desires, their ways of understanding, and their existential values, educational goals, and life. Giroux (2011) argued that pedagogy is inherently political "because it provides the capacities, knowledge, skills, and social relations through which individuals recognize themselves as social and political agents" (p. 16).

Researchers investigating the governing methods of dominant political and economic groups in neoliberal regimes discovered that they tend to utilize distant and indirect governing methods toward their citizens (Hoffman, 2010; Mitchell, 2006; Rose, 1993). To overcome these distant and indirect governing methods, critical educators and researchers point out the significance of students' critical consciousness and comprehensive understanding of the negative systematic impact on who they are and who other marginalized people are within the U.S. and across the globe (Carter & Castillo, 2016). Tuitt (2016) saw students as critical agents capable of deconstructing and reconstructing their understanding and narratives of their individual and group identities.

Critical pedagogy of the humanities recognizes community college students as public intellectuals, able to exert their agency in knowledge production and citizen activities from their perspectives and narratives, which are rooted in their lived experiences and different forms of knowledge. Moreover, they are willing to revisit and advance their knowledge through collaborative works with their peers and instructors in the class. Giroux (2011) noted that "everybody is an intellectual in that we all have the capacity to think, produce ideas, be self-critical, and connect knowledge [where it comes from] to forms of self and social development" (p. 25). Furthermore, students as critical public intellectuals are willing to connect their experiences, knowledge, skills and/or services with broader concerns about humanity, justice, and democracy. More importantly, they are able to develop and enact shared visions of their desirable futures.

In this vein, the critical pedagogy of the humanities pays attention to the relationship between knowledge and power. Apple (1993) argued that dominant power groups have the authority to legitimize certain groups' knowledge as official and exclude other groups' knowledge. In particular, under neoliberal conditions in higher education, Apple observed (1995) that in advanced corporate societies, the production of high levels of technical and administrative knowledge is valued more for economic expansion that is linked to the exploitation of workers and expansion of imperialism abroad. As discussed above, under these situations, I argue that even humanistic knowledge is valued for its profitability rather than "as an end in itself or for its emancipatory effect" (Apple, 1995, p. 118).

In her study of *Burning Man*, Chen (2016) proposed a question of how to foster members' authentic voices and engagement so that all participants are able to share their perspectives and participate in the world. These efforts can be understood as the practice of "decentralizing agency" (Chen, 2016, p. 72). In order to revisit oppressive knowledge and recover the possibility of knowledge as political action, Bourdieu (2001) states that agents, "who are part of the social world, have knowledge of this world" (p. 127) and can act on societies by acting on their knowledge of this world (cited in Giroux, 2011). Structuring humanities classes as critical public spheres where students are educated as critical public intellectuals allows them to engage in structuring their lived experiences and perspectives as counter-hegemonic knowledge.

Conclusion

In this chapter, I attempt to reimagine the role of community college education in creating more democratic and emancipatory social changes. Toward this goal, it is critical to examine the critiques of humanities in terms of the neoliberal cultural politics that subjectify undergraduate students as a means for profit accumulation. Understanding the crisis of humanities in terms of neoliberal politics' objectification of community college students as a means for profit accumulation is the first step. Critical pedagogy of the humanities highlights the institutional and ideological mechanisms that invalidate students' experiences and perspectives and/or silence them by imposing authority, objectivity, or professionalism in terms of knowledge onto them (Giroux, 2011).

Critical pedagogy in the humanities can work to shape classes into a critical public sphere where students and instructors examine the links between power, ideology, politics, common sense, and identity formation, and then to relink this knowledge to citizenry.

Humanities classes could foster students as critical public intellectuals who value and are engaged in structuring their lived experiences and perspectives as counter-hegemonic forces that will bring about new knowledge, emancipatory freedom and rights, social justice, and democracy (see Apple, 1993, 2019; Darder, 2012; hooks, 1994; Giroux, 2011).

Notes

1. This is a pseudonym.
2. This is a pseudonym.
3. Produced by another community college student who was a former fellow of the CUNY Humanities Alliance Program.
4. This is a part of my blog posting entitled, *Inclusive or Exclusive: Reimagining Classrooms as Transnational Spaces* at the Futures Initiative Website (https://futuresinitiative.org/blog/2020/02/06/inclusive-or-exclusive-reimagining-classrooms-as-transnational-spaces-2/) on February 6, 2020.
5. Ssanyoung Auto is one of the most representative automobile companies in South Korea. The company was sold to SAIC Motor Corporation Automobile in 2004. However, after the SAIC took the high-profile technological information from Ssanyoung, SAIC approved massive layoffs due to redundancies. The government executed violent repression on the workers who resisted against the redunancies (H. Jo, April 27, 2021). About 20 union members committed suicide after this process.

References

American Academy of Arts & Sciences. (2013, April). *The heart of the matter: The humanities and social sciences for a vibrant, competitive, and secure nation* (Report of the Commission on the Humanities and Social Sciences).
Apple, M. (1993). The politics of knowledge: Does a national curriculum make sense? *Teachers College Record*, 95(2), 222–241.
Apple, M. (1995). Cultural capital and official knowledge. In M. Bérubé & C. Nelson (Eds.), *Higher education under fire: Politics, economics, and the crisis of the humanities* (pp. 91–107). Routledge.
Apple, M. (2019). On doing critical policy analysis. *Educational Policy*, 33 (1), 276-287.
Aronowitz, S. (2009). *Reflections on class and educational reform.* Routledge
Bickerstaff, S.E., Brock, T., Moussa, A., & Ran, X. (2020). *Exploring the state of the humanities in community colleges.* Teachers College, Columbia University: Community College Research Center.
Bourdieu, P. (2001). *Language and symbolic power.* Harvard University Press.
Carter, D.J., & Castillo, B.M. (2016). Humanizing pedagogy for examinations of race and culture in teacher education. In F. Tuitt, C. Haynes, & S. Steward (Eds.), *Race, equity, and the learning environment: The global relevance of critical and inclusive pedagogies in higher education* (pp. 112–130). Stylus.
Chen, K. (2016). "Plan your burn, burn your plan": How decentralization, storytelling, and communification can support participatory practices. *The Sociological Quarterly*, 57, 71–97.
Davidson, C. (2017). *The new education: How to revolutionize the university to prepare students for a world in flux.* Basic Books.
Darder, A. (2012). Neoliberalism in the academic borderlands: An on-going struggle for equality and human rights. *Educational Studies*, 48, 412–426.
Darder, A., & Griffiths, T. (2016). Labour in the academic borderlands: Unveiling the tyranny of neoliberal policies. *Workplace*, 28, 115–129.
Garrison, U.L., Liu, W.M., Yeung, C.W., Park, S., Shaker, E., & Conrad, M. (2017). The meaning of hakbeol within the context of educational meritocracy and prestige among South Korean college students. *Journal of Asian Pacific Counseling*, 7(2), 105–121.
Giroux, H.A. (2005). The terror of neoliberalism: Rethinking the significance of cultural politics. *College Literature*, 32(1), 1–19.
Giroux, H.A. (2011). *On critical pedagogy.* Bloomsbury.
Hoffman, L. (2010). *Patriotic professionalism in urban China: fostering talent.* Temple University.
hooks, b. (1994). *Teaching to Transgress: Education as the Practice of Freedom.* Routledge
Jo, H. (2021, April 27). 'Ssangyongcha sataet'reul gieokasimnikkattte ... "MBjeongbuui gyeongjejeok sarinte" [Do you remember 'Ssangyoung crisis' ... "The MB administration's economic murder"]. Ohmynews. http://www.ohmynews.com/NWS_Web/Series/series_premium_pg.aspx?CNTN_CD=A0002738623

Kim, S. (2017). *Globalization of a U.S. community college and the politics of belonging in the time of upheaval: Remaking of race and class of Korean international community college students* [Doctoral dissertation, University of Illinois at Urbana-Champaign]. ProQuest Dissertation Publishing.

Kim, S. (2018). Voluntarily exiled? Korean state's cultural politics of young adults' social belonging and Korean students' exile to a U.S. community college. *Higher Education, 76*, 353–367.

Kim, S. (2023). *Space and Subjectivities: A US Community College as a Neoliberal Colonizing Space and the Shift of S. Korean International Students' Subjectivities* [Unpublished anuscript].

Kreighbaum, A. (2018, March 23). *Trump takes another swipe at community colleges.* Inside Higher Ed. https://www.insidehighered.com/news/2018/03/23/president-trump-holds-forth-community-colleges-campus-politics

Levin, J. (2001). Public policy, community colleges, and the path to globalization. *Higher Education, 42*, 237–262.

Levin, J. (2002). Global culture and the community college. *Community College Journal of Research and Practices, 26*, 121–14.

Jung, D., Park, Y., Yoo, J., Kim, C., Kim, J., Jung, D., Lee, G., & Choi, S. (2000). *Pyohyeonui inmunhak: Inmunhagui wigireul neomeoseo* [*The expressing humanities: Overcoming the crisis of the humanities*]. Saenggagui namu.

Ladson-Bilings, G. (2006). It's not the culture of poverty, it's the poverty of culture: The problem with teacher education. *Anthropology & Education Quarterly, 37*(2), 104–109.

Marenne, E.T. (2016). *The case for the humnities: Pedagogy, polity, interdisciplinarity.* Rowman & Littlefield.

Mitchell, K. (2006). Neoliberal governmentality in the European Union: Education, training, and technologies of citizenship. *Society and Space, 24*, 389–407.

Nouwen, C.N., & Vandenbroucke, A. (2013). Meritocracy, deficit thinking and the invisibility of the system: Discourses on educational success and failure. *British Educational Research Journal, 40*, 796–819.

Nussbaum, M.C. (2010). *Not for profit: Why democracy needs the humanities.* Princeton University Press.

Ong, A. (2006). *Neo-liberalism as exception: mutations in citizenship and sovereignty.* Duke University Press.

Rose. N. (1993). Government, authority and expertise in advanced liberalism. *Economy and Society, 22*(3), 327–356.

Sen, A. (1999). *Development as freedom.* Anchor.

Standing, G. (2011). *The precariat: The new dangerous class.* Bloomsbury Acemic.

Tuitt, F. (2016). Conclusion: Inclusive pedagogy 2.0: Implications for race, equity, and higher education in a global context. In F. Tuitt, C. Haynes, & S. Steward (Eds.), *Race, equity, and the learning environment: The global relevance of critical and inclusive pedagogies in higher education* (pp. 205–222). Stylus.

Interdisciplinary Questions that Inform Our Pedagogy: The Who, What, Why, and How that Guide Us

KAYSI HOLMAN

If you dive deep into a conversation with most college faculty about their research, you will undoubtedly receive, at some point, a ten-minute monologue about the most interesting, exciting, cutting-edge research topics that could capture the imagination of almost any passing person. Their excitement shows in the twinkle in their eyes, their intricate hand gestures, and the intonations of their voice. That excitement is catching! On the other hand, if you try to engage with college faculty about their *teaching*, they may confess that they developed their syllabus years ago and basically teach the same thing year after year. Mostly, faculty will groan when you ask about grading, and give some heavy eye rolls or stories of students-behaving-badly when asked about their students' participation. They may tell you about an interesting teaching trick that they use, or a bit more about the topic they teach, if you show some real interest. This difference in reaction can be explained in large part because in academia, we are rarely rewarded for masterful teaching, nor are we encouraged to spend much time innovating and iterating our designs to improve student engagement (Clauset et al., 2015; Milton, 1972; Hiatt, 1981; Schimanski & Alperin, 2018; Walczyk et al., 2006). Even though many of us originally became professors because of our desire to teach, most of us never received formal training in syllabus building or pedagogical development. Whether we are new to teaching or decades into tenure, we rarely talk to each other about our teaching methods or craft conference papers about our praxis. Most of us, who are eager to develop our pedagogy, individually seek out books, articles, or other learning opportunities to innovate out of creativity or necessity.

When considering the evaluation metrics for tenure-track faculty, Deans across the country highly value an instructor's classroom teaching, and yet the primary metric used to evaluate classroom teaching remains to be student evaluations (AAUP, 2014). It's no secret that the numerical scores from teaching evaluations are biased along race and gender, at the very least (Boehmer & Wood, 2017; De Los Reyes & Uddin, 2021; Huston, 2006; Kreitzer & Sweet-Cushman, 2022; Reinsch et al., 2020). And, students rarely fill out meaningful comments to give us more formative feedback than the numerical scores. By this system, the least substantive metric that we have for evaluating professors overall, which is steeped in racism and sexism, is often the only metric used to evaluate a professor's teaching skill (Huston, 2006; Kreitzer & Sweet-Cushman, 2022). It is a wonder that many of us are still motivated to spend our precious few hours available to innovate and cultivate new teaching materials and techniques, when it counts so little for us in terms of our valuation or credit toward tenure.

Those instructors with innate motivation to cultivate their pedagogy are dedicated to meaningfully engaging students and themselves in the classroom, whether or not that work is recognized, acknowledged, or appreciated. This chapter is meant to offer questions that can help move teaching praxis toward a more humanizing collectivist critical pedagogy. Before we jump into those questions, we need to discuss the setting and structural support we had in our pedagogical development program, which included graduate teaching fellows and tenure-track or tenured community college faculty. It was far from easy to develop this sort of intentional space for pedagogical development. It involved carefully negotiated collaboration with administrators, faculty, and graduate student instructors, from a graduate school and a community college.

The Setting, Structure and Resources

As mentioned in the introduction, the classroom activities and theories presented in later chapters are the work of participants in the CUNY Humanities Alliance program, a grant-funded partnership between the Graduate Center and LaGuardia Community College in The City University of New York, generously supported by the Andrew W. Mellon Foundation. In the first iteration of the program, from 2016 to 2020, our pedagogical development program included biweekly workshops with nine graduate instructors and five faculty for each year's cohort, as well as a formal mentorship where the graduate students would attend the faculty's courses in the first semester and have discussions with them about their course syllabus, activities, and pedagogical praxis. The authors in this text are just a small set of those participants. Each participant brought their own disciplinary and scholarly background to the theoretical underpinnings of their pedagogical work. Much of the intellectual and emotional labor of iterating and developing new pedagogical practices happened because the program made intentional space for pedagogical innovation. We had the unique opportunity to create and embed ourselves in an interdisciplinary learning community of mostly experienced pedagogues and be remunerated for spending time working together on teaching and learning practices, with a lot of staff and institutional support. These were the two structural elements that were foundational for our program's success.

First, it was an *interdisciplinary* learning community. The disciplines represented were in the humanities, broadly defined, and included: theater, fine arts, philosophy, linguistics, English literature and composition, creative writing, LILAC (Latin American, Iberian, and Latino cultures), Spanish, (cultural) anthropology, history, sociology, urban education, and (environmental and clinical) psychology. When we talk to other faculty about syllabus drafting and teaching, we often do so with folks in our own discipline, who have been teaching the same course that we are about to teach (Movahhed, 2021; Neumann, 2001). Disciplinary divisions within academia started as deep intellectual differences in the system of organizing knowledge, the questions being asked, and the approaches to answering those questions (Neumann, 2001; Siedlok & Hibbert, 2012; Starkey et al., 2023). In our global interconnected world, disciplinary boundaries also limit the queries and methodological approaches applied to a topic. However, the integration and reconciliation of knowledge and methodologies across disciplines are increasingly necessary to understand and navigate the complexities of our world (Frost & Jean, 2003; Siedlok & Hibbert, 2012).

Breaking disciplinary siloing and creating interdisciplinary connections can catalyze innovation in teaching practices, previously secreted away within disciplines (Frost & Jean, 2003; Siedlok & Hibbert, 2012). In my experience of witnessing an interdisciplinary exchange, there are amazing theater exercises that language professors could be using, and close reading composition exercises that history professors could be using, and debating historical document exercises that philosophy professors could be using. Within the humanities, at least, we found that most classroom practices were able to cross into other disciplines, and actually augment the pedagogical experience for the students. If you are creating intentional groups for instructors to continue their pedagogical development, particularly within the humanities (though I imagine this is true for STEM disciplines as well), it will be more generative to have multiple disciplines together at the same table.

The second key component to our structure was that folks in our program were actually remunerated for the time spent doing this professional development work. For some of you, this may be preaching to the choir, but for those in the back, we cannot simply *add* pedagogical innovation requirements on top of already overworked (or constantly burnt-out) folks. Graduate students are told to expect to work at least 60 hours a week (maybe as high as 80 hours a week) (Tippins, 2020). Many faculty, particularly newer faculty still striving for tenure and driven to take on committees and service work, have the same expectations laid out by their departments, whether the expectation is simply infused into the department culture, or more explicitly dictated (Flaherty, 2014). Graduate students that I have worked with all have coursework or dissertation work, a fellowship where they spend at least 15 hours a week, and teach at least one course as an adjunct to pay the bills, as well as other administrative work of maintaining their positions in the departments. All of that does not include work for conferences, publishing, professional memberships, and extracurricular organizations. Most graduate students are already working 60–70 hours a week, barely getting enough time to do laundry regularly, and are still only getting about 15 hours per week of actual work on their dissertations (Tippins, 2020). Meanwhile, they (and often their committees) are expecting at least 40 hours of work a week on their dissertation. Talk about a losing battle!

Community college faculty are in a similarly difficult position time-wise. In CUNY, faculty carry 4-4 loads, or 24 course hours a year (see Article 15 of the Professional Staff Congress CUNY contract, n.d. psc-cuny.org/cuny-contract). And, they still have department meetings, advising and mentoring students, office hours, committee work, not to mention actual scholarship and writing. Who has time to revise their teaching practices when you are teaching a minimum of four courses (100+ students) a semester on top of all the other expectations of your position?! For faculty in their first decade, who are still attempting to secure tenure, the expectations outside of teaching are incredibly impactful to future career outcomes (Schimanski & Alperin, 2018). When we talk about change in higher education, when we talk about transformative pedagogy, we must acknowledge the climate and expectations already existent in the environment. Given that workloads are already extremely overextended in higher education, we cannot simply *add* pedagogical development responsibilities and expect anyone to either be intrinsically motivated or have the bandwidth to innovate teaching practice (Brownell & Tanner, 2017; Furco & Moely, 2012). The same precepts of pedagogy apply to us as teachers as much as it does to our students; creativity and innovation take dedicated time, mutual support, and intrinsic motivation (Furco & Moely, 2012; Glor, 1998).

Accordingly, our program was not structured as optional workshops with no other benefit for participants than to better themselves and their teaching, nor was it a lunchtime series of talks that folks were expected to attend on top of their already overwhelming workload. Each graduate student instructor had a fellowship, specifically to do pedagogical work with us and to teach iterative sessions of the same course over two years. It still frankly was not enough time or money. One of the most frequent comments I received during the program was that graduate fellows needed more dedicated time to work on pedagogical structure, both individually and together as a group. Many of the graduate fellows still had to adjunct at least one other course each semester to pay their bills in addition to other graduate student expectations.

Similarly, each faculty member in our program was given a course release to mentor graduate fellows, and spend time engaging in pedagogical reflection and iteration with the graduate instructors. That was a *full* course release, three credit hours. Faculty understood and appreciated how rare of an opportunity this was to be given that time. And, at the same time, I had to have conversations with administrators each year to support and justify why we needed all three credit hours' worth of time for this project. Those conversations happened, despite the fact that we had grant money specifically designated for *full* faculty course releases.

Administrators probably do not want to hear this, but in order to run a program like ours, remuneration of the participants is essential! If monetary remuneration is not possible, course credit, both for graduate students and for faculty, is also an option. Obviously, we were extremely privileged to be financially supported by a foundation grant. We were able to create a small group of pedagogues from throughout the humanities and humanistic social sciences, and allow them space to support each other in iterating their pedagogical practice. We hope to share what we gained during that privileged experience with others, who do not have such support from foundations or institutions.

The First Iteration: The Setup of Faulty Assumptions We Started With

Graduate students often serve—during their graduate education and immediately after graduating—as adjunct and future faculty at both community and senior colleges in the area (American Federation of Teachers, 2020). And yet, most graduate students are not required to have any formal training to prepare them to teach, though they are put through an exhaustive gauntlet of research training (Gaff et al., 2003; Lail, 2009; Robinson & Hope, 2013; Ofgang, 2021; Walczyk et al., 2006). Mostly, graduate students are given teaching assignments for a general introductory course, given requirements to use particular textbooks or teach particular topics from the department they are teaching within, and sometimes given an example syllabus—often within 2–3 weeks of being assigned the course. For many unfortunate graduate students, that is the extent of their preparation to teach (Gaff et al., 2003; Ofgang, 2021; Walczyk et al., 2006). A lucky few are given training by their graduate school departments or a teaching and learning center, or are provided with a faculty contact at the institution where they teach. Given that training in pedagogical practice is at a minimum in graduate programs generally, preparation to teach in community colleges, specifically, is typically entirely absent (Lail, 2009; Robinson & Hope, 2013). I think we all—administrators, faculty and students alike—know that teaching is a craft that is not automatically learned through the process of writing a dissertation (Gaff et al., 2003; Ofgang, 2021; Robinson & Hope, 2013). Despite our individual experiences of learning how to teach as new instructors, institutionally and structurally, we still expect the ability to teach to result from being enrolled in a PhD program and having knowledge in particular subject matter (Gaff et al., 2003). The system of higher education teaching is a bundle of seemingly missed connections: if education is important, then instructors' teaching is important, then future instructors should be trained in teaching and given support, and instructors should be incentivized to continue iterating and improving their teaching by the meritorious systems we have in place for faculty evaluation. None of which are currently true in our current higher educational system.

The CUNY Humanities Alliance program was, to our knowledge, one of the first formal relationships between a graduate school and a community college. Its initial mission was to train graduate fellows to teach in community colleges, while increasing access to and engagement in humanities among community college students. The first iteration of the CUNY Humanities Alliance project was built as we were flying it, and nothing changed as much over time as the pedagogical professional development workshops. As the person who would run the program, I was hired less than three months before the graduate fellows would be onboarding with us. We had a Humanities Scholar and a Postdoctoral Researcher, who would later become incredibly helpful intellectual contributors, but they were not set to start until the same day the graduate fellows did. That summer, I spent numerous meetings with the Directors of the Center for Teaching and Learning at LaGuardia, the

Interdisciplinary Questions that Inform Our Pedagogy

Futures Initiative, and the Teaching and Learning Center at the Graduate Center to develop the goals and structure of the fellowship program, including what hours would be dedicated to pedagogical professional development spaces. Every responsibility was measured in a generous estimation of time, and every hour allocated was a careful negotiation of union-agreed rules and regulations for graduate fellow labor, obligations to LaGuardia and the Graduate Center, and the balance of what we hoped fellows would gain from the fellowship. We had to simultaneously navigate comparable negotiations and decisions about the time, resources, and expectations we could have for LaGuardia faculty mentors, who would be working closely with the graduate fellows.

Because the initial planning of the pedagogical professional development program was done in absentia of the graduate instructors and faculty participants, we undertook the work with a few mistaken assumptions: that the graduate fellows would be relatively inexperienced as teachers, that they would not be familiar with community college students, and that these professional development sessions were primarily *for* the graduate student teachers (blind to the participating faculty mentors outside of their contribution as expert pedagogues). We began by developing our learning goals, and came up with five main concepts that would drive the pedagogical professional development program: Knowledge of Community Colleges, Knowledge of Humanities, Pedagogical Experience, Professionalization, and Mentoring (full details in addendum 1). While this may be a good curriculum for folks first learning how to teach, we never got to test it out on a cohort of inexperienced graduate instructors.

Most of the graduate fellows had already taught in CUNY four-year colleges, which meant they had experience with syllabus building and intentional teaching practices. Some fellows had even adjuncted at CUNY community colleges. They had also done the work of connecting their scholarship to their discipline and the Humanities, broadly conceived. Our attempts at broader conversations about pedagogical theory were responded to by folks wanting to delve more into how that theory impacted their praxis, and how to take that theory and make it realized in their lessons and classroom activities. The fourth and fifth areas, of Professionalization and Mentoring, were intended to support graduate fellows with their own career aspirations and leadership development mostly in the second year of the fellowship, but fellows were already deeply concerned with preparation for their futures in academia or elsewhere, and how this program, this work, connected with that future. Nearly all of our carefully crafted curriculum had to be jettisoned and reworked entirely.

What we learned, very quickly in that first year, was that the specific topics we were discussing were not as helpful as who was at the table, what questions we were asking as a group about our teaching, and how we were opening space for folks to discuss their teaching praxis as an interdisciplinary group. Even though we shifted, and changed, and iterated again and again through the years, we always came back to a few key questions in this pedagogical space that were always generative and supported pedagogical development.

Key Questions to Answer about Your Teaching Praxis

In this section, I will be laying out the numerous questions that we asked ourselves and each other as we developed our pedagogy. These are not meant to be merely rhetorical, but to present opportunities for you to clarify your own thinking in approaching your courses.

Who Are You Teaching?

This may seem to be an obvious question, but it may be one of the most crucial questions. As the first iteration of the pedagogical professional development workshops reveals so well, without first knowing who is in the room, a curriculum—as well thought-out, structured and developed as it may be—will not appropriately engage the people in the room. One way of considering this question is to discuss, in general, who is part of the institution. Most campuses have a broad demographic research and information about the students in the institution. What is rarely considered within pedagogical development or academic institutions is the critical history of those demographics (Sciame-Giesecke et al., 2009): who has historically been included at your institution, and who has been excluded? Why did those exclusions exist? The people who have been present in the institution for the past 10–20 years have undoubtedly impacted the structure and content of what has been normalized by faculty as acceptable curricula (Freeman, 2018; Zalaznick, 2022). For example, if the institution has served primarily full-time students who do not work simultaneously to support themselves, then the reading assignment expectations will be higher than if the institution serves students who mostly work full- or part-time while going to school part- or full-time. If the racial demographics have been fairly homogenous, then the need to represent scholars and authors from various racial and ethnic perspectives may not have felt pressing in establishing the department curriculum. As institutions of higher education shift to respond to the urgent needs to create more inclusive curricula, the representation of knowledge and the way it is built into curricula, needs to shift as well (Freeman, 2018; Zalaznick, 2022).

Even more important to consider in shaping your curriculum and syllabus is who is specifically in each class. What is their own history: culturally, socially, structurally, economically? What experiences motivate their learning? Why are they enrolled in college? What do they hope to gain from *this* class? What pressures are they under, from society, family, friends, and themselves? How have they been systematically trained by the education system, and excluded by it? Do they suffer from imposter syndrome, or from a surplus of privilege? What experience and expertise do they bring into your classroom? How are their lives connected to the material that you're engaging in?

You may be curious: how are you supposed to know all of that before they take a step into the classroom? You're not. One of the most generative, engaging, and meaningful topics we discussed as a learning community during our pedagogical professional development sessions was precisely around how to get to know the students and how to integrate their interests, aspirations, and engagement throughout the semester, without imposing an unfair burden of vulnerability and self-disclosure on students. There are a lot of options. Some folks had strategies for the first day of class to gain a lot of information from students about their interests and what they may be excited to learn about. Some instructors had methods of modeling radically brave or vulnerable spaces to invite students to create a learning space in community with one another. Still others intentionally developed part of their syllabus along with the students in the first day or two of the course. And many instructors have methods of weaving students' experience, knowledge, interests, and aspirations throughout their semester-long goals. These are all excellent strategies for attenuating the rigidity of course structure, and intentionally restructuring to better engage the individuals in the room.

What Are You Teaching?

For almost every course taught in academia, there are institutional and department requirements. In an attempt to ensure that education was equivalent across multiple faculty, a group decided, recently or a long time ago, what topics, texts, structures, and evaluations needed to be included in the course. Whether antiquated or modern, rigid or flexible, helpful or detrimental, these are the rules, structure, and parameters within which you must work. Read them carefully. If you do, you will also find all the freedom that you still have within the provided structure—all the decisions that you do get to make.

If the requirements include a list of topics that must be covered, then: What historical lens are you using to teach the topics? Are you repeating centuries-old stories written through cultural domination, oppression, and exclusion, or are you trying to find meaningful ways to represent the other historical perspectives on the topic? What other topics should be added to the required list in order to present a fuller representation of the course focus overall? How much time is allotted for each topic? How are you structuring representation, inclusion, or exclusion by the way you frame, introduce, and discuss each topic? All too often, when we are asked to teach a course, we quickly adopt the most familiar authors, texts, and scripts, and miss interrogating the syllabus in this way. In our experience, class materials need to be revisited, frequently.

If the department or institutional requirements include specific readings that you must present during the course, then: What pieces of that text are the most valuable for the inquiry you wish to lead with your students? What other reading, examples, and activities need to be used to augment the required texts and connect the concepts to students' lives? Of the texts that you have deemed necessary, how naturally accessible are they to students? Students cannot always afford expensive textbooks that are designated as required reading for courses. Students do not always have access to a computer on which to do their reading. What will you do to make the texts truly *accessible* to your students?

If the department or institutional requirements include the modes of evaluation for students' learning (e.g., set quizzes, exams, essays), then: What information and practice are you providing in order to set your students up to succeed within those evaluative structures? We all know that exams and essays can create additional anxiety at the best and detract from learning at the worst. What scaffolding are you incorporating to be inclusive of different writing and thinking processes to create meaningful steps toward the final paper or exam? What systems and supports are you offering students—individually and as a group—to make learning more humanizing and collectivist? Are there ways to demonstrate fallibility and learning as a process? Are there ways to incorporate some peer review or group discussion in the process? What creative, generative activities can you include to support deep learning of the concepts that the exam covers? In what ways are you expanding the scope and curriculum to engage students in the knowledge production of the course? What are the outlets for creativity and generative design that students can contribute?

In addition to teaching requirements, most departments have also prescribed learning goals, which are a combination of skill-based and content-based goals, where skills are a heuristic or lens to interact with the world, and content centers a particular time, topic, or theme. While the wording of these course goals may lean more toward skill-based or content-based (e.g., "After students leave the class, students should know or understand this content" or "After students leave the class, students should be able to do this skill"), we are always engaged in both simultaneously. When we are faced with a content-based goal, we have choice in the way we frame that content, and the skills we utilize to teach that content. When we have a skill-based goal, we have a choice in the ways we model or teach that skill, and what content or material we use to utilize the skill. Accordingly, the questions that should be considered are a bit different for skill-based and content-based learning goals.

For skill-based goals, the questions are: What explicitly are the skills you hope that students leave the class with? Are the skills an unquestioned reproduction of potentially harmful, exclusionary, or oppressive heuristics? What is the legacy of these skills? Who decided on the utilization of these skills? What level of skill development are you expecting students to enter the course with? And what level of skill development are you hoping for them to leave the course with? How were those levels decided in the first place, and by whom? Are you hoping for specific types of improvements in skill development? What space have you created for students to use multiple modalities within skill development activities, or to question the way the skill has developed within the discipline? For example, if we consider critical thinking as a skill, depending on an individual's perspective, goals, and experience, their approach to critical thinking may be entirely different. For an employer, critical thinking may mean analyzing customers' needs. For a political theorist, critical thinking may mean employing agency in a democratic process. As faculty, we should understand our own perspective in defining and teaching these skills, particularly when they sound very neutral to us.

Additionally, what are the ways that students may already be engaging these skills in the world around them? Are you sure students don't already have these skills? For example, in educational settings, utilization of Black English is often seen as a lack of language skill, when it is a perfect example of linguistic elasticity, precision, and creativity. How do students define, develop, and utilize those skills in other contexts? What motivates students to learn these skills, in the classroom and outside of school? What are the students' goals and do they align with yours? What content or activities are you using to support students' engagement in those skills? How much of your course invites students to actively question and engage the skills? Our current heuristics or inherited skills undoubtedly have roots in imperialism, colonialism, misogyny, racism, etc. We must interrogate and question our own practice (and have students question the practice) rather than replicating and teaching the skills as is.

For content-based goals, the questions are slightly different: What is the content that you hope that students will leave the class with? Who decided what content to include and why did they make those decisions? Who is represented in that content? What voices, perspectives, or histories are excluded by that content? How does your syllabus recreate or disrupt those histories? What structure and encouragement are you providing to students to add content, or make choices in the content throughout the semester? How are you supporting students' disruption of, and contribution to, the discipline and the way we consider the content? For example, in a psychology course that requires ten main topics (but not specific authors) that you must include, focusing on non-western and feminist scholars will shift the way the history of psychology is taught. What critical thinking or analysis skills are you incorporating alongside required content or texts to support students in their critical engagement with the content?

Whose viewpoints are you specifically including and excluding? I wanted to separate this out from the overarching question of "What are you teaching?" because it is such a crucial question, and yet somehow gets missed. In every course, we are making decisions about what knowledge—historically, culturally, philosophically, heuristically—gets included in the classroom, and what is purposefully excluded from the classroom (Alim & Paris, 2017). It is an inevitability of being restricted in time; you can only include so much material in a semester. Knowing this, it is important to do this *meaningfully* for each course. What knowledge and perspectives are you privileging by your selection? What have you included and why is it more valuable than other forms of knowledge? What have you excluded and why was it expendable for this course? No one will ever be able to include everything, but creating those boundaries intentionally creates a moment where we have to reflect on what assumptions drive our own intellectual defaults.

Why Are You Teaching It to These Students?

Each student is on their own learning journey through higher education. No matter how many books we assign, or assignments we create, or essays we require, or tests we make students take, students have the ultimate agency in their own education. Students get to choose which major they want, which courses they take each semester, which professor they're going to learn with, and every single day, they decide how much time to commit to the work of each class. Faculty focus so much on accountability, on ways to grade and evaluate, ways that students have proven that they have learned a concept or skill. In many of those cases, students are simply proving that they are good at jumping through academic hoops. Education is a get-what-you-put-into-it experience; deadlines and requirements are only helpful when students want to have accountability checks in their learning journeys. One of the most powerful things we can do as educators is connect students to knowledge and methodologies they want to acquire.

How does the material you are covering or the skill you are trying to develop connect to your students' experiences and lived realities? How does it connect to their aspirations and future career goals? How does it connect with their culture, values and motivations as a person navigating the world? How does it connect to their other studies and activities, within the school and outside of it? As you begin the semester, with your syllabus constructed, you will not know the answers to those questions in their entirety, and yet those are the questions you should be seeking to answer alongside your students. Students are the ones who will fully understand and feel those connections, and it is our responsibility to ensure that those connections can happen.

Before the semester, consider what your own positionality is toward the course content. Why are you motivated to engage with it? What makes you curious and skeptical about the topic? How has it echoed or been contrary to your culture and values? How did it fit within your career goals and research aspirations? These are the starting places of your connection to the topic. By being transparent about that connection, you can begin structuring ways to begin exploring connections students may have with the content.

How Are You Teaching?

Most of this book is dedicated to this question of pedagogy. Indeed, there have been centuries of discussion about the way to teach, to share knowledge with each other. There are volumes to say here about classroom power dynamics, politics of space and voice, and the missions and values underlying higher education institutionally (Emdin, 2016; Freire, 1970; Giroux, 2022; hooks, 1994; hooks, 2003; McLaren, 2003; Shor, 1996; Thompson, 2017). The overarching question here is: how are you making intentional space for the engagement of the humans within the course? How are you recognizing and honoring students' engagement in their own educational journey? How are you inviting students to contribute their insights on the content and skills being centered by the course? Are you making choices for them about which class or content should be the most important in their lives? How are deadlines and scaffolding utilized during the semester? Are you assuming they are irresponsible or lazy unless they prove otherwise to you? We begin communicating these assumptions on the very first day, by the way our syllabus is constructed, what openness there is in the course for students to express their own engagement and knowledge, in the "policies" of the course, and in our demeanor with students.

How are you inviting and supporting students to question and critique the frameworks presented in the course based on their own lived experience and expertise (or are you discouraging it and trying to push through material)? How much are you making space for them to be knowledge producers alongside you during the semester, rather than simply reproducing your methods and style with a topic of their selection? How have you helped students to approach the texts presented in the course? What structure will you offer students to examine text presented in the course? Will you simply put down page numbers for them to read, or will you invite them to use a critical lens or close-reading practice while analyzing and engaging with the text? How have you communicated what the course material is, why they are engaging with it, how to approach it, and the goal of that work? How much deference and credit are you giving to all of the readings in your course? Are you demonstrating that they should be treated as unquestionable, or encouraging students to critically analyze how the text and information presented sits with their own knowledge or external expertise of the topic? How are you making space for students to uncover the motivations and power dynamics embedded in the class materials?

There may also be a lot of things you are implicitly teaching your students based on how you teach—starting with your syllabus and moving through the end of the semester (Zayac et al. 2010). How are you communicating expectations and accountability, for yourself and your students? How have students had the agency to come to an agreement with you about those expectations? How are you requiring, demonstrating and enforcing respect in the classroom? How are you managing speaking time and other modes of participation to allow everyone to have a voice? Are you teaching students that your voice is the most important one in the room? How are you providing alternate modes of "participation" to be inclusive of everyone? Folks who are neurodivergent, suffer from imposter syndrome, have diverse language backgrounds, have survived certain traumatic events, or just interact better in other modes than speaking up in front of a class, can still contribute meaningfully. When we limit "participation" to only one modality, we automatically privilege some and exclude others. How are you centering other modes of communication and engagement in the course materials? Are you teaching that the current white-centered, American, hegemonic, academic traditions way of communicating is the only valid way to express their ideas or communicate?

There are also some deeper and more reflexive questions here: How can you invite students to be critical and aware of the way evaluative structures are hierarchical and steeped in oppression of certain types and styles of knowledge? How can students critically engage with the power dynamics within the course itself? How can they challenge you in unexpected ways, and what kind of receptivity do they encounter when they do so? How does students' knowledge and experience each semester shift the way you understand the content or skills presented in the course? How does it shift your own scholarship and disciplinary orientation?

Conclusion

My goal in presenting these questions has not been to provide answers. Only you can do that for your own courses. These are some of the questions we asked ourselves and each other as we stumbled through a messy, intentional, and structured iteration process of redeveloping our courses each semester. They are questions you could use to reflect on your own work individually, or modify and use to create a professional development learning community (hopefully with some remuneration) to transform your pedagogy. Working across multiple disciplines made these broader questions—of who is included in the classroom, what material is being offered, why it is being offered, and how they're engaging in the material—more obvious (Frost & Jean, 2003). When you bring together a group of folks from different disciplines, research bases, theoretical expertise, lived experiences and positionalities, to offer questions, critiques, methodologies, and praxis to each other within a community, the taken-for-grantedness of assumptions and precepts within our disciplines are suddenly gone. Discussing and explaining our syllabus construction and pedagogical praxis required that we detail and make explicit underlying theoretical foundations, methodologies, and disciplinary histories. The interdisciplinary nature of the group made our differences in perspectives clear.

Speaking from personal experience as a student, being taught that the (frankly myopic) viewpoint that white men have had through the centuries is the unquestionable epitome of our disciplinary knowledge, is equal parts alienating, disheartening, and enraging. And yet, as someone who often builds curricula, I also know how hard it is to disrupt the pattern of passive acceptance of that curriculum that has been passed down to us through the generations. It requires utilizing all of the critical analysis, community-building skills, and pedagogical techniques to create a new direction and structure for a course. It is my hope that these questions offer a good check, a simple moment, where we can each keep ourselves honest about the work that we are engaging in while building our class curricula.

These are the foundational questions: Who are our students and what experience and perspectives do they bring with them? What are the outcomes that the students, faculty and departments want from each course? Why did the student choose this class on their educational journey and how does the material connect to them? How can you make a meaningful and humanizing experience together? They are the foundation of what teaching is, and yet, I find they are so often lost in a granular and rote process of making a syllabus.

References

Alim, S., & Paris, D. (2017). What is culturally sustaining pedagogy and why does it matter? In D. Paris & H.S. Alim (Eds.), *Culturally sustaining pedagogies: Teaching and learning for justice in a changing world* (pp. 1–24). Teachers College Press.

American Federation of Teachers. (2020). *An army of temps: AFT 2020 adjunct faculty quality of work/life report.* https://www.aft.org/sites/default/files/media/2020/adjuncts_qualityworklife2020.pdf#:~:text=This%20new%20report%20from%20the%20American%20Federation%20of,percent%20having%20trouble%20covering%20basic%20household%20expenses.%201

Bird, J., & Sinclair, C. (2019, August 1). Principles of embodied pedagogy: The role of the drama educator in transforming student understanding through a collaborative and embodied aesthetic practice. *Applied Theatre Research, 7*(1), 21–36. https://doi.org/10.1386/atr_00003_1

Boehmer, D.M., & Wood, W.C. (2017). Student vs. faculty perspectives on quality instruction: Gender bias, "hotness," and "easiness" in evaluating teaching. *Journal of Education for Business, 92*(4), 173–178. https://doi.org/10.1080/08832323.2017.1313189

Breuing, M. (2011, May 16). Problematizing critical pedagogy. *The International Journal of Critical Pedagogy, 3*(3). ISSN 2157-1074.

Brownell, S.E., & Tanner, K.D. (2017, October 13). Barriers to faculty pedagogical change: Lack of training, time, incentives, and … tensions with professional identity? *Life Sciences Education, 11*(4). https://doi.org/10.1187/cbe.12-09-0163

Buchanan, S.M.C., Harlan, M.A., Bruce, C., & Edwards, S. (2016). Inquiry based learning models, information literacy, and student engagement: A literature review. *School Libraries Worldwide, 22*(2), 23–39.

Clauset, A., Arbesman, S., & Larremore, D.B. (2015). Systematic inequality and hierarchy in faculty hiring networks. *Science Advances*, *1*, Article e1400005. https://www.science.org/doi/10.1126/sciadv.1400005

De Los Reyes, A., & Uddin, L.Q. (2021). Revising evaluation metrics for graduate admissions and faculty advancement to dismantle privilege. *Nature Neuroscience*, *24*, 755–758. https://doi.org/10.1038/s41593-021-00836-2

Emdin, C. (2016). *For white folks who teach in the hood—and the rest of yall too: Reality pedagogy and urban education*. Beacon Press.

Flaherty, C. (2014, April 8). *So much to do, so little time*. Inside Higher Education. https://www.insidehighered.com/news/2014/04/09/research-shows-professors-work-long-hours-and-spend-much-day-meetings.

Freeman, A. (2018, July 11). *Demographic shifts in higher education: The impact on teaching and learning*. Tambellini Group. https://www.thetambellinigroup.com/demographic-shifts-in-higher-education-the-impact-on-teaching-and-learning/

Freire, P. (1970). *Pedagogy of the oppressed*. Continuum.

Frost, S. H., & Jean, P. M. (2003). Bridging the Disciplines: Interdisciplinary Discourse and Faculty Scholarship. *The Journal of Higher Education*, 74(2), 119–149. http://www.jstor.org/stable/3648252

Furco, A., & Moely, B.E. (2012). Using learning communities to build faculty support for pedagogical innovation: A multi-campus study. *The Journal of Higher Education*, *83*(1), 128–153. https://doi.org/10.1080/00221546.2012.11777237

Gaff, J.G., & Pruitt-Logan, A.S., Sims, L.B., Denecke, D.D., & program participants. (2003). *Preparing future faculty in the humanities and social sciences: A guide for change*. Council of Graduate Schools, Association of American Colleges and Universities. http://www.preparing-faculty.org/PFFWeb.PFF4Manual.pdf

Giroux. (2022). *Pedagogy of resistance: Against manufactured ignorance*. Bloomsbury Academic.

Glor, E. What do we know about enhancing creativity and innovation? A review of literature. *The Innovation Journal: The Pulic Sector Innovation Journal*, Vol 3(1). https://innovation.cc/wp-content/uploads/1998_3_1_2_glor_enhance-create-innovate.pdf

Hiatt, D.B. (1981). Teaching from alternative frames of reference. In J.E. Christensen (Ed.), *Perspectives on education as educology*. University Press.

hooks, b. (1994). *Teaching to transgress: Education as the practice of freedom*. Routledge.

hooks, b. (2003). *Teaching community: A pedagogy of hope*. Routledge.

Huston, T.A. (2006). Race and gender bias in higher education: Could faculty course evaluations impede further progress toward parity? *Seattle Journal for Social Justice*, *4*(2), Article 34. https://digitalcommons.law.seattleu.edu/sjsj/vol4/iss2/34

Kreitzer, R.J., & Sweet-Cushman, J. (2022). Evaluating student evaluations of teaching: A review of measurement and equity bias in SETs and recommendations for ethical reform. *Journal of Academic Ethics*, *20*, 73–84. https://doi.org/10.1007/s10805-021-09400-w

Lail, A.A. (2009). Are new faculty prepared to teach diverse learners? *Inquiry, 14*(1), 29–40. https://files.eric.ed.gov/fulltext/EJ833917.pdf

McLaren, P. (2003). *Life in schools: An introduction to critical pedagogy in the foundation of education.* Allyn & Bacon.

Milton, O. (1972). *Alternatives to the traditional: How professors teaching and how students learn.* Jossey-Bass.

Movahhed, S.S. (2021). Disciplinary culture and effective teaching: A cultural anthropological study. *Higher Education Studies, 11*(2), 179–185.

Neumann, R. (2001). Disciplinary differences and university teaching. *Studies in Higher Education, 26*(2), 135–146. https://doi.org/10.1080/03075070120052071

Ofgang, E. (2021, November 12). *Why aren't professors taught to teach?* Tech & Learning, https://www.techlearning.com/news/why-arent-professors-taught-to-teach

Reinsch, R., Goltz, S.M., & Hietapelto, A.B. (2020). Student evaluations and the problem of implicit bias. *Journal of College and University Law.* https://jcul.law.rutgers.edu/wp-content/uploads/2020/01/jcul-vol45_issue1-final.pdf

Robinson, T.E., & Hope, W.C. (2013, August 21). Teaching in higher education: Is there a need for training in pedagogy in graduate degree programs? *Research in Higher Education Journal.* https://files.eric.ed.gov/fulltext/EJ1064657.pdf

Schimanski, L.A., & Alperin, J.P. (2018, October 5). The evaluation of scholarship in academic promotion and tenure processes: Past, present, and future. *F1000Res, 7,* 1605. https://doi.org/10.12688/f1000research.16493.1

Sciame-Giesecke, S., Roden, D., & Parkison, K. (2009). Infusing diversity into the curriculum: What are faculty members actually doing? *Journal of Diversity in Higher Education, 2*(3), 156–165. https://doi.org/10.1037/a0016042

Siedlok, F., & Hibbert, P. (2012). *Interdisciplinary collaborative research: Course reader (2017).* https://www.researchgate.net/publication/317544578_Interdisciplinary_Collaborative_Research_Course_Reader_2017

Shor, I. (1996). *When students have power: negotiating authority in a critical pedagogy.* University of Chicago Press.

Starkey, L., Yates, A., de Roiste, M., Lundqvist, K. & Ormond, A. (2023). Each discipline is different: teacher capabilities for future-focussed digitally infused undergraduate programmes. *Educational Technology Research and Development, 71,* 117–136. https://doi.org/10.1007/s11423-023-10196-2

Tippins, S. (2020, June 9). *What is the life of a PhD student really like?* Beyond PhD Coaching. https://www.beyondphdcoaching.com/dissertation/life-of-a-phd-student/

Thompson, B. (2017). *Teaching with tenderness: Toward an embodied practice.* University of Illinois Press.

Vasey, C. & Carroll, L. (2014). How do we evaluate teaching? Findings from a survey of faculty members. *American Association of University Professors.* https://www.aaup.org/article/how-do-we-evaluate-teaching

Walczyk, J.J., Ramsey, L.L., & Zha, P. (2006, December 1). Obstacles to instructional innovation according to college science and mathematics faculty. *Journal of Research in Science Teaching.* https://onlinelibrary.wiley.com/doi/10.1002/tea.20119

Zalaznick, M. (2022, November 7). *Student demographics: Big changes are forcing reinvention on campus.* University Business. https://universitybusiness.com/student-demographics-changes-force-reinvention-campus/

Zayac, R., Poole, B., Gray, C., Sargent, M., Paulk, A., & Haynes, E. (2010, September 24). No disrespect: Student and faculty perceptions of the qualities of ineffective teachers. *Society for the Teaching of Psychology, 48*(1).

Addendum 1
Original Graduate Teaching Fellows Professional Development Plan

Graduate Teaching Fellows Background

The Graduate Student Teaching Fellows will be appointed in three cohorts of nine Teaching Fellows with two-year terms for a total of 27 Teaching Fellows over the four-year grant period. A model of the phase-in structure would look like this:

Year 1: 9 Teaching Fellows in Cohort A = 9 Teaching Fellows
Year 2: 9 Teaching Fellows in Cohort B, plus 9 Teaching Fellows in Cohort A = 18 Teaching Fellows
Year 3: 9 Teaching Fellows in Cohort C, plus 9 Teaching Fellows in Cohort B = 18 Teaching Fellows
Year 4: 9 Teaching Fellows in Cohort C = 9 Teaching Fellows

Semester 1 (Fall 2017): Graduate Fellows shadow master faculty mentors in courses taught at LaGuardia Community College. Fellows will be expected to participate in a two-day intensive institute at the beginning of the semester, monthly workshops hosted by LaGuardia Community College, and regular fellows' meetings at the Graduate Center.

Semester 2 (Spring 2018): Graduate Fellows will be assigned to teach their own section of the LaGuardia course they shadowed in Semester 1. Monthly professional development seminars continue, as well as regular fellows' meetings. Fellows' attendance at and participation in these meetings are required in this and subsequent semesters.

Semesters 3–4 (Fall 2018, Spring 2019): Students will continue to teach one course per semester. They will become mentors in the professional development workshops for a new entering cohort of Humanities Alliance Teaching Fellows, and share their reflections about their experiences with a broader audience at the Graduate Center.

Throughout all semesters, Graduate Fellows will be writing public reflections on their work, attending events and meetings to gain exposure to the LaGuardia departments, and collaborating with Humanities Alliance leadership and staff on research about the program. Fellows will also have opportunities to participate in additional professional development opportunities open to the GC and CUNY community.

Goals & Objectives

The following is a structured set of goals and objectives for the Graduate Teaching Fellows during their two-year terms. The motivation behind these goals is to provide the Teaching Fellows with all the information deemed necessary for teaching the Humanities in a Community College setting; train the Teaching Fellows in the most effective student-centered teaching methods; and prepare Teaching Fellows for future careers as Humanities scholars and faculty.

Each of the goals will be introduced in the Institute, and will then be threaded through, experienced, and formalized in professional development workshops, as well as through classroom practice, mentoring relationships, exposure to the First Year Seminars, and humanities enrichment experiences. At the Institutes and workshops, diverse individuals will be responsible for presenting or leading workshops on the segments outlined below.

Semester 1 (Fall 2017)

Knowledge of Community Colleges

Some of the Graduate Teaching Fellows previously graduated from Community Colleges, and even LaGuardia Community College specifically. Others have no personal exposure to Community Colleges. Because the mission, institutional structure, and demographics of LaGuardia Community College are so unique, it is important for any faculty teaching there to have a good understanding of the institution as a whole.

Many of the objectives listed below are also applicable to the "Knowledge of the Humanities" and "Pedagogical Experience" goals, but have been placed here to reduce duplication.

- History of community colleges
  - What it means to be a Community College student now (as opposed to historically)
  - *Prompts for thought:*
    - *What would happen to our country if community colleges were shut down?*
    - *What cultural capital do community college students enter the classroom with? How do you imagine humanities being important for them?*
- Institutional Identity and Mission
  - History of CUNY
  - History of LaGuardia
    - Institutional Mission
      - What was the rationale for creating LaGuardia Community College? What are the historical underpinnings?
      - Humanities and the imaginative possibility for students

- Institutional Structures and Objectives
  - Core Competencies and Assessments ("Outcomes")
  - AA, SA, and ACE (ged, clip, etc.)
  - Developmental education (math, reading, writing)
  - Advisement and First Year Seminar (FYS)
  - College Policies
  - Student goals and outcomes—What percentage of students want to transfer to a senior college? What percentage achieve this goal?
  - Transfer policies
  - Labor structures—TT/adjunct faculty, average course load, number of courses taught across the system, etc.
  - Faculty experience: T&P, balancing teaching/research/service

Knowledge of LaGuardia Community College Students
- Demographic data and identities
  - More than 100 Native languages—ELL/ESL proficiency
  - Stigmas/difficulties that they face: domestic violence, incarceration, hunger,
  - Challenges with Math gateway course
- Teaching in a LaGuardia classroom, and strategies for making space in classrooms for student voices
- Digital Literacies of Community College students
  - Vocational needs
  - E-Portfolios
  - Wordpress
  - Other sites -- where are community college students already engaging (Mobile ready)

Knowledge of the Humanities
Many of the objectives listed below are also applicable to the "Knowledge of Community Colleges" and "Pedagogical Experience" goals, but have been placed here to reduce duplication.
- History of the Humanities
  - Alternate definitions of the Humanities
  - History of the Humanities: tradition and present
  - Disciplinary identity and situation within the Humanities
  - *Prompts:*
    - *What is your understanding of the Humanities?*
    - *How do you think the Humanities has been / is being reconceptualized over time?*
    - *How is your discipline situated within the history of the Humanities?*
    - *How is your subject-matter situated within the Humanities? Does it bridge other disciplines? Are there ways for us to intentionally be more interdisciplinary?*
    - *What do you imagine doing in your classrooms to connect students to the humanities?*

- *What sort of extracurricular activities (for Humanities Classes or the Humanities Cohort) can you imagine might connect students to the Humanities?*
- Humanities at LaGuardia Community College
  - How Humanities are understood and communicated institutionally
  - Current classroom practices in Humanities disciplines
  - Interdisciplinary programs at LaGuardia Community College
- Public Humanities and Public Scholarship
  - Being able to succinctly communicate about the Humanities
  - Performing public scholarship
  - Encouraging students to engage in public scholarship

Graduate Teaching Fellows will gain experience with these objectives during:
- Institute, August 25–26, 2016
- Professional Development workshops
- Experience shadowing mentors
- Mentoring relationship with their faculty mentors
- Mentoring relationship with Humanities Student Leaders
- Exposure to first-year seminars
- Attendance at Department meetings
- Engaging in Humanities Enrichment activities with Humanities Student Leaders

Pedagogical Experience

Many of the objectives listed below are also applicable to the "Knowledge of Community Colleges" and "Pedagogical Experience" goals, but have been placed here to reduce duplication.

- Reflecting on Your Teaching Methods
  - Teaching your own research in a public forum (before teaching in a course), and being able to describe other people's research
  - Presentations/Public speaking
  - Educational Autobiography (which will later be workshopped into the Teaching Philosophy)
  - Using educational technology
- Purposeful/Intentional Teaching
  - Syllabus Creation
  - Design for educational activities
  - How to encourage student voices in classroom
  - How to Integrate Student Interests
  - Integrating families/communities into learning
  - Understanding cultural differences
  - Assessment
    - Grading efficiencies

- Teaching Structure
  - Certification
  - Teacher Observations
  - Attendance policies & How to take attendance
  - Transfer and Pathways (and Majors)—how do your classes fit in?
  - WIT
- Digital Literacy
  - LaGuardia Digication ePortfolio training
    - Editing content (e.g., posting syllabi, posting summative reflection)
    - Helping students with their "About Me" on e-Portfolios
  - Graduate Center Wordpress training
    - Posting monthly blogs (with images and potentially videos)
    - Creating a subsite (course website)
  - Hybrid/Online Teaching (probably a bootcamp)

Professionalization
- Market Readiness
  - CV
  - Teaching Philosophy
  - Syllabuses
  - Writing sample
  - Teaching Observations (from Mentors)
  - Teaching Demo
  - Giving developmental advice
  - Student evaluations/letters
  - Interview Skills (in different contexts)
- Understanding Departments
  - Attending Department Meetings
  - Exposure to First Year Seminars
  - Opportunities for Community College jobs and what departments look for
  - Shifts in space over time
  - Handling conflicts with students and other scholars
  - Requirements of Service
- Professional online presence
  - Website of one's own
  - Contribute to Public Scholarship on Community Platform (i.e., blogging)
  - Social Media presence
  - Email Professionalism
- Scholarship
  - Writing Journal Articles
  - Presenting at Conferences
  - Helping to produce/develop public events

Mentoring

- Teaching your skills to others
  - Peer-to-peer mentoring
  - Peer mentoring (with incoming cohort)
- Mentoring College students
  - In Classes (LaGuardia Advisement program)
  - Selection/identification of the Humanities Cohort
  - Mentoring the Humanities Cohort

A Toolkit for Questioning Everything: Collaborative Deep Reading for Critical Thinking

DAVIDE GIUSEPPE COLASANTO

As a historian, teaching for the first time a new course outside of my discipline seemed quite daunting at the beginning. What would I say to my students? What would they expect? Would I be able to spark their curiosity and learn with them something unexpected at the end of the semester? These sorts of questions were floating in my mind as I was approaching the first course of Critical Thinking I had ever taught. Critical Thinking has traditionally been taught and identified as a philosophy course, especially for its focus on the reasoning process and its strong logic component. However, at LaGuardia Community College, the course is often taught by professors from varying humanities disciplines. As a short introduction, these are some of its core components: definition of community, knowledge-making process, meaning of perception and belief, practices of argumentation, developing problem-solving skills, analyzing language, and building self-awareness of one's own reasoning and creative processes. The following is the official description from LaGuardia Philosophy program in the Humanities department:

> The goal of this course is to help students become thoughtful and effective critical thinkers, applying the intellectual abilities and specialized reasoning skills to themselves and their society. Students will also learn to identify, evaluate, and solve problems on an individual and societal scale. They will gain self-awareness and a deeper knowledge of the ways in which they interact, change, and are changed by society in order to analyze their role as responsible citizens in a globalized world. (LAGCC—Philosophy Courses Offered, n.d.)

I was lucky enough to observe an already experienced educator who kindly introduced me to the specificities, structures, and methods of a philosophy course. The first semester as a CUNY Humanities Alliance Fellow was a full dive in critical pedagogy. It was divided into two major activities: weekly workshops with other fellows and instructors on pedagogy, and observations of the class I was going to teach in the spring semester. I jumped into this course and attended almost all classroom hours. It was an incredible chance for me because I was able to see how an experienced educator was teaching this course while, at the same time, I could experience it as a student. Finally, I could discuss and exchange on what I learned with other committed educators during our weekly workshops.

And then there were the students: I had never taught in a community college. Something was different from my previous teaching experience. It seemed as if their questions had a tone of urgency, of passionate and genuine curiosity, all along with a sense of deep awareness of life's struggle, a living testimony of the harshness and creativity of New York City (NYC). It was an exciting discovery, a breath of fresh air in my academic life, a new human and intellectual journey.

But still, when it was my turn, when I was on my own, when the weight of 60 eyes would gaze at me, when the fear of letting down the intellectual interest of my students was rising, when the anxiety of being a stale, boring facilitator lurked into my mind, I felt lost. Of course, I had concrete examples of the kinds of lessons I could provide, and there was a textbook always ready for reference. But I wanted to *feel* the course, to make it fit better with my teaching persona (who I am as an instructor/facilitator) and positionality (my identity in terms of gender, sexuality, and race), in order to offer a more genuine and passionate input to my students. It was at this moment that critical pedagogy principles of subjectivity of knowledge, co-creating learning spaces with students, and students' agency in learning helped me a lot in understanding how to move forward (Davidson, 2017; Foucault, 1966; Freire, 1985; hooks, 1994; Kim, 2021; Woldeyes & Offord, 2018). It was essential to critically assess who my students were, how my teaching persona could interact with them, and how I could question the content of the course itself in order to develop a student-centered inclusive teaching environment.

I started thinking about my previous teaching experience, which gave me a first exposure to the incredible diversity of CUNY students. It was not hard for me to feel at home. For the past ten years, while keeping a strong link with my place of birth (Italy) and culture, I have lived in different foreign countries. The feelings of displacement and hardship along with excitement for new possibilities have always accompanied me in my journeys. It is with this awareness that I tried to present myself to NYC and LaGuardia students. Because many of them are multilingual and have multicultural backgrounds,

I have always found it easy to connect with them and we often talked and exchanged stories on our personal and family belongings.

In addition, passing as a white cis-gender male, I was very aware of how I could easily reiterate an unbalanced power dynamic within the classroom. Therefore, my stance was always to present myself as a facilitator, who is in the classroom not to impart knowledge upon, but to create it with the students (Darder, 2012; Freire, 1970; hooks, 1994). My objective was to make apparent that the methods, ideas, and values that I was presenting were not the ultimate truth, that they had to be questioned as well, and that it was upon the students themselves to decide how to best adopt, or not, the course's principles.

I decided to start from what I already knew, from my experience as a historian. And what I had to do became quite suddenly much clearer. To think critically means to intentionally explore our thinking process in order to "understand and make more intelligent decisions" (Chaffee, 2019). It involves self-awareness, analysis, questioning, researching, argumentation, and creativity. Similarly, as a historian I investigate the past in order to track change over time and to understand how we came to be the way we are. I was applying the same skills involved in critical thinking: analyzing primary sources, researching their specific historical context, and elaborating an overarching argument that could answer a specific question about our present state. But I had internalized this process to the point it became invisible. Thus, my initial disorienting sensation when I had to reflect on how to teach this course.

Critical thinking adds a deeper layer of awareness and clarity to any cognitive activity. It makes evident the structure governing reason and how we can make it more effective. It is a set of skills and principles that can aid any intellectual endeavor. According to Birjandi et al. (2019):

> In any field of knowledge there are dissenting ideas and theories proposed by prominent scholars. Young scholars are expected to decide which approach to adopt as their own and develop their own unique perspective. This necessitates the development of the ability to think critically about ideas they come across in their fields of study. Instead of memorizing some unlinked facts to be reproduced in a test or exam, learners are expected to be involved in critical analysis of ideas. (p. 35)

I could see critical thinking as a guide, a method to question everything, even the questioning process itself. Thanks to this realization, I could now see my history training as implicit critical thinking training. Therefore, I could use the methodologies I developed in researching the past also in the new critical thinking course. In addition, I could now address more directly the evolving and unresolved issues the society we live in is facing, such as the impact of increasing economic and racial inequality in modern societies (Giroux, 2005).

In this chapter, I present an assignment originally developed in my past history courses that I was able to adapt to teach key critical thinking skills. I will clarify the learning objectives driving the class design, the humanizing pedagogical principles applied, and the assignment's scaffolding (the different concrete steps instructors could adopt to implement the assignment). The conclusion returns to this need to think more intentionally about the broader and creative application of one's own academic disciplinary practices, the invaluable insights graduate students can learn by teaching in community colleges, and the relevance of critical pedagogy in guiding any teaching endeavor.

Primary Sources 101

Analytical skill—dissecting and breaking a complex piece of information into smaller parts in order to make it more understandable—is crucial to critical thinking and to any cognitive activity (Chaffee, 2019). It is also crucial for students to recognize the significance of their agency, and to create broader social change. All human beings possess different levels of analytical skills. However, we often lack awareness of our analytical abilities. Critical thinking helps develop this consciousness and provides a structural approach and guidance to the analytical understanding of any piece of information (Chaffee, 2019). Chaffee (2019) defines critical thinking as "the ability to think clearly and rationally, understanding the logical connections between ideas" (p. 6). While critical thinking goes beyond textual understanding, to include creative and ethical thinking as well (Birjandi et al., 2019), the foundation of critical thinking begins with analyzing arguments, evaluating the evidence available, and assessing claims for validity and reliability. Starting from these assumptions, I was facing the question of how to communicate this awareness to my students in a direct and concrete way. That is when my historical training came into help.

The raw and essential material historians use are primary sources: without them nothing is possible. Within the discipline, primary sources are any piece of information that was generated at the time under scrutiny and that provide direct knowledge about the historical topic researched (Brophy et al., 2016; see also Kishlansky & Victor, 1995). *Sources of the West: Readings in Western civilization*). Primary sources could be anything, from a newspaper article to a video clip, from an autobiography to a public speech (Brophy et al., 2016). It is by putting together all the primary sources that the interpretation of the past comes to life. Like puzzle makers or detectives, historians try to explain the past with the evidence they can find.[1]

What if these primary sources are not about the past? What if these sources come from our time and society? The method for understanding and interpreting them would not change at all. This is why the way historians look at primary sources can be applied to teach critical thinking.

A main goal of the critical thinking course is to raise awareness and understanding of analytical thinking. A way to reach it is to design a pedagogical activity with the following learning objectives: provide an accessible and versatile model of analysis; show students how to utilize "deep reading" (Bean, 2011); expose them to different kinds of primary sources; and develop an overarching explanation of a primary source in connection to other sources and their broader context. This progression allows the students to move from a basic phenomenological understanding of the text itself, to a critical social understanding of the politico-historical context of knowledge production (Birjandi et al., 2019; Chaffee, 2019).

The whole activity is centered around practicing 'deep reading' of primary sources in incremental steps. It is divided in two major phases: the first one, done on an individual level, is focused on the analysis of one source; for the second phase students work in groups and are exposed to a larger number of sources. Overall, it is a low-stakes assignment done in the class and it is not graded, which allows students to feel less anxious and to gradually approach a primary source analysis, an exercise most of them have rarely done before.

The very starting point of the whole activity is a list of questions designed to accompany the reader into a deeper understanding of the text. The list is based on questions found in history collections of primary documents, usually used by history professors as aid materials for their courses (Brophy et al., 2016). In most cases, the prefaces of these collections provide ideas, suggestions, and tips on how to practice deep reading of primary documents. They all stem from the classical journalist rule: who, what, when, where, why, and how. But it is possible to enrich this basic line of analysis by organizing the questions on an incremental reading level. Here is an example of the line of questioning I give to my students to answer as part of this first individual layer of analysis:

1st Reading Level: understand what your source is
- Who wrote the document?
- What is the intended audience?
- What is the storyline?

2nd Reading Level: get yourself inside the text
- What type of source is this?
- Why was this source produced?
- What are the author's basic assumptions and biases?

3rd Reading Level: interpret and produce knowledge
- Can I believe this document?
- What can I learn about the society that produced this document?
- What does this document mean to me?

The first level of questioning provides a quick framing of the text. It is focused on grasping its author, intended audience, and its basic message/narrative. This basic level of information is often something we take for granted when quickly scrolling through information, and yet making this explicit, it is necessary for any reader to begin the critical thinking process. The second level deepens the readers' understanding by fostering an inquiry on the nature of the source, the reasons why it was produced, and the author's assumptions and biases. This invites students to explore the subjective nature of the primary source, questioning how it fits in a larger schema of societal motivations and power dynamics. The final level guides the student to an original interpretation of the source. This is achieved by expressing a judgment on the reliability of the source, the connections to its context, and finally how the document resonates with the reader. While encouraging students' agency and voice in creating their own scholarly and grounded explanation of the primary source, this activity also highlights the significance of critical thinking in interpreting any text. By progressing from simple questions of who wrote the primary source, to understanding what goals those authors had, and how that artifact fits into our political landscape, students engage in this practice of questioning everything.

Phase 1: Deep Reading

For the following step, the instructors need to find one appropriate sample source that will be read in class with the students. Each instructor should choose whatever text fits best the level and interests of their students. Newspaper opinion editorials (op-eds) are usually helpful sources for this kind of activity because they often have a clear, direct message, and an identifiable author.

In my Critical Thinking courses, I used the "I Am Part of the Resistance Inside the Trump Administration" op-ed published in *The New York Times* (Taylor, September 5, 2018). I chose this piece for various reasons: it tackles current and unresolved political and social issues; everyone could relate to its content because it addresses moral and societal questions, such as the definition of what a U.S. president should do; the author's assumptions and biases might be more apparent because of the intrinsic nature of op-eds; and it fosters a confrontation on the reliability of the source because it juxtaposes the anonymity of the author and the newspaper's reputation.

On the day of the activity, if not done previously, the class can start by introducing what a primary source is and how it is different from a secondary source (the instructor can easily explain this difference by discussing with the students concrete examples of both types of sources). Next, each student should receive one printed copy of the analysis questions and the sample source.

Before starting with the actual reading, the instructor can quickly go over each analysis question and clarify possible doubts. At the end of this process, students can start reading the primary source alongside the analysis questions. Their task is to highlight, mark, and note any element of the primary source they think might help answer the analysis questions. Students should use different colors for each specific reading level, for instance, black for level one, red for level two, and blue for level three. Students can work individually or in pairs.

When the first reading is over, the instructor can engage students question by question, level by level. It is important to encourage students to point out the specific elements of the text (words, sentences, paragraphs, etc.) that answer the different analysis questions. The collective reading and discussion of students' answers could be extended as much as the instructor sees fit, but it should allow time for the second activity phase. Indeed, some questions might take more time than others depending on the nature and content of the chosen primary source. For instance, this might happen with the question about biases and assumptions. It is useful to clarify the difference between the two, and to point out that often certain beliefs are not clearly stated in the source. The role of critical thinkers is exactly to make evident the beliefs hidden through the lines.

Phase 2: Difference and Connecting the Dots

The second part of this activity requires extra materials and group work. Its main objective is to build on the analysis practiced in the first phase, to expose students to the idea that sources can come in many different forms, and that a single topic can be approached from multiple points of view.

The instructor should identify and reproduce in advance a small number of primary sources of different natures. They could be of any type: the lyrics of a song, a photo, a page from a comic book, a governmental document, a post from social media, etc.

In my critical thinking course, I built this primary source activity around NYC because the course's main assignment and defining theme were focused on students' semester-long research project called "Real World Problem Solving." Students could choose among a series of different topics all related to NYC and covered by the LaGuardia & Wagner Archives (n.d.), hosted on campus and at www.laguardiawagnerarchive.lagcc.cuny.edu. Once the topic was chosen, students had to narrow down their research to a specific problem and start looking for relevant primary sources in the archive. The city was the common denominator for all the sources I chose for the group activity. The other criteria driving my choice were accessibility via the internet and variety in the type of source.[2] Having all of this in mind, I selected the following sources:

- Comic book preface: Will Eisner (2016), A Contract with God, (www.en.wikipedia.org/wiki/A_Contract_with_God)
- Song Lyrics: Grandmaster Flash & The Furious Five, The Message (www.youtube.com/watch?v=PobrSpMwKk4)
- Photo: Thomas Hoepker, New York City 9/11 (www.theguardian.com/commentisfree/2011/sep/02/911-photo-thomas-hoepker-meaning)
- Governmental document: New York State, Enumeration of Inhabitants (www.tenement.org/wp-content/uploads/2019/01/Primary-Source-Lesson-Plan-High-School.pdf, pages 13 and 14)
- Comics: Amy Hwang, People Who Can Afford to Live Here (condenaststore.com/featured/people-who-can-afford-to-live-here-amy-hwang.html)
- Social Media Post: Brandon Stanton, Humans of New York (www.facebook.com/humansofnewyork)

The instructor should choose the number of sources depending on the classroom size. A ratio of 1 source to 4 students should be enough. Once printed, each source reproduction should provide enough space for students to write on the paper.

Once everything is ready, the class can be divided into groups of four students. Each group receives one source and three markers of different colors (each one corresponding to a specific reading level). The instructor can now ask each group to answer the questions of the first reading level, using the respective marker, to highlight the relevant elements of the source. Students should write their answers on the paper. This process should take no more than 10 minutes.

As soon as students have finished answering all level 1 questions, each group can swap their source with another group's source. Every group can now work on level 2 questions having available all the information gathered by a different group that was previously working on the same source. When level 2 is done, groups swap sources for the last time and complete level 3 questions. By doing this practice collaboratively as groups, and layering the activity between groups, the activity creates a dynamic collaborative model of textual interpretation.

Analysis and source exchange should take 30 minutes in total. When this part is over, the instructor can go over each source examining the analysis written by the students with the whole class. Another option is to ask each group to talk about the last source they worked on. Either way, by the end of the class all students will have been exposed to all the different sources including those they did not directly analyze. Finally, the instructor can ask students what the common characteristics among the sources are. This has the potential of fostering a discussion about the variety of points of view, and the multiple forms knowledge can take. In fostering the skill of deep reading and critically interpreting primary sources, students are able to move beyond merely accepting texts as truth, and are encouraged to reevaluate and reinterpret primary sources, and to build their own understanding. This development of agency in students is at once humanizing for students who are historically excluded and marginalized by most production methods of dominant primary sources; and also critical in providing them broader context and the ability to question and reinterpret the given primary resources.

Conclusions

When I started teaching at LaGuardia, I had two main objectives: rethink my previous disciplinary knowledge and experience in a different—general education or philosophical—framework, and foster my student's curiosity and intellectual engagement in content that seemed to be highly theoretical. The first step that allowed me to pursue these aims was the realization that coming from a different academic background was not an obstacle. Rather, it was an advantage. I had first to understand what critical thinking and history shared, that inquiry, analysis, and creativity were the core common components. While history is more concentrated on the study of the past, critical thinking is not bound to a specific time and it offers a more methodologically oriented approach to knowledge. I then tried to combine the best aspects from history and philosophy in order to satisfy the main learning objective of my course: providing an analytical toolbox able to increase awareness of our thinking process and to approach problem solving in a systematic way.

Teaching in a community college was a new experience as well, thus a challenge of its own kind. As written earlier, a sense of urgency seems to characterize my new students. Despite their average young age, they are fully invested in their adult lives, in charge of onerous responsibilities (family and work), and often facing social injustices and traumas (the majority of them come from underrepresented social-economic groups), all of which are heightened by the metropolis lifestyle and costs. They do not take college for granted. Community college students are already critical in questioning the reason behind curricula and content presented in each course that they take, in each semester's worth of tuition paid (by them). The instructors have to make their courses relevant to students' lived experiences–provide students the tools and create a class culture to co-create, reframe and share their knowledge within the class—for it to be meaningful and worthy of students' time and effort. This requires instructors to reposition themselves as co-creators of knowledge alongside students. And this is something I had to realize and understand in order to effectively teach there. Throughout questioning what they're taking, why they're taking it, how they co-create knowledge, students are engaging in critical thinking. Birjandi et al., (2019) discusses:

> critical thinking became an educational ideal across the world and many educational institutions mentioned it as a major goal in their mission statements. Having become an educational idea, critical thinking strives to take another step and emerge as an educational reality. (p. 36)

Interpreted in this context, critical thinking courses are not meant to teach students how to think, but instead to encourage the students to reflect on and become more aware of the ways in which they are already thinking critically, creatively, and ethically. This includes thinking critically about the authority of knowledge production, presented in colleges and elsewhere. In other words, to invite them to question everything!

I had all these ideas in my mind as I was designing the deep reading of primary sources activity described in this chapter. In the end, it can be summed up as a history and philosophy practice aimed at making intellectual discovery and reasoning comfortable, unpretentious, enticing, and, most importantly, fun.

Notes

1 On the contrary, a secondary source could be any document that studies, interprets, and analyzes information about a certain topic or historical event. For instance, manuals, academic books and journals' articles are clear examples of secondary sources. A secondary source can become a primary source as well. All depends on the questions and object of research. For instance, modern historians of early twentieth-century education might consider school manuals of the time as primary sources, while researchers of that time considered the same books as secondary sources. Likewise, a contemporary historian of science might consider previous scientific research as primary sources in order to understand how science and knowledge was produced in the past. This same book, today a secondary source, could as well be used as a primary source by future historians of American Education.
2 By accessibility I mean materials that can be easily found on the web. Variety refers to the kind of source.

References

Bean, J.C. (2011). *Engaging ideas: The Professor's guide to integrating writing, critical thinking, and active learning in the classroom.* Jossey-Bass.

Birjandi, P., Bagheri, B.M., & Maftoon, P. (2019). Towards an operational definition of critical thinking. *The Journal of English Language Pedagogy and Practice, 12*(4), 17–40.

Brophy, J.M., Cole, J., Robertson, J.F., Safley, T.M., & Symes, C. (2016). *Perspectives from the past: Primary sources in Western civilizations* (6th ed., Vol. 1; 2 vols.). W.W. Norton.

Chaffee, J. (2019). *Thinking critically.* Cengage Learning.

Darder, A. (2012). *Culture and power in the classroom: Educational foundations for the schooling of bicultural students.* Routledge.

Davidson, C. (2017). *The new education.* Hachette Book Group.

Eisner, W. (2016). *A contract with God.* W.W. Norton.

Foucault, M. (1966). *The order of things: An archeology of the Human Sciences.* Éditions Gallimard.

Freire, P. (1970). *Pedagogy of the oppressed.* Continuum.

Freire, P. (1985). *The politics of education: Culture, power, and liberation.* Bergin & Gravy Publishers.

Giroux, H.A. (2005). The terror of neoliberalism: Rethinking the significance of cultural politics. *College Literature, 32*(1), 1–19.

hooks, b. (1994). *Teaching to transgress: Education as the practice of freedom.* Routledge.

Kim, S. (2021). Empowering students & creating social change through the humanities. *CUNY Humanities Alliance.* https://cunyhumanitiesalliance.org/2021/01/04/empowering-students-creating-social-change-through-the-humanities/

Kishlansky, M.A., & Victor, S. (Eds.). (1995). *Sources of the West: Readings in Western civilization* (2nd ed., Vol. 2; 2 vols.). HarperCollins College Publishers.

LaGuardia Community College. (n.d.). *LAGCC—Philosophy courses offered.* https://laguardia.catalog.cuny.edu/programs/PHL-AA

LaGuardia & Wagner Archive. (n.d.). https://www.laguardiawagnerarchive.lagcc.cuny.edu/

Taylor, M. (2018, September 5). I am part of the resistance inside the Trump administration. *The New York Times.* https://www.nytimes.com/2018/09/05/opinion/trump-white-house-anonymous-resistance.html

Woldeyes, Y.G., & Offord, B. (2018). Decolonizing human rights education: Critical pedagogy praxis in higher education. *International Education Journal: Comparative Perspectives, 17*(1), 24–36.

Addendum 2
Primary Source Analysis Questions (Example)

Level 1: Understand what your source is

1. Who wrote this document?

2. What is the intended audience?

3. What is the storyline?

Level 2: Get yourself inside the text

1. What type of source is this?

2. Why was this source produced?

3. What are the basic assumptions and bias of this source?

Level 3: Interpret and produce knowledge

1. Can I believe this document?

2. What can I learn about the society that produced this document?

3. What does this document mean to me?

Teaching Linguistics to Promote Social Justice: Ending Exclusionary Language Practices

OLIVER SAGE AND LEIGH GARRISON-FLETCHER

In a linguistics class, language is, of course, in the forefront. But whose language is it? The vast economic, racial, cultural, religious, gender, sexuality, and multilingual diversity in our classrooms does not reflect the White Formal Standard American English,[1] majority-based resources and interests presented in most college-level textbooks. Many of our students are multilingual and speak English as an additional language, and many also speak historically marginalized varieties of English. As difficult as it is, we include all the language varieties of our students in the classroom, which are all worthy of academic inquiry. Excluding students' language sends the message that there is only one form of correct language and that all other forms of language are wrong, bad, and don't belong in higher education. That's discriminatory. When we exclude their language, we are excluding them. When we include all students' language varieties, it welcomes their identity, their being, into the class and into academia.

    This chapter is based on our experiences in the CUNY Humanities Alliance (HA) as a faculty mentor (Leigh) and a fellow (Oliver) teaching the course ELL101: Introduction to Language, which is a survey course in the field of linguistics. We will each discuss activities we use in our courses designed to teach linguistics with a focus on social justice. We both feel the need to teach linguistics using our students' diverse language backgrounds as resources and believe the course is a perfect place to counter discriminatory language ideologies. Linguistics, as the scientific study of language, reveals that all languages and varieties of languages have the same expressive ability and follow their own set of complex rules, each being a systematic means of communication (Fromkin et al., 2019; Sandoval & Denham, 2021). All-too-common labels of incorrect or "broken" language do not have scientific backing, in that varieties of language that are labeled broken or incorrect are not breaking any rules; they are just distinct and follow their own rules (Lippi-Green, 2012; Reaser et al., 2017; Wolfram & Schilling, 2016). One goal of our course is to raise student awareness of this, talking about students' own language practices, not focusing on just White Formal Standard American English, and thus critically engaging students in the study of language.

At LaGuardia, the course ELL101 is required for students majoring in Liberal Arts: Social Science and Humanities, which is one of the largest majors at the college. It is also a required course for all Education majors. Furthermore, ELL101 is an elective that fulfills the General Education requirements for all majors. Thus, the course has multiple sections every semester, with about 1,000 students taking the course each year. It's unique that a linguistics course is a core course taken by so many, and as such has a huge potential to contribute to students' sense of belonging in the college. The course proposal lists the following instructional objectives: familiarize students with the nature and general properties of language; provide the students with an overview of what it means to know a language; introduce students to the major fields of general linguistics: phonology, morphology, syntax, and semantics; enable students to understand the nature of first and second language acquisition; familiarize students with the relationships between language and society; reinforce students' writing skills through a written paper; introduce students to historical linguistics and its methods of inquiry; and enable students to understand the relationship of language to the brain.

Linguistics is often considered a technical discipline, but by isolating it from our social body, we risk losing sight of the reason that language takes such primary importance in our lives. Language is a critical tool used by humans, and linguistics is a multifaceted field with connections to almost every other discipline. All of us have experience with language and bring in our own perspectives and ideas. By allowing for a mix of the structural and the social, we can help students put names and concepts to their lived experiences of language and to continue to apply that knowledge critically throughout their time as scholars, as well as in the larger world. By facilitating our students' understanding of how and why we communicate in the ways that we do, without judgment, while simultaneously acknowledging differences and difficult histories of language use, we are allowing for a different type of study—one that stretches far beyond the actual lesson. In the words of Harvey and Moten (2013), "[S]tudy is already going on, including when you walk into a classroom and before you think you start a class ... " (pp. 111–112). When learning about the mechanisms of language itself, the complexities of the world (inside and) outside the classroom are never far away. Walking through their neighborhood, reflecting on the street names, the tensions of gentrification wrapped in a changing skyline, a pharmacy sign written in six languages, eavesdropping on grocery store check-out line gossip, ... these are the ways in which knowledge, study, becomes part of the landscape of students' everyday lives. So much of this, of course, is wrapped up in language. Harvey and Moten (2013) extend the idea of study from the classroom and into the streets, hair salons, and subway platform conversations. For them, study is a coming together, "a mode of thinking with others" that is not solely a classroom activity, but an everyday, everywhere, and anytime activity (p. 11). This stretching of 'study' is crucial to creating new forms of teaching and learning rooted in social justice and radical change.

Language is a fundamental aspect of ourselves and our communities, and one that does not exist in a socioeconomic or cultural vacuum. Our approach to teaching linguistics uses an interdisciplinary and student-centered approach, with students' concerns, backgrounds, and areas of interest sought out and integrated into the lesson plan, in order to make the content relevant and accessible to students within a wide array of disciplines. By using a humanities-based approach to a social-science field, students can more fully understand the power of language in their lives, personally, professionally, and politically.

In the sections below, we will describe methods we use in the classroom that focus on empowering students to bring in their experiences and think about linguistics from a social justice perspective. We will also discuss how working together in the HA, with the opportunity to share ideas and have a designated space to talk about pedagogy and course goals, helped us improve our approach to teaching the course ELL101.

Global Learning Language Attitudes Assignment (Leigh Garrison-Fletcher)

Teaching linguistics for social justice is an important endeavor. The support from the HA helped me improve my pedagogy and focus on this crucial point. As a mentor, I needed to convey the logic of the course and reflect on my teaching practices in order to explain how and why I teach the course the way I do. I had honestly not taken the time to articulate clearly and reflect on why I had arranged the curriculum, assigned certain class activities, readings, etc. for the course. Doing so, especially at the time we as a department were developing an assignment for college-wide assessment, was invaluable.

At LaGuardia, we have core competencies across the curriculum that we assess to measure student learning. One of those is called Global Learning[2] and ELL101 is a course that is used in assessing the competency college-wide. I worked with colleagues in my department to create an assignment for ELL101 that develops this competency, called the Language Attitudes assignment (Garrison-Fletcher et al., 2017). I was developing this assignment with my colleagues in my department when I joined the HA, and I got a lot of help from my fellows in implementing the assignment. As a result, I was able to integrate the new assignment into my class, and focus on the social justice aspect of the course from the start of the semester, which I had not been doing previously.

I integrated the topics of phonology, morphology, and syntax into our broader theme of linguistic diversity, valuing all of the languages in the class by asking students to bring in their language backgrounds into the study of each of these topics. For example, while the textbook that we commonly use in ELL101 mainly looks at the sounds of American English, when we discuss phonology, students look at the entire International Phonetic Alphabet and try to find phonemes that exist in another language they are familiar with. In morphology, our textbook discusses the most common ways new words are formed in English, but we work together to think through how those processes do or do not work in the other languages in our classroom. Thus, I decenter White Formal Standard American English throughout the entire class by bringing in students' languages; we form a community of linguistic scholars trying to understand the systems that underlie the languages present in our community.

The major goal of the course is to understand the complexity of language—that all languages are governed by a system of rules (for instance, the rules of phonology, morphology, syntax) and that we all acquire language based on the input we receive (Clark, 2017; Yule, 2020). There is a prevalent myth in our society that some languages and language varieties are better than others (Bauer & Trudgill, 1998), and often in the U.S. that plays out in thinking that one form of English, White Formal Standard American English, is inherently better than other languages or varieties of English. Baker-Bell (2019) discusses that this abstract, hypothetical form of English "legitimizes white, male, upper middle-class, mainstream ways of speaking English" (p. 11). The myths and misconceptions about language in our society can foster linguistic discrimination, too often seen in schools, with the devaluing of multiple languages and varieties that are not White Formal

Standard American English (Baker-Bell, 2019; Lippi-Green, 2012; Love, 2019; Lyiscott, 2017; Reaser et al., 2017). The misconception that some dialects of English are "improper" often leads to the belief that the speakers of these dialects are unintelligent and do not know the rules of English. But this is incorrect because judgments about "proper" and "improper" are not based on linguistic facts; rather, these judgments are related to the principle of linguistic subordination: "the speech of a socially subordinate group will be interpreted as linguistically inadequate by comparison with that of the socially dominant group" (Wolfram & Schilling, 2016, p. 7). From a linguistic perspective, all languages and varieties of languages have equal value, and all are governed by a system of rules. We think that this understanding is crucial, especially since linguistic discrimination is all-too-common in our society.

The student population at LaGuardia Community College is extremely diverse; only 11 percent of students identify as white, while 45 percent identify as Hispanic, 19 percent as Asian, and 16 percent as Black. Furthermore, 60 percent of students are foreign-born (LaGuardia Community College, Office of Institutional Research and Assessment, 2020). Therefore, the majority of our students come from language backgrounds that differ from the White Formal Standard American English that is the norm in college and many have experienced forms of linguistic discrimination. As a white American professor, at the beginning of the semester my students make assumptions about me; they begin by saying they want to learn to speak "properly" in the class. Before they step into the class, students experience pressure to speak in a certain way. This ideological pressure has the ability to silence students and disempower them in an academic setting. My goal is to engage students in questioning these linguistic pressures and realizing the value in their linguistic repertoires. By the end of the semester, students should be empowered by linguistics to counter the narrative that only a certain group of people speak "properly." Furthermore, I hope they also come away with the notion that no one really fully speaks the "standard" as it is an idealized variety. I use my background, as being from Missouri, to highlight aspects of my English that most people in New York would think were "incorrect," like how I pronounce caramel with only two syllables.

In many ways, I view teaching linguistics for social justice as one of the most important roles I have in teaching ELL101, and our Global Learning assignment deals directly with these issues. The assignment has two parts: the first part asks students to write about their own and societal attitudes that exist toward a language or dialect the student uses; the second part asks students to do a small amount of research and write about different attitudes that certain groups of people have about a different language or dialect, and give some reasons for the existence of these attitudes. Having these two overlapping papers, students must consider more than one language in the language attitudes assignment, thus raising awareness of language diversity and understanding multiple viewpoints about language. This also encourages students to understand that the way they view a language isn't necessarily the same way everyone throughout the world would view the language, and begin to see the false link between language and worth, while realizing the link between language and power.

From the first day of class, I encourage students to share their linguistic practices. Our first topic covered is how to define language, and to discuss the difference between a language and a dialect. To do this, we use students' own language practices—we count how many languages are spoken in our class, for example, as we try to define our unique speech community. Very often we encounter a case where a student labels one of their language practices "broken" or "improper." Students critically examine this notion through the complex definition of language and the sociolinguistic norms that come up in discussion. In the words of one student, who claimed to speak "improper" English on the first day of class, from part 1 of their Global Learning assignment:

> The prestige way of speaking in America is associated with white, middle to upper class Americans and taught or assumed to signify a higher intelligence. The commonly stigmatized way is African-American Vernacular English or some variant and gets associated with black or minority Americans, poverty, crime and a lower intelligence. This not only causes a misunderstanding of the people and their circumstances but creates a feeling of internalized oppression when we teach people to view themselves as less than because of their dialect or accent. The largest misconception is that every person in this speech group has a lower level intelligence because their vocabulary and tone is so much different from what has been established as "proper". One's accent or dialect is not a signifier of intelligence, only a different form of communication when compared to another. However, when one group of speakers holds power or prestige in society it becomes that much easier to claim superiority and marginalize those "below".

This student has reflected on the social status of languages and counters the idea of "improper" language, although they started the class with this feeling of internalized oppression due to the way they used language.

Another student writes about Spanish:

> There are many differences between how people speak Spanish in Mexico and the place where it truly originated, Spain. Some people believe Spain's Spanish is better because it is a western European country giving it more of an important

and prestigious outlook. Also, these people believe since it is the place where Spanish originated from, it is better. This is untrue. These two countries just have very distinct ways to say the same thing ... .we need to respect other people's way of communicating instead of criticizing those for not knowing a language. We should appreciate the diversity we have in the world!

This student's writing highlights their understanding that no variety of language is inherently better than another, but there are links between language and power.

One area of difficulty I have encountered in part two of the assignment is helping students narrow their options and clarify whose attitudes they are discussing. Oliver offered an excellent solution, and had their students focus on endangered languages for Part 2. I am now also focusing on this, especially since the United Nations declared 2019 the International Year of Indigenous Languages. There is a lot of information and clear reasons why certain languages are endangered related to societal attitudes toward different languages and the roles the languages have in society. One student chose to write about Quechua and in the following excerpt of their paper discusses an article about Quechua in Ecuador:

> Grzech (2017) identifies Quechua as an endangered language and how the views of people thinking the language is unnecessary have led to more and more people disassociating themselves with the language. The author begins by focusing on Tena Kichwa, a minority variety of the language. Rather than all speaking the same form of Quechua, there are many different dialects .... Because of languages like Spanish and the socio-economic and political changes in the region, there have been many varieties of the language that have developed. However, this creates conflict within regions. ... Moreover, the language policies implemented by the local and state authorities do not respond to the needs of the local population, and contribute to the increasing marginalization of the local dialects. Language policies like the need to learn Spanish because of its use in society further supports Ecuadorian people's views on the language's disuse. With different dialects used by different classes of people, it further complicates the people's ability to work through policies and reform for the country.

This student gives political and societal explanations for the disuse of Quechua in Ecuador. Furthermore, she notes the diversity within Quechua itself, and that there are multiple dialects of Quechua. The student who wrote this paper speaks Spanish in addition to English and wanted to raise awareness that there are many indigenous languages spoken in countries where Spanish is the dominant language. She brought her own background and interests into her decision to research Quechua and shared with me that she had never really thought about issues related to education and endangered languages, and is now very interested in this topic.

When students in ELL101 analyze their own linguistic practices and complete the Language Attitudes assignment, they are developing their agency and critical awareness of language. For each part of the Language Attitudes assignment, students share their drafts and ideas with one another through peer feedback sessions. This gives them the opportunity to learn with each other, share ideas, and build community. While the Language Attitudes assignment was developed for an introductory linguistics course, some professors at LaGuardia use similar assignments in first-year composition, having students tell their language stories. Language courses could also implement a similar assignment, with a focus on varieties of the target language.

ELL101 raises language awareness for our students. However, it is also essential for instructors to be language-aware. In a professional development workshop at LaGuardia called Language Across the Curriculum, my colleague and I have shared the Language Attitudes assignment with instructors across departments and have asked them to do their own language reflections in order to put language at the center of their approaches in the classroom (McNair & Garrison-Fletcher, 2022). In order to be inclusive of all students, we need to include all of their language practices in our classrooms, and more work must be done across higher education to question the hegemony of White Formal Standard American English.

Teaching Language Survival and Linguistic Rights (Oliver Sage)

Before coming to LaGuardia and teaching linguistics, I had almost exclusively been teaching French language courses at a four-year public college. I found that the real challenge of teaching language was not conveying the material itself, but finding a way to connect the lessons to concepts that were relevant to my students' daily interests and struggles. This felt crucial to me, not only because of the required textbook's disturbing white-washing and erasure of French colonial history and the ongoing racial, economic, and political complexities of the francophone world, but also because of the assumptions that it made about *who was in the classroom and why.*

The vast economic, racial, cultural, religious, gender, sexuality, and class-based diversity in my classrooms has never reflected the white and upper-middle-class majority-based resources and interests presented in the required material. As a white educator, I try to remain aware and critical of my own racial positionality in the classroom, and how that affects the (already) hierarchical relationship that I have with my students and colleagues. Alongside this awareness, however, is the knowledge that as a visibly transgender person walking with a cane, my presence in the classroom, especially as the instructor, is fairly unexpected. Living with overlapping areas of marginalization has become a space of ongoing reflection for me, and while there is danger that comes with the vulnerability of constant visibility, I have tried to turn it outwards as a way to move toward solidarity with others who experience different or overlapping forms of oppression than my own.

In my ELL 101 course at LaGuardia, language, identity, and structural inequality were able to enter the conversation in much more explicit, and often more personal ways. Learning 'someone else's' language is one thing, but to reflect on our own world of language is another. To engage students in reflecting on their own positionality, I found that it often helped to take the first step myself. In class, when relevant, I bring up topics such as growing up in a very rural mixed-working and lower-middle-class home, my work as a house cleaner to pay for school, the difficulties involved in socially transitioning, and living with chronic pain and fatigue. I related these personal nodes of struggle to larger, structural issues of racial and socioeconomic injustice and to students' own histories, whether openly told or held private.

In this gesture of vulnerability, I try to express to my students that while I may not know what they are going through, nevertheless we exist together in an ongoing and shared struggle. My hope is that by coming together as a community to understand the structural forces that shape our lives and our identities, everyone involved develops a deeper sense of solidarity with each other, which can, ideally, reach beyond the classroom and into the larger world.

A low-stakes assignment that I give my linguistic students, in an effort to tease out this broader scope of study, as Harney and Moten (2013) define it, is to ask my class to research the Indigenous people(s) local to their neighborhood or borough. To frame this assignment, I ask them to come in having read and listened to materials created by Indigenous scholars, specifically around racist histories of research on Indigenous populations, the difficulties of keeping Indigenous languages alive, and what Indigenous activists and scholars are doing to protect and preserve indigenous languages and cultures. Because I know that my students' time and energy is often limited, I assign a reading and a short podcast, so that they can both read and listen to the material.

One podcast episode that I've assigned in the past is "Jenny L. Davis on Indigenous Language Revitalization" on *Imagine Otherwise*. Davis, a citizen of the Chickasaw Nation and an assistant professor of anthropology at the University of Illinois, Urbana-Champaign, discusses Chickasaw language revitalization and Indigenous activism centered around language.

In addition, students also read from Linda Tuhiwai Smith's *Decolonizing Methodologies: Research and Indigenous Peoples*. Tuhiwai Smith (2005), a professor of Indigenous education at the University of Waikato, and affiliated with the Ngāti Awa and Ngāti Porou iwi, writes that,

> Although in the literary sense the imagination is crucial to writing, the use of language is not highly regarded in academic discourses which claim to be scientific. The concept of imagination, when employed as a sociological tool, is often reduced to a way of seeing and understanding the world, or a way of understanding how people either construct the world or are constructed by the world. As Toni Morrison argues, however, the imagination can be a way of sharing the world. This means, according to Morrison, struggling to find the language to do this and then struggling to interpret and perform within that shared imagination. (p. 39)

What does it mean to interpret and perform within that "shared imagination"? How can we guide students toward a notion of a shared, but not homogenous, existence, especially with other marginalized groups? This can be especially difficult with topics that have often been taught as 'history,' such as slavery and the genocide of Indigenous peoples, even though those processes and their ongoing legacies are still central to our world.

The following exercise, done for homework in conjunction with listening and reading contemporary Indigenous scholars, is meant to bridge destroyed and forgotten Indigenous histories with the continued effects of physical and cultural genocide and the forced dislocations of Indigenous peoples, who are actively fighting for their rights, cultures, and languages, as well as for the earth, as water protectors and activists of all sorts. For this assignment, students researched the following questions and then reported their findings during our next class:

- Research what tribes/Indigenous peoples live(d) where you grew up (and/or where you are living now) and find out the answers to the following questions. Write down what you find and bring the information into class.
- Note: if you lived/grew up outside of the United States and can find information about the Indigenous groups from those areas, that's completely acceptable.
- Who were the Indigenous groups that lived/are living in the area you're discussing? Are there still tribal members living in these areas? If not, where did they go and why did they leave their original territory?
- Find out what languages they speak/spoke, and how many speakers there are of these languages currently, or whether they are now dead languages.

- Are there resources available to learn these languages or efforts happening to revitalize these languages? What kind of resources are they?
- Finally, write a few sentences on your reaction to what you learned. Did your findings surprise you? Why or why not?

The next class, we went around and discussed the people and languages from the area they live. Though most of my students lived in Queens, they gave a diverse array of answers, with several members of the class researching Indigenous cultures from their native countries, including Uzbekistan and Bangladesh. Often, however, information about the specific Indigenous peoples that were native to that location were limited, and information on the languages they speak/spoke were even more so. We discussed the social and historical reasons for this lack of information, including the cultural elements of Indigenous genocide facilitated by boarding schools intended to "kill the indian [and] save the man" (generally attributed to General Richard Henry Pratt) (Richie, 2008).

After students shared their reflections and research, I shared some videos and resources to highlight the central importance of language to concerns of Indigenous rights, colonization, and related issues of social and structural marginalization. We began with definitions of what it means for a language to become endangered or extinct, and students reflected on everything that is lost when a language dies. To give a specific example on how linguistic extinction occurs, I played a video of Dennis Banks, cofounder of the American Indian Movement (Worldbeat Productions, 2016), discussing being separated from his mother at a young age, being forced to live at a boarding school where he was beaten and abused, and denied access to his language and culture. We also watched excerpts from the documentary *Our Spirits Don't Speak English: Indian Boarding School* (Richie, 2008). Learning that these boarding schools were funded by the United States government was clearly a stunning moment for many students, who responded in shocked silence, anger, and disbelief.

To shift their energy toward a sense of possibility and potential for action, I shifted us toward the idea of language survival and renewal. Together, as a class, we came up with a "Language Bill of Rights" as a way to create a sense of agency around what we can do to combat linguistic discrimination, endangerment, and death, and work toward strengthening and rebuilding endangered languages. This activity also gave them an opportunity to discuss their own relationship to dominant and/or marginalized forms of language, and to hear their classmates' thoughts as well. After working on this theme together in small groups and then coming back together for a discussion, we came up with ten main declarations. Our "Language Bill of Rights" reads as follows:

- Signage in all languages!
- Announcements in different languages
- Right to a translator
- Protection against linguistic discrimination- can't be denied a job, resources, or housing because of the language you speak
- Wide availability of languages taught in schools
- Language appreciation celebrations!
- Learning languages through culture/songs, sharing languages through culture
- Technology and media available in variety of languages
- Funding and grants to promote linguistic diversity and learning
- Education to counteract stereotypes and create sharing of variety and depth of different linguistic cultures

Though my LaGuardia students came from a variety of different linguistic and cultural backgrounds, all of them have dealt with social marginalization of some sort, be it because of their race, class or cultural background, immigration status, gender, sexuality, and/or dis/ability. I make sure to leave as much time as I can for my students to find their own relation to language (in)justice and articulate it throughout the course, and how language can both be a tool and a weapon. Finding how to connect and create change through a shared desire for justice, not for one, but for all of us, is always the end goal for me, no matter what the subject matter.

This assignment was developed for a linguistics course, but it could also be modified for use in other classroom contexts. For instance, history or geography courses could ask their students to research the Indigenous communities who live and lived nearest to their geographical area and to trace their geographical, political, and historical trajectories pre- and post-colonization. As a French instructor, I show maps of the language diversity that existed in (what is now) France throughout history, discuss the processes through which French became the dominant language of the colonial nation-state, and highlight the ways in which France, similarly to the United States, has attempted to wipe out the native languages spoken within their colonies, and even within France itself, through systems of (re)education, cultural dominance, and physical violence.

While one of the goals of this chapter is to provide concrete resources for instructors, I also want to emphasize that incorporating Indigenous content and history into our course materials is only one small piece of our work as educators invested in social and linguistic justice. As a non-Indigenous white person, I believe that my larger responsibility is to continue the process of unlearning cultural white supremacy, strive to center anti-colonial and anti-racist strategies and methodologies in my work, and, most crucially, to follow the lead of Indigenous and First Nation researchers, scholars, and activists, who have been doing this work for many generations.

Conclusion

These two approaches to teaching linguistics, taken together, allow students to connect to their own use of language, endangered languages, and Indigenous languages. Both promote critical reflection on the ideology behind centering White Formal Standard American English and the suppression and intentional extermination of other languages. Both are done in ways that connect with students' present-day experiences and lives, and encourage them to understand their linguistic positionality and to move forward with linguistic advocacy. These are just two reexaminations of critical pedagogy in linguistics classes within the contemporary context.

We hope that our examples from our introductory linguistics course help generate ideas in how to approach a course with an eye toward social justice and in engaging our diverse student population. Along with our material, our own pedagogical practices must be designed to empower our students and take into account who our students are and what they bring with them to the classroom. Furthermore, we need to work on including the voices of our students and making our course content and experience meaningful and relevant to them. We must continue exploring and reflecting on our classroom practices and developing new ways to meet the needs of our diverse student body. By making our classrooms a reflection of what we want our society to look like, we can move one step closer to a more just world.

Notes

1 We are combining the terminology of Formal Standard English (Reaser et al., 2017) and the notion of White American English (Baker-Bell, 2020) for the idealized language variety that society in the U.S. deems as the appropriate form of language.
2 As stated on the Assessment page of the LaGuardia website (LaGuardia Community College, n.d.), "Global Learning asks students to approach the world's challenges and opportunities from multiple perspectives and engage with issues of diversity, identity, democracy, power, privilege, sustainability and ethical action."

References

Baker-Bell, A. (2019). Dismantling anti-black linguistic racism in English language arts classrooms: Toward an anti-racist black language pedagogy. *Theory Into Practice*, 59. https://doi.org/10.1080/00405841.2019.1665415

Baker-Bell, A. (2020). *Linguistic justice: Black, language, literacy, identity, and pedagogy*. Routledge & National Council of Teachers of English.

Bauer, L., & Trudgill, P. (1998). *Language myths*. Penguin.

Clark, E.V. (2017). *Language in children*. Routledge.

Fromkin, V., Rodman, R., & Hymes, N. (2019). *An introduction to language* (11th ed.). Cengage Learning.

Garrison-Fletcher, L., McCormack, B., & Sistrunk, W. (2017). *Language attitudes [Linguistics]*. CUNY Academic Works; Open Educational Resources. https://academicworks.cuny.edu/lg_oers/7/

Grzech, K. (2017). ¿Es necesario elegir entre la estandarización de las lenguas minoritarias y la vitalidad de sus variedades? Estudio de caso del kichwa de Alto Napo. Onomázein Revista de lingüística filología y traducción. 37. 16-34. 10.7764/onomazein.amerindias.02.

Harney, S., & Moten, F. (2013). *The undercommons: Fugitive planning et black study*. Minor Compositions.

LaGuardia Community College. (n.d.). *Assessment*. https://www.laguardia.edu/assessment/

LaGuardia Community College, Office of Institutional Research and Assessment. (2020). *Institutional Profile*. LaGuardia Community College, Office of Institutional Research and Assessment. https://www.laguardia.edu/uploadedfiles/main_site/content/ir/docs/institutional-profile-2020.pdf

Lippi-Green, R. (2012). *English with an accent: Language, ideology, and discrimination in the United States*. Routledge.

Love, B. (2019). *We want to do more than survive: Abolitionist teaching and the pursuit of educational freedom*. Beacon Press.

Lyiscot, J. (2017). Racial Identity and Liberation Literacies in the Classroom. *The English Journal*, 106 (4). http://www.jstor.org/stable/26359462

McNair, L., & Garrison-Fletcher, L. (2022). Putting languages at the centre: Developing the Language Across the Curriculum (LAC) faculty seminar at LaGuardia Community College, Queens, New York. *Language, Culture and Curriculum*. https://doi.org/10.1080/07908318.2022.2047196

Reaser, J., Temple Adger, C., Wolfram, W., & Christian, D. (2017). *Dialects at school: Educating linguistically diverse students*. Routledge.

Richie, C. (Director). (2008). *Our spirits don't speak English: Indian boarding school* [Documentary]. Rich Heape Films.

Sandoval, J.B., & Denham, K.E. (2021). *Thinking like a linguist: An introduction to the science of language*. Cambridge University Press.

Smith, L.T. (2005). *Decolonizing methodologies: Research and indigenous peoples.* Zed.
Wolfram, W., & Schilling, N. (2016). *American English: Dialects and variation.* Wiley Blackwell.
Worldbeat Productions. (2016). *American Indian Movement: Dennis Banks interview* [Video]. YouTube. https://www.youtube.com/watch?v=4-_2MW6S5fY
Yule, G. (2020). *The study of language.* Cambridge University Press.

Visualizing Identity, Fandom, and Representation

MICHEAL ANGELO RUMORE

Figure 1. The Professor

The artifact from my time as an educator I think about most often isn't any statement on teaching, observation report, publication, or the like. It's a hand-drawn sketch included in a student's final portfolio from a 2015 section of College Writing at Queens College, CUNY. This was back when I inexplicably still asked students to dump stacks of physical portfolios on my lap at the end of every semester. But if the strain of carrying dozens of overstuffed folders back to Manhattan was the cost of receiving this drawing, so be it. Picture me giving a sardonic stare, clutching a sword and adorned with the Triforce of *Legend of Zelda* fame, speaking the simple injunction to "WRITE!" I often think of this image not just out of an inescapable sense of amusement. (For example, is my command to take up the writing process depicted as akin to *Zelda*'s Hero of Time and his stand against Hyrule's forces of darkness or, instead, his fairy companion Navi's constant nagging interruptions that only seem to get in the way of the hero's journey? It depends on the class, I suppose . . .) But I also return to this image for how it prompts me to reflect on how I "visualize" myself as an educator and how I bring not just my scholarly interests to class, as well as how I incorporate my more banal interests and quirks to the Very Serious work of teaching literary analysis. For this reason, the image was very much on my mind as I prepared for teaching my first section of Writing Through Literature at LaGuardia Community College, part of my assignment as a fellow of the CUNY Humanities Alliance.

Visualizing Identity: Drawing the Syllabus

The syllabus I developed, eventually titled "Visualizing Identity," grew out of a desire to extend these kinds of reflections to the arc of an entire course, which seemed to be enabled by a turn to visual culture as an organizing theme. The focus on visuality, on one hand, became a strategy of unpacking the baggage that comes with capital-L Literature and instead emphasizing textuality, which of course includes but doesn't only encompass literary texts. This is perhaps a basic point, but still an important one given how "English" class can present as a dispossessive discipline for a stunningly broad array of students. For many, "English" still operates as a shorthand for a coercive process of replacing the vulgarities of everyday culture with some "higher" standard that—as traditions of postcolonial and critical ethnic studies clearly teach—derives from colonialist and classist histories.[1] On the other hand, I hoped the heuristic of visualization might allow us to interrogate how identity necessarily shapes textual reception and also how we come to conceive of identity *through* textual representation.

Thus, attending to how we translate the experience of "reading" across textualities—the processes by which we visualize written texts or, vice versa, textualize the visual—became something of a metaphor for the push and pull of identity formation.

The focus on visual style was also influenced by the opportunity, in the previous semester, to shadow LaGuardia Professor Jacqueline Jones' section of Writing Through Literature. Many things impressed on me throughout the semester, but among them was the use of a visual syllabus that not only framed course materials but also set a welcoming "tone" for the entire class. I learned that, far from simply gilding a traditional syllabus, creating a visual style for course documents did enormous work in subverting the notion of the syllabus as an imposing contract. Ultimately, my own visual syllabus took on a comic book look in its panels, fonts, and color scheme, all of which allowed me to experiment with the overall tone of the course by eschewing the legalistic language of the syllabus as a genre in favor of a more informal voice. Looking back, the design was fairly rough, but still worked to establish a particular feel for the course. This tone-setting went beyond just the syllabus, as I also incorporated the comic book style for all other course materials, housed on a website and blog used often during class.

Figure 2. Syllabus Page

Course themes seemed to organically grow out of the comic book visual style. One particular topic, "fandom," emerged as a recurring theme in readings and assignments for the course. In addition to a desire to expand notions of the literary and textuality, this theme also developed as an attempt to think through questions of centering and situating student experience at a time in which "identification" is often linked to the consumption of intellectual properties. One can identify as a "comic book nerd," a Trekkie, a member of the Fighting Game Community, and so on. Given the unprecedented popularity of comic book-inspired film franchises such as the Marvel Cinematic Universe, I anticipated comic book fandom, broadly conceived, would constitute a primary site—at least initially—from which students would engage discourses concerning cultural representation and media stereotypes. To students' credit, many interpreted "fandom" much more broadly than this framing. But, in any case, the double-sided questions of representation in franchise filmmaking—the simultaneous contestation and perpetuation of circumscribed conceptions of cultural identity—influenced my understanding of the fandom theme.

I must admit, however, that trepidations did exist. For one, I worried whether my own nostalgic feelings for comic book aesthetics would obscure ways these images might come across to students as condescension. I also wondered whether focusing on such texts might in the end reproduce consumerist and corporatist ways of thinking about identity. For example, the increasingly monopolistic role of Disney, which owns Marvel Studios as well as many other lucrative franchises, in setting the cultural terms for these discourses on popular representation stuck in my mind. What Henry Giroux years ago described, in the documentary *Mickey Mouse Monopoly: Disney, Childhood, and Corporate Power* (Picker, 2002), as Disney's "spectacle of innocence" that justifies a long history of racist, sexist, and classist representations in classic children's films through an "apolitical" conception of childhood has given way to a more multifaceted discourse of diversity in popular media representation. While certainly an important part of the necessary work of addressing the long-standing exclusions and stereotyping of numerous marginalized groups in Hollywood films, critics such as Roderick Ferguson have demonstrated why it is also important to question the neoliberal, even sometimes "humanistic," rhetorics by which corporatized forms of minoritized representation may reflect the biopolitical "management" of difference ultimately serving the status quo (2012). I hoped to capture such tensions as topics of discussion in the course, all of which I refer to with the term "politics of representation," but I was not sure if I would adequately do so. This is another reason that I ultimately focused on the Marvel series *X-Men*, which I thought fairly explicitly encompassed the opportunities and pitfalls of these kinds of questions of identity and representation.

Some tension also exists in how we as instructors might imagine fan practices and the common connotations of "fandom" in mainstream culture. For example, Linda Zygutis has recently complicated the assumption that fandom simply encourages democratic reading practices:

> Teaching with fandom—and fandom itself—is often presented specifically as a salve to singular and authoritative readings of a text. Instructors who use fan studies in the classroom are likely to make use of transformative works and theories as a way of encouraging students to produce their own readings of a text. (2021)

Despite this preconception (which I too carried into my course), Zygutis found that students were surprisingly more likely to express a conception of fandom as essentially "affirmational," reflecting a "particularly enthusiastic form of close reading that rewards deference to an authorial voice." This is fandom in its most 'fanatical' sense, denoting practices that, even when participatory, claim to defend a canon or authorial tradition from interlopers (whether a corporate exploiter of an intellectual property or a segment of a fan base itself). While affirmational fan practices can be mobilized toward critical ends, often they represent (at best) an uncritical consumerism or (at worst) a justification for toxic gatekeeping. Any collection of students might more naturally embody the more critical or affirmational fan across the semester, but what we do with this tension relates directly to the critical thinking goals of a first-year writing course. As Zygutis provocatively points out, affirmational fan practices reflect formalistic literary methods that encourage "authoritative readings" at the expense of critical agency. Thus, asking students to think like fans can also risk reinforcing problems inherited from traditional literary pedagogies, ironically the very methods one might assume "fandom" as a theme would undermine.

Addressing this tension required reflecting on the relationship of literary studies conventions to my deliberately "non-literary" framing for the course. My thinking here engages the foundational debates defining what we now call cultural studies, broadly focused on applying the analytical and theoretical techniques associated with literary studies to so-called popular culture. Thus, the cultural studies tradition challenges the emphasis in literary studies on "high" cultural productions and, consequently, inaugurates a debate on the relationship of popular cultural productions to political struggle and social change. Though excavating the debates around cultural studies would necessitate a more careful intellectual history than I can fully provide here, one can trace this debate to the foundational work of Frankfurt School critics that institute popular culture as a key site of political contestation, yet sometimes also haughtily dismissed popular culture as offering little possibility for enacting social change (Adorno & Horkheimer, 2001). As a result, by the

1980s, a number of "culturalist" theorists, especially those associated with the Centre for Contemporary Cultural Studies at Birmingham University, such as Stuart Hall, instead foregrounded the creative ways oppressed and marginalized groups engage pop cultural forms in subversive ways (Hall, 2019).

I chose the first orienting reading for the course, poet Derrick Austin's essay "In the Name of the Femme: A Queer Boy's Voyage with Sailor Moon," in the spirit of this critical tradition (2018). In the essay, Austin describes how his fandom of the "magical girl" anime series *Sailor Moon* enabled an exploration of Black, queer identity.[2] Austin demonstrates the creative ways that "seeing oneself" in a cultural property—in this case, a Japanese anime intended primarily for young girls—isn't necessarily a predictable or obvious process. For Austin, *Sailor Moon*'s celebration of relationships between women also provided "a space to learn that masculinity isn't a rejection of femininity." Additionally, as Austin writes, the show also offered a lens through which to negotiate the vexed intersections of race, gender, and class in a white supremacist and heterosexist society:

> If Blackness already marked me with a target, then effeminacy would double that. Queer, even while nascent sexual desires fumbled, inchoate, I found myself closeted, walled-in really, both the prisoner and the bricks-and-mortar itself. I wore the masks and flat affects I needed to live. But at home, all it took were three words to let in some light and sweet air and—in my head at least—a glamorous costume change: Moon Prism Power! (2018)

In an accessible way, Austin's essay demonstrates how the consumption of cultural representations does not merely "reflect" hegemonic narratives and imperatives: this is the fundamental mistake Adorno and Horkheimer make in their noted critique of the culture industry, a mistake that would be repeated in some variants of critical discourse analysis that would follow. Rather, the politics of representation involves a much more complex struggle between hegemonic and counter-hegemonic reading practices. I hoped that the critical interrogation of fan consumption would ultimately encompass both of these senses.

However, the ways popular cultural representations *do* reflect hegemonic ideologies must not be elided either. While clearly offering avenues for creative identification and community-building, the terms "fandom" or "fan culture" often rightly circulate as shorthands for some of the most toxic aspects of online culture. To offer one demonstrative example, the reactionary backlash to the *Star Wars* sequel *The Last Jedi* (2017), a franchise now also owned by Disney, often portrayed the film as antagonistic to "Star Wars fans" in a sleight of hand identifying "true" Star Wars fandom with a politics of white male resentment to diversity. While I do not wish to amplify any particular examples, a cursory trip to YouTube will quickly reveal a multitude of video essays by disgruntled "fans" about how so-called "social justice warriors" are ruining your favorite intellectual properties. Before teaching this course, I believe I greatly underestimated the extent to which many fan cultures circulate, especially in online forums, as forms of white supremacist, sexist, homophobic, and transphobic identity politics. At the very least, raising the topic of fandom runs the risk of exposing students to these discourses as legitimate debates.[3] This disquieting reality is often elided in the push toward cultivating digital literacies and public-facing assignments in writing classrooms. While I wished to emphasize counter-hegemonic fandoms, and most students ultimately did, there was no guarantee that they would necessarily do so. For this reason, I wonder if a student[4] in my inaugural Fall 2018 this theme was in some sense justified in his reticence to "identify" with a fan culture. "I have no idea what I 'identify' with," this student wrote:

> It was suggested that I think about the things I like, so let's start with that. What show do I identify with? I don't know. What game do I identify with? I don't know. What character do I identify with? Okay, that one ... I still don't know. What am I supposed to identify with? ... [Anime] has what I like, but I don't identify with it. I don't see something that feels like it has "myself" in it. Maybe I don't really have a proper "self."

Student resistance is always insightful. I had asked students to craft a personal narrative on the model of Austin's essay describing how a "fandom" influenced their sense of identity and belonging. While the majority of students supplied creative and unexpected answers—mentioning everything from the *Kill Bill* films as feminist inspiration, the chain-restaurant review podcast *Doughboys* as a way of approaching questions of class difference and food cultures, the experience listening to Mariah Carey on Chinese radio, even an aspiration to ride every different subway car in New York City—this one response stood out as the only overtly resistant one. While, by the end of his essay, the student did come to an "unexpected" identification with what he called the "concept of hype" in anime fandoms, he consistently rejected the notion that he needed to "see himself" in any particular anime series or character. I took the reticence as in part a negotiation of the notion that identification in the way I had posed the essay assignment might be too restrictive a way of approaching the representation of identity.

Others, particularly international students, interpreted the essay prompt in terms of cultural translation. Another student, who grew up in Nepal and was in her first semester studying in the United States, narrated her long-standing fandom of Alicia Keys dating back to childhood listening to Radio Nepal. She wrote that Alicia Keys' music, especially the song "Superwoman," provided a soundtrack to a conflict between her parents about whether she would study at a "government school" or an "English school." As a result of fighting to attend the "English school," she gradually learned to understand the lyrics of her favorite Alicia Keys song, which seemed to have cheered on her ambitions all along even though she could not at first understand them. She also related Alicia Keys' music to resisting patriarchal expectations in her community:

> Everyone in my neighborhood said that I was aggressive just because I behaved differently than other girls (I was not aggressive though)—I, a Nepali girl should be soft, sweet, compliant, reliant and button up my lips even if I was right. Who knew? I had "Superwoman" hanging in my mind in which Alicia Keys taught me to stand up and search for "the better part of me," to be independent, to do what is right, and not to stop trying if we fall down or get weak because I knew "I can fly."

Many students, because they related fandom to experiences of learning new languages (particularly English) and, ultimately, studying in New York City, interpreted the prompt not in terms of self-reflection, but in terms of processes of self-creation. I knew, going forward, that the more analytical assignments and activities to follow would have to explicitly negotiate these multiple ways fandom signified questions of identity for students writing from vastly different experiences, standpoints, and cultural contexts.

While the LaGuardia classes this chapter reflects on primarily concerned writing, as they served as a bridge between a three-class composition sequence beginning with argumentative writing and concluding with the research paper, they nevertheless focused on analyzing primary literary texts. While I have already mentioned above how I theoretically grounded the course in the tradition of cultural studies rather than capital-L Literature per se, this does not mean that I eschewed more traditionally literary texts completely. Rather, I wanted the framing of the course to address the unique baggage that literary studies carries. It's no surprise that two oscillating stereotypes about English studies prevail in the popular imagination: one focusing on rote standards of grammatical correctness and the other assuming that studying literature disseminates some kind of "humanizing" cultural essence. As alluded to earlier, both of these notions derive from colonial pedagogies that take on an especially sinister bent for marginalized and minoritized students for whom traditionally canonical English studies can feel highly dispossessive. As a white educator teaching predominantly students of color in the CUNY system, I always strive to, at the very least, demystify these colonial structures. And, yet, I feel that I have sometimes unwittingly reproduced these structures even when rendering them as objects of critique if by doing so I have erased the presence of resistant student voices. Part of the structure of the LaGuardia courses alluded to in this essay emerged from ongoing reflections on how to hold these two aspects of engaging the politics of representation in writing classrooms—both the centripetal and centrifugal—in a productive, potentially empowering tension.

X-Men and the Politics of Representation

Before elaborating on how students responded to, challenged, and refashioned my framing of the literary texts to follow, I want to say a bit more about how I conceived them and why I did so. The first literary text explored in the course drew, perhaps selfishly, from one of my own "fandoms": the Marvel series *X-Men*, which depicts a world in which superpowered "mutants" are subject to popular prejudice and legalized discrimination. I chose this series, in large part, because I found it a productive universe for continuing to explore the double-edged sense with which I conceptualized the theme of the politics of representation—in both its political and aesthetic senses. In distinction to many other superhero concepts, the mutants of this facet of the Marvel universe are born with their superpowers as a result of natural genetic mutations and, thus, are treated with distrust by the general public and structural discrimination by the state. As a result, the series has been popularly understood as reflecting the liberation movements of the 1960s from which the comic emerged, such as the civil rights, feminist, and gay rights movements. The rather unwieldy series tends to be glossed in relation to the political conflict between Charles Xavier, a.k.a. Professor X—who organizes and names the X-Men—and his primary antagonist, Magneto, leader of the more radical Brotherhood of Mutants. The relationship between these two characters has often been related (sometimes in an overly simplistic way) to that between Martin Luther King, Jr. and Malcolm X, in that Charles Xavier perpetuates a reconciliatory response to anti-mutantism while Magneto advocates for a revolutionary response. "Is Magneto Right?," a video by Abigail Thorn (2016) of the YouTube channel PhilosophyTube that I used in part to frame our discussion of the X-Men, more provocatively situates the conflict between Charles Xavier and Magneto in terms of political responses to structural violence, which emerged as another primary theme as the course progressed. While I will return in more detail to this framing of the X-Men shortly, for now I want to point out that I found making the shift from themes of stereotyping and prejudice to questions of structural violence to help the class move from "personal" to "analytic" writing without presenting this as a flight from self-interested and politicized thinking.

At the same time, our discussion of the X-Men series continued to pose questions about how and what kinds of identities can appear under hegemonic ways of thinking about representation. On one hand, the X-Men series has long been one of the most "diverse" casts in Marvel Comics in terms of race, gender, class, religion, and national origin since its inception in 1963. On the other hand, however, the series has been critiqued for reducing these intersections of oppression to the metaphor of mutantism and describing structural discrimination in terms of mere prejudice. As the fourth wall-breaking titular protagonist of the X-Men universe film *Deadpool 2* (Leitch, 2018) quips, the X-Men could be characterized as "dated metaphors for racism in the sixties." Despite the diversity of its ever-expanding cast, the metaphor of 'anti-mutantism,' which tends to be interpreted as a stand-in for any number of oppressions of race, class, and gender, can be characterized as doing so in an abstracted way palatable for a white, middle-class readership. In particular, the comparison of anti-mutantism to racism, a common analogy parodied by the aforementioned *Deadpool* quote, alludes to one of the more serious failings of the mutant metaphor: by "naturalizing" mutants and presenting them as a global minority, anti-mutantism is in significant ways a poor analogy for the socially constructed character of racism, colonialism, and white supremacy. As critical race and postcolonial scholars have continually shown, there is nothing "natural" about race and the global "minority" perspective involved in the colonial production of racialized otherness belongs to whiteness itself (Delgado & Stefancic, 2019). For this reason, I felt that the X-Men series continued the dialectical notion of representation implicit in the theme of fandom and posed the politics of identification with the X-Men as more ethically complicated.

To get more specific, I asked the class to read the 1982 graphic novel *X-Men: God Loves, Man Kills* (Anderson & Claremont, 2011). I chose this graphic novel for a number of reasons, the first being its relatively self-contained position within the sprawling X-Men continuity. More importantly, however, the graphic novel is notable for being one of the first instances in which the series' traditional villain, Magneto, appears as an uneasy ally of the X-Men and as representing a persuasive political alternative to Charles Xavier. To give a quick synopsis, *God Loves, Man Kills* concerns the X-Men's conflict with the Stryker Brigade, an anti-mutant vigilante group led by the fundamentalist televangelist William Stryker. After Stryker kidnaps Charles Xavier, planning to use his telekinetic abilities to conduct a mutant genocide, the X-Men team up with Magneto to defeat Stryker and rescue Professor X. While reflecting the then-contemporary political rise of the so-called Moral Majority, the graphic novel also grapples with the efficacy of Charles Xavier's reconciliatory political sensibilities in the face of a genocidal enemy: the graphic novel ends with a rescued Charles Xavier very nearly abandoning the X-Men and joining Magneto's more radical Brotherhood of Mutants.

More so than many other X-Men storylines, *God Loves, Man Kills* does some work to address the limits of anti-mutantism as a metaphor in an "intersectional" way. The graphic novel opens, for example, with the murder of two young Black mutants by the Stryker Brigade, visually depicted in a way clearly reminiscent of the lynching of African Americans in the U.S. South. Other scenes in which the X-Men confront popular supporters of the Stryker Brigade's anti-mutant "crusade" plainly acknowledge the existence of racism as well as anti-mutantism in the world of the X-Men and don't merely substitute the latter as a metaphor for the former. Along these lines, Abigail Thorn's aforementioned YouTube video "Is Magneto Right?" argues for a reading of *God Loves, Man Kills* as a meditation on political responses to structural violence, particularly around the political philosophy of Magneto: a notion I adapted for the class's discussion of the graphic novel and the writing assignment to follow.

Thorn (2016) recasts Magneto as akin to Frantz Fanon, who famously argued that colonized subjects had the right to resist their colonial oppressors with direct violence (Fanon & Philcox, 2005). In her reading, Charles Xavier's dream of peaceful coexistence between humans and mutants fails to recognize the reality of structural violence under which mutants live and assumes, falsely, that anti-mutant prejudice results from the humans' *fear* of mutants rather than overt exploitation. As Thorn puts it:

> Professor X rejects direct violence in favor of peace, where peace is the absence of violence. But in so doing, he assumes there can be an absence of violence whilst the systems he lives under are still standing, which is impossible if genoism [that is, anti-mutantism] is central to how they operate. He rejects direct violence but in doing so he effectively sides with the systems that maintain structural genoism and all the violence that they inflict.

In other words, Thorn's framing allowed for the class to extend discussions of representation beyond "stereotyping" and into the realm of political structures and questions of resistance.

Thorn casts Magneto, by contrast, as a revolutionary figure bent on upending all systems of oppression. This characterization of Magneto finds dramatic support in *God Loves, Man Kills* in a famous scene (disquietingly taking place atop the Twin Towers) in which Magneto lays out his political vision to the reluctant X-Men. As Magneto says, "I am not your enemy, X-Men, nor do I consider you mine. True, my goal has been the conquest of earth—but solely to create a world where [mutants] can live in peace. Look at yourselves, risking your lives for a humanity that would rather see you behind bars, or dead. Why do you persist?" (Anderson & Claremont, 2011, p. 55). When challenged by the earnest Cyclops about whether Magneto's "conquest of earth" amounts to a dictatorship, Magneto shoots back by alluding to his origins as a Holocaust survivor:

> I have lived under dictatorship ... and seen my family butchered by its servants. When I rule, it will be for the betterment of **all**. Contentment breeds tranquility—discontent, rebellion. Therefore, I shall ensure the one by eliminating the root causes of the other: hunger, poverty, disease, war. The freedoms lost will not be noticed, even in the most libertarian of states. And the material benefits should more than balance the scales. (Ibid.)

Directly echoing Marx's famous maxim that "to be radical is to grasp the root of the matter," this incarnation of the Magneto character is antagonistic in the most dialectical sense of the word in its calling into question the possibility of Professor X's dream of peaceful coexistence under the violent status quo. Thus, the writing assignment building from this framing of the central political conflict in *God Loves, Man Kills* asked students to respond to the titular question of Thorn's video: Is Magneto right? And, furthermore: Can the "mutant metaphor" of the X-Men be analogized to other real-world forms of oppression?

Students responded in a multitude of ways, some arguing more forcefully for Xavier or Magneto's point of view, others arguing for some sort of middle ground. I was struck, whatever the position, about how students connected careful readings of Magneto's character to historical and contemporary social struggles. For example, one student directly connected Magneto's conception of mutant resistance as self-defense given the structural violence of the status quo to the then-recent white nationalist "Unite the Right" rally that took place in Charlottesville, Virginia in 2017. Comparing the villain Stryker to President Trump's embrace of the "fine people" at Charlottesville, this student found Stryker's potent combination of charisma, fanatical following, and a xenophobia cloaked in moral language sounded disturbingly contemporary. He concluded that Xavier's reformist position, like those in contemporary struggles, had failed, writing that, "with a monster like Striker, there is no room for civility." He continued: "Stryker is charismatic, he is a powerful person of faith, and an influential media figurehead. Mutants, as ironic as it may seem, have little to no power as it relates to politics and media influence. The rules are in Stryker's favor, which means rules have to be broken in order for the X-Men to simply live." Thus, the student argued for Magneto's more revolutionary position, that "in order to fix the system it has to be broken first."

While other students were sympathetic to Magneto's characterization of structural violence, they found Xavier's methods of passive resistance more effective. Take, for example, another student's argument that "Magneto contradicts himself by stating that he wants to eliminate the causes of war." Similarly to other students, she argued that Magneto's vision of a "mutant dictatorship" that would eliminate the root causes of inequality fails to be revolutionary because it replicates the social forms that had oppressed mutants, even if the power dynamics were overturned. By the end of this assignment, it became clear that students had, in a sophisticated manner, developed a firm grasp of the vexed issues connecting questions of identity and representation to ongoing structural violence.

Representing Claudia Rankine's Citizen *in Splash Pages*

These engagements with themes of structural racism continued into our discussions of a more real-world, but no less visually innovative text, Claudia Rankine's (2014) book-length poem *Citizen: An American Lyric*. The accompanying essay assignment involved a critical analysis of how the poem represents the structural violence of American racism. However, to frame the essay, I asked students to represent a scene from *Citizen* in the form of a comic book "splash page," a one-panel comic page. Having students represent *Citizen* in a visual form required them to reflect on their own varied positionalities in relation to the depictions of racism in the poem. Readers of *Citizen* will recall how the poem itself raises questions of positionality in its use of a second-person speaker. In other words, the poem's address to "you" deconstructs notions of the (assumed white) "ideal" reader and instead forces readers to confront how their lived experiences of race structure different responses to the poem. In addition to helping students "visualize" a specific focus for the critical essay, the Splash Page activity served as a way to bring these issues of social positioning into their writing. *Citizen* itself is a highly visual text, including supplementary images in the margins of the poem. Thus, engaging *Citizen* in a visual way also helped to highlight the intertextuality contained within the poem.

The model splash page offered to students came from Marvel's *America Chavez* (2017), written by queer Puerto Rican author Gabby Rivera and illustrated by Joe Quinones. The series follows the titular America Chavez, a multiversal migrant who takes up the moniker Miss America. The image from *America* #1 depicts the Latina superhero protecting the barrio from extraterrestrial attack, saying, "America's Got You!" Simultaneously, bystanders flee the destruction, save for two teenage girls taking a selfie. I chose this particular image because of how it plays on the doubled sense of America as at once the nation and the name of a queer Latina superhero, thus succinctly suggesting larger themes of multiculturalism, national belonging, queer diaspora, and the dignity of migrant identity. It also not so subtly recalls the nationalistic and perhaps jingoistic connotations of the Captain America archetype, recasting and problematizing them for students reading in the context of Trump-era mainstreamed xenophobia. Reinforces these themes, but also demonstrates a practice of close reading, which ultimately represented the mode of literary analysis highlighted in this section of the course: the assignment built into a more traditional close reading where they would offer an interpretation of the passages they had "visualized" in the form of a splash page.

While some students' splash pages were more technically achieved than others, ranging from doodles on loose-leaf to full photoshopped productions, all demonstrated a keen engagement with the major images and themes of *Citizen,* especially its challenges to white normativity in representation. Many students, in fact, focused on a section titled "Stop and Frisk," which impressionistically depicts a Black man's encounter with police during a frivolous traffic stop using a number of repetitive phrases that blur the lines of interior monologue, police commands, and the voice of the Black speaker. Standout engagements of this particular scene showed how various mediums and skill-levels in graphic designs could provide compelling representations that, nonetheless, worked the muscles of interpretation we in literary studies associate with the practice of close reading. One especially simple, but no less powerful, example came in the form of a student's drawing on loose-leaf paper. This splash page depicts a young man in a hoodie, clearly evocative of Trayvon Martin, whose face is obscured by a large question mark. Coming from outside the panel, a voice speaks a central repeated line from "Stop and Frisk": "And you are not the guy, but still you fit the description because there is only one guy who is always the guy fitting the description." In quite a succinct way, this splash page distilled class discussions exploring two key terms Rankine employs to describe the rendering of Black bodies as "deviant" in white normative spaces: that the white gaze alternately renders the humanity of Black people as "invisible" while at the same time policing Blackness as "hypervisible." In presenting her splash page as an exploration of these two important concepts, this student also helped clarify their use as lenses for the close reading essay she later wrote based on her visualization.

Figure 3. Stop & Frisk

Another standout engagement with "Stop and Frisk" came from a student with a background using Photoshop. This experience is evident in his splash page, titled "Terry Stop." This image incorporates additional lines from *Citizen*, the injunction to "Get on the ground now!" and images of sirens. The splash page pictures two police officers detaining a Black man with a target on his back. However, this student also creatively added context and story content not contained in *Citizen*, depicting the officer as shouting, "Terry, stop!" while the Black man being detained replies, "That's not even my name." Here, the splash page plays on the term "terry stop," a more formal name for stop and frisk. The detained Black man, mirroring the impressionistic aspects of Rankine's source text, hears this term as the name Terry: a

Visualizing Identity, Fandom, and Representation 111

Figure 4. Terry Stop

violent act of misrecognition and, ultimately, renaming. This student, like many others, explained the design in relation to the concepts of "invisibility" and "hypervisibility," linking them to how stop and frisk policies are based on both willful 'misrecognition' of the individuality of People of Color while constructing their bodies as potentially criminal in white normative spaces.

Many other students found interest in a section focused on Serena Williams' struggles with racial microaggressions on and off the tennis court, which reengaged the fandom theme (i.e., sports fandom) in a way I didn't entirely anticipate. This section, written in an expository style that highlights the unfair sanctions that Williams has faced as a Black woman in a "white" sport. Beneath the surface, nonetheless, these passages also work as a poetic meditation on the interpellation of Black bodies in "white" normative spaces. In other words, Rankine shows how Williams' body has been already constructed as "breaking" the rules of tennis by officials, and thus this disciplining of her body on the tennis court becomes, in the context of *Citizen*, also a larger comment on the broader logics of racialized policing in a normatively "white" American society. In this sense, though the section more literally concerns the ethics of consumption between Black athletes and white spectators, in a figurative sense it continues the larger themes of Black embodiment and policing explored throughout *Citizen*.

To exemplify how students represented contrasting "readings" of this section, let's highlight two submissions. One, a multi-paneled collage of athletic images of Serena Williams on the tennis court contrasted with an image of an incident, recounted in *Citizen*, in which a rival, white tennis player named Caroline Wozniacki stuffed her breasts and buttocks in an apparent racist mimicry of Williams' physique. The creator of this splash page juxtaposes these images with key phrases from *Citizen*, such as "What does a victorious or defeated Black woman's body in a historically white space look like?" and a quote from Zora Neale Hurston, "I feel most colored when I am thrown against a sharp white background." Here, the student highlighted how Rankine's representation of Serena's body on the tennis court mirrors the larger racial imagination of Black bodies in white supremacist spaces, as well as the white innocence that decries resistance to this policing of Blackness as "bad sportsmanship." Another standout example, presented a cut-and-paste splash page on a poster board that directly confronted and challenged the white normative imagination that Rankine exposes. Instead, this design emphasized Serena Williams' "confidence," "strength," and "drive," in essence pushing for a deconstruction of the structures of white normativity explored in *Citizen*.

Figure 5. Serena Williams

These are just a few examples, but what struck me in all of them is how students' visualizations did, in fact, perform and ultimately inform close readings. Through visualization, students were able to isolate themes, recurring literary elements, and concepts from *Citizen* while offering competing interpretations—interpretations that were debated in the informal and low-risk environment of simply sharing their splash pages with the class. They were also able to link the questions regarding structural violence in the

Figure 6. A Self-Made Woman

metaphorical X-Men graphic novel that preceded *Citizen* using the ideas and concepts introduced in Rankine's aesthetic representation of the racist structures of white normativity and the way the poem's very form calls attention to how our experiences of race necessarily structure our reception of the text. Thus, it also recalled and complicated the questions of representation, identity and, importantly, consumption from which the course began.

The Five-Paragraph 'Exam'

The final essay, taking the form of an "exam," was mandated by the English department. Though I ordinarily would shy away from a timed, five-paragraph essay format, nonetheless I was surprised by how many students produced some of their best writing in this format. Treating it as a chance to show off the forms of literary analysis built throughout the semester, students wrote about the final dramatic work we read together: in Spring 2018, Kristoffer Diaz's *The Elaborate Entrance of Chad Deity* (2011) and in Fall 2018, Matt Barbot's *El Coquí Espectacular and the Bottle of Doom* (2018). Both works, in different ways, explore Nuyorican identity, with Diaz's play following a Nuyorican wrestler who is continually scripted to lose while playing stereotypical characters and Barbot's play presenting the misadventures of a Puerto Rican superhero.[5] In short, the final exam prompt asked students to show how the play represents experiences of cultural identity and alienation. In the process, students also recapped their engagement with these themes throughout the course. While I had to return these hand-written exams to the English department and, thus, no longer have access to them, suffice to say that there was something about stripping away everything except a blank page and the text at hand that resulted in many students producing some of their most clear, organized, and focused work of the semester, even if they took more productive risks on other assignments. In short, I would just say here that this experience underscored the usefulness of in-class writing.

Also, though it's outside the scope of this chapter, I also experimented in my final semester with switching up the intertextual medium, trying a similarly constructed course organized around sonic textuality titled "Literary Listening." While doing justice to this course would require a separate chapter, and thus I'm excising it from this one, I mention it primarily to highlight the adaptability of assignments and framings that began in "Visualizing Identity" but have influenced subsequent courses I have taught that have little to do with visual culture, fandoms, or comic books. For example, all of my subsequent courses at LaGuardia and Lehman College, and later even at a quite different institution in Georgia Tech, have used visual syllabi as tone-setting devices and explored centering textualities and sensibilities beyond traditional framings of literary studies.

Final Thoughts

So, about my final takeaways. Beyond the specific themes of identity, representation, and resistance to structural violence, on which students produced socially engaged and sophisticated writing, issues of *form* have stuck with me. For example, while many interlocutors were supportive as I shared early drafts of the visual materials for this course, some did wonder whether their informality would appear less "rigorous" to students than a traditional syllabus. While the course materials certainly did loosen *me* up in how I present as a human being in the classroom, I got the sense that this was also true for students. Ultimately, this looseness provided the opportunity for highly rigorous writing and exploration, not just because students were encouraged to incorporate their own interests. Rather, students took their own standpoints and experiences as serious groundings for creative academic inquiry and social transformation. They became humanists in the broadest possible sense: not in the spirit of solipsism, but in a socially engaged inquiry into human liberation and freedom.

Notes

1 For two paradigmatic examples, see Ngũgĩ wa Thiong'o's (1986) *Decolonizing the Mind* or Gauri Viswanathan's (2015) *Masks of Conquest*.
2 Austin, a dear friend, also hosted, in his words, a "queer and fabulous" poetry reading for students in the Spring 2018 class and the LaGuardia community at large. The reading spanned poems on themes from *Sailor Moon* and *Legend of Zelda*, through to a student-favorite series on the hip hop artist Drake. Invite him to your institution! And pay him handsomely!
3 In retrospect, I did not foresee how such rhetoric would quickly make the jump from the comments section to mainstream right-wing discourse, as evidenced by Florida Governor Ron DeSantis' ongoing retaliation against Disney over their opposition to the state's utterly noxious and discriminatory 2022 "Don't Say Gay" bill. We are now seeing what happens when the toxic fanboy occupies a governor's mansion.
4 The names and identifying details of students have been removed for privacy.
5 Barbot himself was kind enough to visit the Fall 2018 class to discuss the play and run a writing workshop. The workshop asked students to adapt and restage two passages from Shakespeare's *Romeo and Juliet* in genre styles such as horror, science fiction and Westerns. The horror group, turning Romeo into a homicidal maniac, was especially hilarious. Do invite Barbot to run this workshop if you get the chance. And also pay him handsomely!

References

Adorno, T., & Horkheimer, M. (2001). The culture industry: Enlightenment as mass deception. In V. Leitch (Ed.), *The Norton anthology of theory and criticism* (pp. 1223–1239). Norton.

Anderson, B., & Claremont, C. (2011). *X-Men: God Loves, Man Kills*. Marvel.

Austin, D. (2018, August 20). *In the name of the Femme: A queer boy's voyage with Sailor Moon*. Black Nerd Problems. https://blacknerdproblems.com/in-the-name-of-the-femme-a-queer-boys-voyage-with-sailor-moon/

Barbot, M. (2018). *El Coquí Espectacular and the bottle of doom: A superhero play*. Theatrical Script.

Delgado, R., & Stefancic, J. (2019). *Critical Race Theory: An introduction* (3rd ed.). New York University Press.

Diaz, K. (2011). *The elaborate entrance of Chad deity*. Samuel French.

Fanon, F., & Philcox, R. (2005). *The wretched of the Earth*. Grove Press.

Ferguson, R. (2012). *The reorder of things: The university and its pedagogies of minority difference*. University of Minnesota Press.

Hall, S. (2019). Notes on deconstructing the popular. In *Essential essays* (Vol. 1). Duke University Press.

Leitch, D. (Director). (2018). *Deadpool 2* [Film]. Twentieth Century Fox.

Ngũgĩ wa Thiong'o. (1986). *Decolonising the mind: The politics of language in African literature*. Heinemann.

Picker, M. (Director). (2002). *Mickey Mouse monopoly: Disney, childhood, and corporate power* [Film]. Media Education Foundation.

Rankine, C. (2014). *Citizen: An American lyric*. Graywolf Press.

Rivera, G., & Quinones, J. (2017). *America Vol. 1: The life and times of America Chavez*. Marvel.

Thorn, A. (2016, July 29). *X Men: Is magneto right? | Philosophy tube ft NerdSync*. YouTube. https://www.youtube.com/watch?v=7xE6Pb5y9hs

Viswanathan, G. (2015). *Masks of conquest: Literary study and British rule in India*. Columbia University Press.

Zygutis, L. (2021). Affirmational canons and transformative literature: Notes on teaching with fandom. *Fan Studies Pedagogies, 35*.

Subverting White Androcentrism in Psychology Curricula

Mike Rifino

As a psychology instructor in a community college, what it means to introduce students to psychology entails orienting students toward psychology's diverse feminist, queer, and Black liberation traditions, which continue to be marginalized within mainstream, Euro-American psychology. Most of my students, who often represent historically marginalized communities, welcome these traditions and recognize them as legitimate psychological knowledge. Thus, I was shocked when my student shared with me (during class discussion) the skeptical and dismissive feedback she received from her presentation on the androcentric history of psychology in her advanced psychology course. According to Stella,[1] although some of her peers appreciated her work, the majority, including her professor, were critical of the idea that feminism is a legitimate topic in psychology. In fact, one of her peers claimed that her presentation was "too feminist for psychology" claiming it felt more relevant for sociology. This experience was disheartening for Stella, and me, and our class validated her efforts and feelings. Later, Stella would present this work in a student club, which won her the "Best Presentation" award.

What Stella's contentious encounter represents is the illumination of the ethical and political orientation of hegemonic psychology, embedded in the teaching and learning of undergraduate psychology education. Specifically, psychology is taught from an orientation that historically reflects specific geographies, ontologies, epistemologies, ethics, and politics as its disciplinary pillars while dismissing and denigrating others. As has been widely documented, hegemonic psychology and undergraduate psychology education have been historically oriented toward Euro-American traditions that foreground the perspectives of white, male, upper-class, Christian, heterosexual, and nondisabled individuals (Adams et al., 2015; Bhatia, 2018, 2021;

Canham et al., 2021; Kiguwa & Segalo, 2018; Macleod et al., 2020; Ratele et al., 2018; Readsura Decolonial Editorial Collective, 2022a, 2022b; Reddy & Amer, 2022). Situating its origins in European colonization, hegemonic psychology's embrace of positivism, universalism, and individualism have been complicit in reinforcing racist and ableist science that views the majority of the world through a lens of the Other grounded in deficit, inferior, or problematic assumptions (Bhatia, 2021; Kessi et al., 2021; Simango & Segalo, 2020). These tenets undergird curriculum in undergraduate psychology education, and constitute a significant portion of key psychological knowledge. Thus, undergraduate psychology education, as it is currently constructed, entails a politics of orientation, that is the implicit ways students are influenced to embrace Western conceptions of being, knowing, and doing, while orienting away from those that may represent their own local knowledge, traditions, and perspectives. Given that one of the goals of first-year seminars is to introduce, or orient students toward the discipline, it is my contention that these courses serve as a fertile ground for exploring the following questions: what does it mean to provide students an orientation to psychology, how might we pedagogically illuminate the hegemonic Euro-American canon and facilitate resistance? Considering how Stella's experience represents an explicit interrogation about what is, and is not, legitimate psychological knowledge, Sara Ahmed's (2006) queering of the concept of orientation is potentially generative in these questions.

As Ahmed asserts, "To educate is to orient" (p. 54). Drawing from Plato's *Republic* (1998), Ahmed (2010) argues that education as a form of orientation involves "turning minds around" to face the proper way, thus implying students are misaligned prior to receiving formal education (p. 54). To become oriented, then, is to "know where we are when we turn this way or that way" entailing "different ways of registering the proximity of objects and others" (Ahmed, 2006, pp. 1–3). Thus, orientation involves understanding where one is situated in relation to objects known or recognizable and those that are unknown or foreign. According to Ahmed (2006), the way that some objects feel near and others feel far away can illuminate an orientation. In Stella's experiences with her peers, what is being said about the orientation of psychology when feminism is dismissed as unrecognizable or irrelevant, whereas individualistic, experimental, and biological essentialist approaches are felt as familiar and foundational? Additionally, what might be the affective dimensions of orientation and disorientation (Ahmed, 2014)? The first-year seminar for psychology, a course that entails providing students a series of orientations, namely toward the discipline, college life, and student success, offers a unique site to explore with students how psychology is oriented toward certain mainstream traditions and how we can promote alternative ones. This chapter suggests a politics of orientation in psychology that is a process of orienting *toward* hegemonic psychology's Euro-American traditions, while becoming oriented *away from* the local and indigenous ones. However, decolonial and decentering pedagogies can critically examine and disrupt this, fostering liberatory conditions for teaching and learning.

This chapter is divided into three parts. First, I review the relevant literature on recent apology letters and resolutions the American Psychological Association (APA) has made regarding psychology education, and then I shift to exploring the growing movements toward decolonizing and decentering psychology curricula. Second, I present how I implement the Psychology's Feminist Voices' Imagined Conversations research paper along with my scaffolded assignments that took place in a first-year seminar in psychology at LaGuardia Community College, CUNY. Third and final, I assess the merits of this project and how it can provide students a critical introduction toward psychology.

APA Apology Letters and Recommendations for Psychology Curriculum

Despite the many decades of unheeded calls for transforming undergraduate psychology education, the global COVID-19 pandemic and international counter-hegemonic movements toward racial, ecological, and reproductive justice have ignited activists and scholars into widespread critical examination of undergraduate education (Cranney et al., 2022). In this context, the APA issued various apologies to historically disenfranchised communities for its contributions to perpetuating systemic racism and hierarchy, cultural oppression, white supremacy, eugenics, and indigenous erasure (APA, 2023a). Specifically, one of the issued apologies was addressed to People of Color for psychology's contributions to systemic racism and hierarchy (2021a), and a resolution for examining its support of racial injustice across a range of domains, starting with education, stating that psychology has "distorted the lives of People of Color, omitted their contributions in history, and portrayed them in pathological and stereotypical ways" (APA, 2021b, p. 2).

As a response to these resolutions, including the Equity, Diversity, and Inclusion framework (APA, 2021c), many critically oriented voices, such as the Association of Black Psychologists (ABPsi), have expressed their distrust in APA actually holding itself accountable to its own claims. ABPsi issued an official statement that the APA "cannot simply dismiss the full history of Euro-American psychology that is rooted in a legacy of the pathology of Whiteness with a simple apology and questionable claims to now combat racism, oppression, and white hegemony" (2021, p. 1). Furthermore, ABPsi pointed out that APA, at the time of this resolution, did not consult with them or any ethnic Associations on these matters and highlighted its inactions toward dismantling the dominant, white-centered psychology curriculum in undergraduate and graduate programs. Echoing a similar sentiment, Desai et al. (2023) point out APA's and psychology's blatant disregard for Dr. Martin Luther King Jr.'s (1968) APA address on the intersections of structural oppression, psychology, and mental health and Franz Fanon's (1967/1952) groundbreaking works on internalized colonial oppression (see also Fanon, 1963/1961). Indeed, the pedagogical struggle is to rework the entirety of the psychology curricula so that these important contributions (including many others, like E. Kitch Childs' activist legacy; Mulvale, 2020) are foundational, rather than marginal in psychology (Rifino, 2022). These are deeply rooted issues embedded in psychology as exemplified by Robert Guthrie's (2003) landmark book, *Even the Rat was White: A Historical View of Psychology*.

Occurring in the backdrop of these issued statements, APA has also initiated a series of committees to update its principles and guidelines for quality curricular experience in psychology (APA, 2022, 2023b), including a concentrated effort for addressing national inconsistencies concerning Introduction to Psychology (Boysen & Becker-Blease, 2021; Carolissen et al., 2015; Gurung & Neufeld, 2022). However, psychologists on the margins remind us that these initiatives have not only excluded critical perspectives, but also support psychology's orientation toward emulating itself as a STEM discipline (Bachik & Kitzman, 2020; Tyrell et al., 2023)Yakushko & Hook, 2017). This entails psychology curricula to further entrench itself within western paradigms, thus centering a "stats-and-rats" curriculum where biological-based explanations of psychological processes are prioritized over contextual understandings (p. 174). This may render students in psychology ill-equipped to address issues of social justice, and even may deter others from committing to psychology altogether. As a psychology instructor, it is imperative to show students these conceptual, yet deeply practical debates as part of their orientation toward psychology. The current decolonial turn in psychology and decentering approaches offer a rich landscape for speaking to students' values, perspectives, and worldviews.

The Decolonial Turn in Psychology

Recent movements for decolonizing knowledge production and curricula in higher educational institutions, such as #RhodesMustFall in South Africa (Hussain, 2015) and 'Why is my curriculum white?' at Oxford University

(Maxwele, 2016), have generated massive interest in what Nelson Maldonado-Torres (2011) defines as 'the decolonial turn.' Rooted in a long lineage of diverse, contradictory, and divergent traditions, the decolonial turn foregrounds perspectives from Latin America, the Caribbean, Africa, and other historically marginalized sectors of the world that "share a view of coloniality as a fundamental problem in the modern (as well as post-modern and information) age, and of decolonization or decoloniality as a necessary task that remains unfinished" (Maldonado-Torres, 2011, p. 2 as cited in Sonn & Stevens, 2021, p. 2). Coloniality, drawing from Quijano (2000), interpenetrates with capitalism, gender, sexuality, sex, and race, and denotes the continuing legacy of European colonization that ubiquitously informs being, doing, and knowing, and defines culture, gender, sex, labor, socioeconomic systems, social relations, and more (Maldonado-Torres, 2007). Thus, the rise of Euro-Western modernity, especially its modern gender system, is based on colonial capitalist violence and exploitation as it imposed essentialized and immutable categories of difference over colonized communities suggesting there is "no modernity without coloniality" (Mignolo, 2007, p. 3; Bohrer, 2020; Lugones, 2007; Rodrigues, 2022). Unsurprisingly, the development and expansion of the discipline of Psychology is connected to colonialism, with scholars of the Global South[2] illuminating the colonial dimensions of Euro-Western psychology. Critical and decolonial feminist psychologists in Africa, and in particular South Africa have been the most generative in producing decolonial thought and practice in psychology and have long highlighted that "the discipline of psychology cannot be divorced from its colonial history" (Segalo & Simango, 2021, para. 4; Armero et al., 2022; Nsamenang, 2007; Segalo, 2016).

Although the manifestation of Euro-Western psychology's coloniality differs depending on socio-historical, temporal, and geographical contexts, there are common themes to be gleaned from a specific case (e.g., Armero et al., 2022; Bhatia, 2018). Simango and Segalo (2020), for instance, understand Euro-Western psychology's colonial history in Africa in three ways. First, the violent importing of Euro-Western psychology knowledge systems to African contexts coincided with European colonization and Christian missionary education. Colonial mentality emerged from the perpetuation of epistemic violence and scientific racism that not only promoted racist ideologues about African inferiority and white superiority but attempted to undermine local knowledge systems and traditions, thereby legitimizing the adoption of Euro-western psychology (Adams et al., 2018; Adams et al., 2020; Biko, 2002; Fanon, 1967/1952; Sonn et al., 2017; Ngũgĩ wa Thiong'o, 1986). Second, the expansion of Euro-Western intellectual imperialism in Africa and other parts of the world continued, through the use of the eugenics movement, and imposed its system universally, thus rendering Euro-Western psychology to appear as a neutral body of knowledge that can be applied regardless of context. This has led critical and decolonial scholarship to suggest that Euro-Western psychology is a WEIRD discipline as its worldviews and knowledge systems derive almost exclusively from Western, Educated, Industrial, Rich, and Democratic societies, yet it positions itself as the universal standard for humanity to conform to (Bhatia, 2018; Henrich et al., 2010; Thalmayer et al., 2021). Third, the popularization of mental health testing and intelligence test research in the early 1900s supported and contributed to oppressive laws and policies, such as segregation policies and apartheid laws, that aimed to "govern black bodies and black people's intellectual capabilities, physical movement, and knowledge" (Simango & Segalo, 2020, p. 71). As scholars from the Global South continue to illuminate this history, these colonial foundations are still intact in Euro-Western psychology, and much burgeoning literature on the decolonial turn in psychology has been concentrated on this area.

In fact, current decolonial literature in psychology is focused on examining the ongoing forms of colonization persistent within present disciplinary psychology. In general, much of this work is twofold: (1) challenge hegemonic psychology for its Euro-western imperialism, positivism, individualism, and universalism in its theories, methods, and approaches, and (2) envision possibilities and implement pathways for decolonizing psychology (Adams et al., 2015; Canham et al., 2021; Kessi et al., 2021; Kiguwa, 2023; Malherbe & Ratele, 2022; Ratele, 2019; Readsura Decolonial Editorial Collective et al., 2022 a, 2022b; Reddy & Amer, 2022; Simango & Segalo, 2020).

Decolonizing and Decentering Undergraduate Psychology Curricula

Calls for decolonizing and decentering hegemonic psychology curricula suggest a wide-ranging set of approaches, with specific orientations and philosophical commitments. Similar to decolonial approaches to disciplinary psychology, the Global South and in particular South African psychologies have produced an extensive and diverse range of literature on decolonial approaches to teaching and learning in psychology often representing commitments to the field of community psychology. Although it is beyond the scope of this chapter to present the breadth and depth of this multiplicity of perspectives, it can be argued that many of these works have asserted that challenging and transcending the hegemonic, Euro-western psychology curricula requires a transformation in pedagogy, suggesting a decolonial approach to teaching and learning in psychology (Canham et al., 2021; Carolissen et al., 2017; Fernández, 2018; Fernández et al., 2021; Gomez-Ordonez et al., 2021; James & Lorenz, 2021; Kiguwa & Segalo, 2018; Schmidt, 2019; Seedat & Suffla, 2017; Silva et al., 2022). As Terre Blanche et al. (2021) assert "to teach decolonially requires a transformation in the teaching *process* as much as in the ideas being communicated" (p. 370). For them, decolonizing psychology education entails explicating the critiques of Euro-Western psychology and the biases inherent in its knowledge production and argue for a decolonial pedagogical approach to psychology that foregrounds reflexivity, dialogue, and an inclusivity of historically marginalized knowledge systems.

This literature has also challenged how we view curricula as not only a textual artifact but also entailing "psycho-social biographies" (Kiguwa & Segalo, 2018, p. 310). Drawing on Le Grange (2016), Kiguwa and Segalo (2018) explore Eurocentric psychology's curricula in three dimensions: explicit (what we teach), null (local knowledges excluded from institutional curricula), and hidden (the implicit values dictating the socio-emotional norms and expectations). To address all three dimensions, Kiguwa and Segalo (2018) suggest a centering of multiplicity of situated knowledge systems that challenge eurocentric epistemic traditions while avoiding superficial attempts of merely adding critical voices to a western curricula. Other works, specifically in a special issue focused on decoloniality and psychology (Carolissen & Duckett, 2018), have explored what might entail a decolonizing psychology curricula (Castell et al., 2018). Specifically, these works have demonstrated the decolonial necessity for critical reflectivity (Castell et al., 2018), diagonal affectivity (Bell, 2018), and solidarity as key for decolonial resistance vis-à-vis hegemonic psychology curricula (Watkins et al., 2018). This suggests that decolonizing psychology entails more than epistemological transformation, but also ontological transformation. Carolissen et al. (2017) assert that destabilizing the centrality of Euro-Western knowledge would allow for the coexistence of multiple knowledge systems. Drawing on Santos (2007), Carolissen et al. (2017) argue that this may challenge the 'abyssal lines' in which Euro-western history of psychology is centered and universalized, while all other psychologies particularly from the Global South, are erased contributing to epistemicide (p. 497). These works are diverse in their positionings, commitments, and visions in what entails a decolonizing psychology curricula.

Although not all critical, liberatory, transformative work does not always center itself within decoloniality, it is important to acknowledge this other strand of literature as it also attempts to challenge systemic injustices in psychology curricula (Costa & Bedir, 2022; Gillborn et al., 2021; Jankowski et al., 2022; Kelly et al., 2022; Kontopodis & Jackowska, 2019; Pownall, 2022, 2023). Gillborn et al. (2023), for instance, connect how race-neutral psychology curricula reproduce pathologizing accounts of Black, Indigenous, People of Color based on not conforming to whiteness. Similarly, Kontopodis and Jackowska (2019) explore how a decentering of the psychology curricula entails challenging white supremacist histories through centering "polyphonic and polycentric psychologies" (p. 508) representing alternative frameworks that reflect the interests and values of students from historically marginalized backgrounds. Importantly, these ongoing critiques on undergraduate psychology education are not limited to the psychology curricula, but also to its textbooks. This is crucial because textbooks are heavily relied upon in psychology and also serve to naturalize disciplinary assumptions, and values (Apple & Christian-Smith, 2017). Much critical psychology textbook scholarship examines how androcentrism (George et al., 2020; Hill, 2019), Euro-western-centricism (Kiguwa & Segalo, 2018; Uluğ & Acar, 2022), and positivism (Costa & Shimp, 2011; Moke & Bohan, 1992) are encoded in most Global North produced psychology textbooks. These works have highlighted how systemic inequalities are encoded in psychology curricula and textbooks. This chapter attempts to contribute to the literature on decolonizing and de-entering the psychology curricula by offering a pedagogical project that afford students a critical examination of their psychology curriculum that they contrast with alternative epistemic traditions of psychologies on the margins featured on *Psychology's Feminist Voices* database and their Imagined Conversations research paper (Young et al., 2015).

First-Year Seminar for Psychology

Given that a first-year seminar is typically one of the first classes students take, it offers a fertile ground to invite students into a critical examination of the curricula that they are in the process of becoming oriented in. Higher educational scholarship has consistently recognized first-year seminars as essential for promoting student engagement and retention (Kuh, 2008). First Year Seminars (FYS) are designed to introduce students to the college, their majors, and the skills, dispositions, and values necessary for college success.

The current research paper project takes place at LaGuardia Community College (LaGuardia), which is part of the City University of New York (CUNY) system. LaGuardia prides itself on serving students primarily from historically marginalized communities, representing a highly diverse, non-traditional student body. Specifically, among the approximately 19,000 students in academic programs in Fall 2019, there were over 160 countries represented and over 90 different native languages (LaGuardia Community College, Office of Institutional Research and Assessment, 2020). In LaGuardia, FYS courses are credit-bearing, discipline-specific, and are supported by student affairs staff and student peer mentors (Battle et al., 2017). The current research paper project takes place within my FYS in Psychology, which has a maximum roster size of 25 students. In this course, all students are psychology majors. The majority of students are either freshmen or transfer students.

My Pedagogical Positionality and Context

As Kiguwa and Segalo (2018) argue, "positioning matters for how we choose what we teach, how it is packaged, and how it is presented ... Engaging the socio-history of the discipline—its worldviews and philosophical underpinnings—is linked to our specific orientations and view of the self-in-the-world" (p. 13). As a critical response to Eurocentric psychology, positionality challenges the assumption that knowledge can be produced from a neutral viewpoint (Decolonial Psychology Editorial Collective, 2021).

Two major experiences of my psychology education inspired me to take the position of teaching a critically oriented introduction to psychology. First, as an undergraduate student earning a bachelor's degree in psychology, I noticed that my education was rooted in a Euro-Western orientation to psychology in which (neuro)biological topics, quantitative research methods, and theories based on individualism and linear models of development were centered as natural facets of psychology. Pedagogically, these psychology courses were typically taught based on a transmission model in which learning was based on memorizing overly simplified bits of information that came from a textbook. Even though I would participate with critical ideas in these courses, I would often feel isolated as it was rare to find psychology students who were also critically oriented. However, in my humanities courses, I was learning conceptual theories based on primary sources that emphasized social context and social issues. Even though the (white-male dominated) issues present in psychology were common in some of these courses, these humanities-based classrooms offered a space to address this critically and creatively with my peers. Upon becoming a lecturer in psychology in the same community college that I was once a student, I wanted to develop my pedagogy based on my humanities courses that emphasized reflexivity, participation, and multiplicity. Second, as a doctoral student at the Graduate Center, I remember vividly when I first came across the thesis room that is named after Ignacio Martín Baró (1994). When I learned who he was, a Salvadoran social psychologist-activist, and central figure of Liberation Psychology, I felt strong emotions about my understanding of psychology education. I felt deeply validated to learn about psychologists who I was able to identify with, both politically and because of my Dominican background. At the same time, I also felt angry because I had already invested a considerable amount of years studying psychology, and this was the first time I had the opportunity to learn from a psychologist who represented my worldviews and political-ethical commitments. As a psychology instructor, I did not want my students to have to wait until graduate school just to learn that there are psychologists who may look and sound like them and care about the issues that concern their lives (Rifino, 2022).

I came across the Psychology's Feminist Voices (PFV) multimedia archive (https://feministvoices.com) (Ball et al., 2013) and their research paper, The Imagined Conversations, amid the COVID-19 pandemic in which remote learning was hastily imposed on us (Rifino & Sugarman, 2022). In the midst of international Black Lives Matters protests and fights for ecological justice, I wanted to take bolder steps toward infusing my psychology courses with an explicit stance against the Euro-American, male, and white-dominated curricula. Additionally, it was also my priority to find zero-cost materials that offered critical knowledge in psychology. The PFV addressed both of these concerns and I first used their Imagined Conversation research paper assignment and archival database in a virtual FYS course in Spring 2021.

Imagined Conversations: A Feminist Voices Research Paper

A consistent omission in mainstream narratives about psychology's history is the neglect and devaluation of women and feminist contributions in the discipline (MacArthur & Shields, 2014; Unger, 1998). To address psychology's non-inclusivity, Dr. Rutherford initiated the PFV to preserve and promote the legacies and contemporary figures of feminists in psychology and feminist psychology (Vaughn-Johnson & Rutherford, 2019). PFV offers a range of materials, including oral histories, teaching resources, interactive exhibits, and original profiles of over 250 psychologists across the world (Ball et al., 2013; Young et al., 2015). One of the teaching resources, the Imagined Conversations research paper, invites students to engage with the ideas of prominent women and feminists within the field.

The Imagined Conversations assignment invites students to explore the PFV database, pick a pair of psychologists to research, and then construct a hypothetical conversation between them. Additionally, a rationale for pairing their chosen psychologists is included. For the conversation, students are encouraged to engage their chosen psychologists in discussions about similar or opposing positionings on a range of issues such as research foci, intersectional experiences as members of marginalized social groups, and political, epistemological, and ethical commitments (Ball et al., 2013). Based on my pedagogical positionality, I slightly modified the Imagined Conversations research paper in the following ways: First, I encouraged students to pair one psychologist from the PFV database with one psychologist from any of their psychology courses. This was intended to provide the opportunity for students to see the contrasting epistemological, ontological, and ethical commitments between mainstream (i.e., Euro-Western white men) and critically oriented psychologists. Second, I implemented the Imagined Conversations research paper in phases in my FYS, and below, I detail the scaffolded low-stakes assignments I used to support collaboration, reflection, and criticality.

Phase 1: Illuminating Eurocentric Androcentrism in Psychology

The purpose of this phase is to invite students to explore the psychology curricula and the voices and perspectives it typically privileges and those that it might leave out and exclude, creating an initial awareness of androcentrism and eurocentrism in the curricula. This phase, which typically takes the first month of the semester, consists of a collaborative reading, two low-stakes assignments, and a high-stakes assignment.

Collaborative Reading. First we read the journal article, "Disrupting Androcentrism in Social Psychology Textbooks" (George et al., 2020), a case study of social psychology textbooks analyzing the implicit and explicit ways that androcentrism persists and is presented to students. In the class, students are assigned a section of the article to read in small groups and later present their sections to the class. The purpose of reading this is to understand androcentrism as a systemic issue underlying psychology and psychology education. Importantly, I focus on the empirical study of this article and specifically the methods that the research team used to analyze androcentrism in social psychology textbooks. For the first low-stakes assignment "Exploring Your Psychology Courses," students are asked to research their own psychology courses to examine to what extent androcentrism (and Eurocentrism) persist in their own psychology courses.

Exploring Your Psychology Courses. This assignment invites students to critically examine whose voices and ideas are most represented in their psychology courses. Students examine each of the psychology courses they are taking and respond to the following questions: What is the title of this psychology course? Who are you studying in this course and what are they known for? What is their geographic location and can you identify their racial/ethnic and gender identity? Students are encouraged to research online and review any teaching materials provided by their psychology courses to find this information (e.g., syllabi, textbook, readings, etc.). Students submit their responses on a google form that compiles all submissions into a single spreadsheet that will be later collectively analyzed along with the following low-stakes assignment.

Exploring Psychology's Feminist Voices. This assignment is an opportunity for students to begin exploring the PFV database and the content it offers. After familiarizing themselves with PFV, I ask students to pick two potential feminist psychologists for their research paper, and detail why they are considering either one. Similar to the first assignment, I ask students to include psychologists' race/ethnicity, gender identity, geographic location, and research foci. Also, student submissions are uploaded onto a single spreadsheet. Then, we segue into the research paper proposal.

Analyzing the "Exploring" Assignments and Proposal. As a class, we collaboratively interpret our collected responses from the first two "Exploring" assignments. The purpose is to identify patterns about what perspectives, geographies, social identities are most and least prominent across their psychology courses and the PFV database. I present their submissions in raw form and I ask students open-ended questions that help guide their analytical thinking, such as: based on this graph, do you notice any patterns or inconsistencies? Do you notice any patterns occurring in terms of geographic locations, racial/ethnic and gender identities? If so, what might this suggest about whose voices are being represented in our courses? Mostly, our collective analysis leads to an interpretation that their undergraduate psychology courses typically promotes white, male psychologists who study topics that are often decontextualized and masquerading as depoliticized, whereas the PFV consists of an alternative to mainstream psychology that centers social issues, women, Black psychologists, and psychologists of color who explore issues related to living in an unjust world. Given that psychology is a highly popular major particularly among Black, Latinx, and women students at LaGuardia, when students arrive at this conclusion, many express either shock or disappointment. During these potentially discomforting moments, I share with my students my alienating experiences with studying psychology (Sawyer & Rifino, 2020), but I affirm to them that having the opportunity to pass down this critical knowledge to community college students, instead of it being reserved for so-called more advanced sectors of higher education, fosters a sense of hope and joy to continue my pursuit of psychology on the margins.

Students are then assigned to write a proposal stating their key ideas for their research paper. Specifically, students discuss the psychologists that they are considering to use, and their rationale for pairing them. Also, a brief academic and personal biography of each of the psychologists is required. I provide individual feedback on this proposal, which will serve as an early draft for the introduction section of their research paper.

Phase 2: Research and Collaboration Through a Political Lens

In phase 2, students are introduced to the basics of academic research and explore writing a conversation for their research paper. We first attend a library orientation that introduces the library's academic databases and resources. After the library workshop, I introduce students to APA formatting. I often feel challenged teaching APA formatting in a way that is contextual without overemphasizing memorization of technical details. What seems to be effective is to first discuss citational politics as an entry into why academic formatting should be taken seriously. To illustrate, I discuss debates within affect studies (my own field) that illuminate the role that western citational practices play in proliferating an overrepresentation of Eurocentric male voices in the field, while downplaying contributions from Black feminist, queer, and third-world womxn (Garcia-Rojas, 2017; Rogers, 2019). The aim is for students to understand that learning how and what to cite carry vast ethical and political implications. By this stage, students begin the first research-based assignment.

Reflective Annotated Bibliography. The first assignment of phase 2 is the Reflective Annotated Bibliography (RefAnnBib) assignment (McBeth, 2014). The RefAnnBib is a medium-stakes assignment that serves as a comprehensive device for evaluating a research artifact that students will likely use for their research paper. In addition to a conventional annotated bibliography that requires a bibliographic entry and objective summary, the RefAnnBib also asks students to produce "subjective editorial remarks" that entail the readers' initial reactions, and to select key terms and excerpts from the research artifact that they deem relevant (McBeth, 2014, p. 1). For my RefAnnBib assignment, I ask students to complete a RefAnnBib for two relevant sources, one for each of their respective psychologists. Next, we begin practicing our literary skills in writing a conversational exchange.

Mock Dialogue Between Two Psychologists. For this in-class assignment, I provide students with a handout that features two psychologists, each with a brief biography and excerpts from their magnum opus. In pairs, students produce a conversation between these two psychologists based on the research provided. Feedback on their mock dialogue is based on how well students can translate content about their psychologists into a dialogical format. By the end of this phase, students should have committed to two psychologists for their paper. In addition, they should have produced some research on them, via the RefAnnBib assignment, and be a bit familiar with writing a conversation. The last phase entails applying these lessons learned to compile a full draft of the research paper.

Phase 3: Writing As an Iterative and Social Process

This last phase emphasizes the iterative and collaborative process to writing process. Specifically, students will submit a first draft of their Imagined Dialogue, receive peer and instructor feedback, and then revise and resubmit their draft as the final submission.

First Draft of the Research Paper. For the first draft of the research paper, which is considered a high-stakes assignment, students are required to complete a cover page, introduction, dialogue, conclusion, and a reference page in APA format. As writing is an iterative process, I encourage my students to use their proposal (completed in phase 1) and annotated bibliography (completed in phase 2) to help them write their first draft. To assess the merits of this multistage research paper (and to improve my pedagogy), students write a conclusion about what they liked about this project, the challenges they encountered, and how it can be improved. Importantly, feedback is an essential component of this research paper, especially during this phase. I usually implement a peer editing session so students can pair up with one another, read each other's drafts, and provide constructive feedback.

Peer Feedback workshop. The peer editing assignment is conducted in-class on the day that the first draft is due. I ask students to bring a digital or hard copy of their paper to class. Students pair up in groups of three for peer editing. Each student receives two peer editing handouts (one for every draft that they edit) that feature questions to be responded to after reading their peers' drafts. The questions featured on the handout are:

- Based on the criteria provided for the first draft assignment, did the writer's introduction include all required sections?
- What was their rationale for pairing their psychologists and to what extent was it convincing?
- How can they improve their introduction?
- Summarize the writer's dialogue. Be sure to note what topics were discussed, and what each psychologist contributed to the dialogue.
- What was one aspect from their dialogue that interested you the most?

- What may be improved for their dialogue?

I also suggest students write questions or ideas that their peer editor(s) can consider when providing feedback. After students read and provide feedback on each of their peers' drafts, they discuss within their groups, the feedback that was suggested. I also encourage students to talk about any challenges that they encountered while completing the assignment.

Conducting a peer editing activity on the day that students submit their first draft research paper has several pedagogical advantages. One, it provides students with immediate feedback about the quality of their work. Two, having students provide initial comments on their peer's research paper drafts lessens the time it takes me to provide feedback on their papers. Three, the peer editing assignment reminds students that writing is an embodied (i.e., emotional) and collaborative process.

After the discussion, students submit the feedback handouts that they received from their peers with their research paper draft. The comments that I provide for each of their papers build off of the feedback that they received from their peers. For the first draft, I grade according to completion and my feedback is strictly comments and suggestions. I consider each peer editing handout as I provide feedback. The goal is to provide ample feedback that does not overwhelm students, but provides them with a clear sense of what they did well and the direction that they should go in to improve their paper for the final submission.

Revised, Final Submission. After students receive instructor and peer feedback, I decide, on a paper-by-paper basis, whether a paper requires revisions or not. I used to require revisions for all first drafts, but this became a daunting task that prevented me from providing deeper feedback for papers that genuinely needed them. Thus, depending on the quality of their first draft, students may or may not need to revise.

Discussion and Conclusion

This chapter explored the Euro-American psychology curricula and how decolonial and decentering pedagogical efforts can disrupt them. Ahmed's notion of orientation (2006, 2010, 2014) was used to explore how the politics of orientation in psychology is in many ways connected to becoming oriented toward Euro-American knowledge systems and worldviews at the expense of becoming oriented away from local knowledge systems and worldviews. This notion of orienting away from one's local knowledge and perspectives may entail a sense of estrangement vis-à-vis one's sociocultural background. What must be emphasized in first-year seminars, or any course, are pedagogical practices that support students' critical examination in illuminating hegemonic disciplinary assumptions and worldviews. This certainly entails foregrounding "psychology's shameful past" in one's introduction to psychology including the ongoing legacies of Euro-American psychology's complicity with scientific racism, sexism, ableism, eugenics, war, and cis-heteronormativity (Stetsenko, 2020, p. 6). This can prepare them for critical examination across their future courses within and beyond psychology. Importantly, diverse traditions of critically oriented psychology psychologists and knowledge needs to be centered not just promoting recognition and validation, but also that students will be in a better position to challenge Eurocentric knowledge systems and worldviews embedded in their curricula within and beyond psychology. This can be a way that we reclaim our orientations as central to knowledge production and ethical commitments.

This chapter also outlined how I use interrelated pedagogical activities to facilitate a critically oriented approach to introducing students to psychology. Specifically, I relied on the Imagined Conversations research paper, scaffolded assignments, and the PFV database to promote criticality, reflection, and collaboration as we become oriented in various ways in psychology. Based on student reflections, many students expressed that they enjoyed the Imagined Conversations research paper and favored how the scaffolded assignments afforded them ample space for their intellectual curiosity and creativity. These pedagogical activities offered the opportunity to tailor the paper according to one's evolving interests about psychology. Virtually all students expressed that they had not expected to study psychologists and theories that represented their knowledge systems, traditions, and concerns for specific social issues. Indeed, many students focused their research papers on pairing Sigmund Freud with a feminist psychologist (e.g., Naomi Weisstein) who was critical of his theories on gender development. For these students, this paper represented an opportunity to critique Freud's theories and find alliances with like-minded psychologists. Other students used this paper to explore the conceptual principles of psychology paradigms that they were learning from in their courses. Importantly, there were also students who did not enjoy the creative dimensions of this paper and preferred a more traditional approach to writing a research paper. Decolonial and critical pedagogical work in psychology has also demonstrated how students might resist non-western pedagogies and assessments (MacPherson et al. 2022; Terre et al., 2021). This suggests that pedagogical practices should always offer space for student feedback about how they experienced learning and what they might suggest instructors to do differently.

A suggestion that students made that I implemented in my future FYS courses is to offer more psychology databases to choose from in addition to PFV that offered additional psychologies and psychologists from the margins. While the PFV website does provide an extensive coverage on Black feminist psychology and women of color across the global majority world, it has been fruitful to offer students the following online projects and databases: the BME (Black, Asian, Minoritized, Ethnic) Psychology multimedia database, a project that centers "diversifying psychology away from its white, western bias" (https://bmepsychology.com). The "Black History in Psychology" resource on the Cummings Center for the History of Psychology, an internationally recognized research and humanities center that preserves and interprets the history of psychology and associated human sciences, also examines the contributions of Black psychologists and the historical role of racism in psychology (https://www.uakron.edu/chp/education/black-history). Carmichael-Murphy and Dr. Danquah (2022), "Hidden Histories: Black in Psychology," a resource that offers a substantial overview of Black trailblazers in psychology and illuminates their history and contributions to psychology. Together, these resources provide a considerable amount of psychologies and psychologists to explore.

It is our responsibility as faculty to introduce students to our disciplines, and how we perform that introduction—the biases, lenses, and orientation inherent in our approach—is often carried from previous generation of scholars and is seldom questioned. To challenge the hegemonic, imperialistic history of Androcentrism and Eurocentrism, we must evaluate our own teaching practices and the inclusion of diverse knowledge bases and expertise from our own disciplines.

Notes

1 Stella is a pseudonym.
2 The term 'Global South' is used to describe countries on the grounds of socioeconomic and political dimensions, implying that wealthier countries tend to be located in the "Global North," whereas poorer countries are located in the Global South. As Zembylas (2022) writes, these terms are too simplistic; however, they are used in this chapter to illuminate how oppression, marginalization, and Eurocentrism are central to the western colonial legacies.

References

Adams, G., Dobles, I., Gómez, L.H., Kurtiş, T., & Molina, L.E. (2015). Decolonizing psychological science: Introduction to the special thematic section. *Journal of Social and Political Psychology, 3*(1), 213–238. https://doi.org/10.5964/jspp.v3i1.564

Adams, G., Estrada-Villalta, S., & Ordóñez, L.H.G. (2018). The modernity/coloniality of being: Hegemonic psychology as intercultural relations. *International Journal of Intercultural Relations*, 62, 13–22.

Adams, G., Osei-Tutu, A., & Affram, A.A. (2020). Decolonial perspectives on psychology and development. In *Oxford research encyclopedia of psychology*. Oxford University Press. https://doi.org/10.1093/acrefore/9780190236557.013.514

Ahmed, S. (2006). *Queer phenomenology: Orientations, objects, other.* Duke University Press.

Ahmed, S. (2010). *The promise of happiness.* Duke University Press.

Ahmed, S. (2014). *The cultural politics of emotion* (2nd ed.). Edinburgh University Press.

American Psychological Association. (2021a). *Apology to People of Color for APA's role in promoting, perpetuating, and failing to challenge racism, racial discrimination, and human hierarchy in U.S.* American Psychological Association. https://www.apa.org/about/policy/racism-apology

American Psychological Association. (2021b). *Role of psychology and APA in dismantling systemic racism against People of Color in U.S.* American Psychological Association. https://www.apa.org/about/policy/dismantling-systemic-racism

American Psychological Association. (2021c). *Equity, diversity, and inclusion framework*. https://www.apa.org/about/apa/equity-diversity-Inclusion/equity-division-inclusion-framework.pdf

American Psychological Association. (2023a). *Report on an Offer of Apology, on behalf of the American Psychological Association, to First People's in the United States.* https://www.apa.org/pubs/reports/indigenous-apology.pdf

American Psychological Association, APA Board of Educational Affairs Working Group to Revise the APA Principles for Quality Undergraduate Education in Psychology. (2023b). *Principles for quality undergraduate education in psychology*. https://www.apa.org/about/policy/principles-qualityundergraduate-education-psychology.pdf

American Psychological Association. (2022). *APA guidelines for the undergraduate psychology major: Version 3.0.* https://apps.apa.org/CommentCentral2/attachments/Site97-Undergrad%20Guidelines.pdf

Apple, M., & Christian-Smith, L. (2017). *The politics of the textbook*. Routledge.

Armero, Y., Costilla, A., & Hwang, J. (2022). Whom does psychology serve? Neocolonialism in Peruvian psychology. *Psychology from the Margins*, 4(5). https://ideaexchange.uakron.edu/psychologyfromthemargins/vol4/iss1/5

Association of Black Psychologists. (2021). *ABPsi's official statement to the APA apology*. https://abpsi.org/wp-content/uploads/2021/11/ABPsi-Full-Statement.pdf

Ball, L.C., Bazar, J.L., MacKay, J., Rodkey, E.N., Rutherford, A., & Young, J.L. (2013). Using psychology's feminist voices in the classroom. *Psychology of Women Quarterly*, 37(2), 261–266. https://doi.org/10.1177/0361684313480484

Bachik, A.K., & Kitzman, M.J. (2020). The case for including personal development in undergraduate psychology curricula. *Scholarship of Teaching and Learning in Psychology*, 6(2), 150–162. https://doi.org/10.1037/stl0000153

Battle, T., Chandler, L., Eynon, B., Francis, A., Radhakrishnan, P., & Quish, E. (2017). LaGuardia Community College, CUNY. In T.L. Skipper (Ed.), *What makes the first-year seminar high impact? An exploration of effective educational practices* (pp. 59–64). National Resource Center for the First-Year Experience & Students in Transition.

Bell, D. (2018). A pedagogical response to decoloniality: Decolonial atmospheres and rising subjectivity. *American Journal of Community Psychology, 62*(3–4), 250–260.

Bhatia, S. (2018). *Decolonizing psychology: Globalization, social justice, and Indian youth identities*. Oxford University Press.

Bhatia, S. (2021). The pandemic is a mirror: Decolonizing psychology and racism in times of COVID-19 crisis. In I. Strasser & M. Dege (Eds.), *The psychology of global crises and crisis politics* (pp. 65–89). Springer.

Biko, S. (2002). *I write what I like*. University of Chicago Press.

Bohrer, J.A. (2020). Toward a decolonial feminist anticapitalism: María Lugones, Sylvia Wynter, and Sayak Valencia. *Hypatia, 35*(3), 524–541.

Boysen, G.A., & Becker-Blease, K.A. (2021). An introduction to the special issues on teaching the introductory psychology course. *Scholarship of Teaching and Learning in Psychology, 7*(3), 161.

Canham, H., Baloyi, L., & Segalo, P. (2021). Disrupting the psychology canon? Exploring African-centered decolonial pedagogy. In G. Stevens & C.C. Sonn (Eds.), *Decoloniality and epistemic justice in contemporary community psychology* (pp. 193–212). Springer.

Carmichael-Murphy, P., & Danquah, A. (2022). *Hidden histories: Black in psychology*. University of Manchester. https://documents.manchester.ac.uk/display.aspx?DocID=62182

Carolissen, R., Shefer, T., & Smit, E. (2015). A critical review of practices of inclusion and exclusion in the psychology curriculum in higher education. *Psychology in Society, 49*, 7–24. https://dx.doi.org/10.17159/2309-8708/2015/n49a2

Carolissen, R., Canham, H., Fourie, E., Graham, T., Segalo, P., & Bowman, B. (2017). Epistemological resistance towards diversality: Teaching community psychology as a decolonial project. *South African Journal of Psychology, 47*(4), 495–505.

Carolissen, R., & Duckett, P.S. (2018). Teaching toward decoloniality in community psychology and allied disciplines. *American Journal of Community Psychology, 62*(3–4), 261–271.

Castell, E., Bullen, J., Garvey, D., & Jones, N. (2018). Critical reflexivity in indigenous and cross-cultural psychology: A decolonial approach to curriculum?. *American Journal of Community Psychology, 62*(3–4), 261–271.

Costa, R.E., & Shimp, C.P. (2011). Methods courses and texts in psychology: "Textbook science" and "tourist brochures". *Journal of Theoretical and Philosophical Psychology, 31*(1), 25.

Costa, N.C., & Bedir, N. (2022). A call for antiracist foundations of teaching: Ideas for socially conscious psychology education. *Scholarship of Teaching and Learning in Psychology*. https://doi.org/10.1037/stl0000320

Cranney, J., Morris, S., Norris, K., & Connolly, C.E. (2022). Charting the psychological literacy landscape: Systematic review highlighting psychology education. *Frontiers in Education, 7*, Article 913814. https://doi.org/10.3389/feduc.2022.913814

Decolonial Psychology Editorial Collective. (2021). General psychology otherwise: A decolonial articulation. *Review of General Psychology, 25*(4), 339–353. https://10.1177/10892680211048177

Desai, M.U., Laubscher, L., & Johnson, S. (2023). Perspectives (of People of Color) on psychological science: Does psychological science listen?. *Review of General Psychology, 27*(2), 155–163. https://doi.org/10.1177/10892680221118038

Fanon, F. (1963/1961). *The wretched of the earth*. Grove Press.

Fanon, F. (1967/1952). *Black skin, white masks*. Grove Press.

Fernández, J.S. (2018). Decolonial pedagogy in community psychology: White students disrupting white innocence via a family portrait assignment. *American Journal of Community Psychology, 62*(3–4), 294–305.

Fernández, J.S., Sonn, C.C., Carolissen, R., & Stevens, G. (2021). Roots and routes toward decoloniality within and outside psychology praxis. *Review of General Psychology, 25*(4), 354–368, 1–15. https://doi.org/10.1177/10892680211002437

Garcia-Rojas, C. (2017). (Un)disciplined futures: Women of color feminism as a disruptive to white affect studies. *Journal of Lesbian Studies, 21*(3), 254–271.

George, M., Mulvale, S., Davidson, T., Young, J., & Rutherford, A. (2020). Disrupting androcentrism in social psychology textbooks. *Awry: Journal of Critical Psychology, 1*(1), 15–33.

Gillborn, S., Woolnough, H., Jankowski, G., & Sandle, R. (2023). "Intensely white": Psychology curricula and the (re)production of racism. *Educational Review, 75*(5), 813–832.

Gomez-Ordonez, L., Adams, G., Ratele, K., Suffla, S., Stevens, G., & Reddy, G. (2021). Decolonizing psychological science: Encounters and cartographies of resistance. *The Psychologist, 34*, 54–57.

Gurung, R.A., & Neufeld, G.E. (2022). *Transforming introductory psychology: Expert advice on teacher training, course design, and student success*. American Psychological Association.

Guthrie, R. (2003). *Even the rat was white: A historical view of psychology*. Pearson.

Henrich, J., Heine, S.J., & Norenzayan, A. (2010). The weirdest people in the world? *Behavioral and Brain Sciences, 33*(2–3), 61–83.

Hill, D.B. (2019). Androcentrism and the great man narrative in psychology textbooks: The case of Ivan Pavlov. *Journal of Research in Gender Studies, 9*(1), 9–37.

Hussain, M. (2015). Why is my curriculum white. *National Union of Students blog*. https://www.nus.org.uk/en/news/why-is-my-curriculum-white/

James, S., & Lorenz, H. (2021). Back to the source: Moving upstream in the curricular rivers of coloniality. *Review of General Psychology*, *25*(4), 385–404.

Jankowski, G., Sandle, R., & Brown, M. (2022). Challenging the lack of BAME authors in a psychology curriculum. *Psychology of Women Section Review*, *5*(1), 18–36.

Kelly, A.E., Laurin, J.N., & Clinton-Lisell, V. (2022). Making psychology's *hidden figures* visible using open educational resources: A replication and extension study. *Teaching of Psychology*. https://doi.org/10.1177/00986283221108129

Kessi, S., Boonzaier, F., & Gekeler, B.S. (2021). *Pan-Africanism and psychology in decolonial times*. Palgrave Macmillan.

Kiguwa, P. (2023). "The world looks like this from here": Kopano Ratele's African psychology. *American Psychologist*, *78*(4), 496–511. https://doi.org/10.1037/amp0001131

Kiguwa, P., & Segalo, P. (2018). Decolonising psychology in residential and open distance e-learning institutions: Critical reflections. *South African Journal of Psychology*, *48*(3), 310–318.

King, M.L. (1968). The role of the behavioral scientist in the civil rights movement. *American Psychologist*, *23*(3), 180–186. https://doi.org/10.1037/h0025715

Kontopodis, M., & Jackowska, M. (2019). De-centring the psychology curriculum: Diversity, social justice, and psychological knowledge. *Theory & Psychology*, *29*(4), 506–520.

Kuh, G.D. (2008). Excerpt from high-impact educational practices: What they are, who has access to them, and why they matter. *Association of American Colleges and Universities*, *14*(3), 28–29.

LaGuardia Community College, Office of Institutional Research and Assessment. (2020). *Institutional profile*. LaGuardia Community College, Office of Institutional Research and Assessment. https://www.laguardia.edu/uploadedfiles/main_site/content/ir/docs/institutional-profile-2020.pdf

Le Grange, L. (2016). Decolonizing the university curriculum. *South African Journal of Higher Education*, *30*, 1–12.

Lugones, M. (2007). Heterosexualism in the colonial/modern gender system. *Hypatia*, *22*(1), 186–209.

MacArthur, H.J., & Shields, S.A. (2014). Psychology's feminist voices: A critical pedagogical tool. *Sex Roles: A Journal of Research*, *70*(9–10), 431–433. https://doi.org/10.1007/s11199-014-0349-9

Macleod, C.I., Bhatia, S., & Liu, W. (2020). Feminisms and decolonising psychology: Possibilities and challenges. *Feminism & Psychology*, *30*(3), 287–305. https://doi.org/10.1177/0959353520932810

MacPherson, A., Patev, A., Ghose, S., Reid, M., Sabet, S., Williams, C., & Dautovich, N. (2022). Using photovoice to teach an undergraduate psychology of women course: An intersectional-feminist approach. *Psychology of Women Quarterly*, *46*(4), 531–535. https://doi.org/10.1177/03616843221106081

Maldonado-Torres, N. (2007). On the coloniality of being: Contributions to the development of a concept. *Cultural Studies*, *21*(2–3), 240–270. https://doi.org/10.1080/09502380601162548

Maldonado-Torres, N. (2011). Thinking through the decolonial turn: Post-continental interventions in theory, philosophy, and critique—An Introduction. *Transmodernity*, *1*(2), 1–15.

Malherbe, N., & Ratele, K. (2022). What and for whom is a decolonizing African psychology?. *Theory & Psychology*, *32*(1), 116–130. https://10.1177/09593543211027231

Martín-Baró, I. (1994). *Writings for a liberation psychology*. Harvard University Press.

Maxwele, C. (2016). Black pain led me to throw Rhodes poo. *Business Day Live*, https://www.businesslive.co.za/bd/opinion/2016-03-16-black-pain-led-me-to-throw-rhodes-poo/

McBeth, M. (2014, October 14). The reflective annotated bibliography. https://blogs.baruch.cuny.edu/teachingenglish/files/2014/11/Mark-McBeth-RefAnnBib.pdf

Mignolo, W.D. (2007). Introduction: Coloniality of power and de-colonial thinking. *Cultural Studies*, *21*(1), 155–167. https://doi.org/10.1080/09502380601162498

Moke, P., & Bohan, J.S. (1992). Reconstructing curriculum: Psychology's paradigm and the virtues of iconoclasm. *Women's Studies Quarterly*, *20*(1/2), 7–27.

Mulvale, S. (2020). Takin' it to the streets. *Psychology's Feminist Voices* digital exhibit.

Ngũgĩ wa Thiong'o. (1986). *Decolonising the mind: The politics of language in African literature*. Heineman.

Nsamenang, A.B. (2007). Origins and development of scientific psychology in *Afrique Noire*. In M.J. Stevens & D. Weddings (Eds.), *Psychology: IUPsyS global resource*. Psychological Press.

Plato. (1998). *Republic* (R. Waterfield, Trans.). Oxford University Press.

Pownall, M. (2022). Encouraging feminist discussion in asynchronous online teaching. *Psychology of Women Quarterly*, *46*(1), 111–117. https://10.1177/03616843211027479

Pownall, M. (2023). Supporting students to reimagine social psychology through a critical feminist lens. *Psychology Teaching Review*, *29*(1), 51–55. https://10.53841/bpspsr.2023.29.1.51

Quijano, A. (2000). Coloniality of power, Eurocentrism, and Latin America. *International Sociology*, *15*(2), 215–232. https://doi.org/10.1177/0268580900015002005

Ratele, K. (2019). *The world looks like this from here: Thoughts on African psychology*. Wits University Press.

Ratele, K., Cornell, J., Dlamini, S., Helman, R., Malherbe N., and Titi, N. (2018). Some Basic Questions About (a) Decolonizing Africa (n)-Centred Psychology Considered. *South African Journal of Psychology*, *48*(3), 331–342.

Readsura Decolonial Editorial Collective. (in random order), Ratele, K., Reddy, G., Adams, G., & Suffla, S. (2022a). Decoloniality as a social issue for psychological study. *Journal of Social Issues*, *78*(1), 7–26.

Readsura Decolonial Editorial Collective. (in random order), Adams, G., Ratele, K., Suffla, S., & Reddy, G. (2022b). Psychology as a site for decolonial analysis. *Journal of Social Issues, 78*(2), 255–277.

Reddy, G., & Amer, A. (2022). Precarious engagements and the politics of knowledge production: Listening to calls for reorienting hegemonic social psychology. *British Journal of Social Psychology, 62*, 71–94.

Rifino, M. (2022, November 30). Shifting out of neutral into OER. *The Graduate Center's Mina Rees Library blog.* https://gclibrary.commons.gc.cuny.edu/2022/11/30/shifting-out-of-neutral-into-oer/

Rifino, M., & Sugarman, K. (2022). Loneliness with the lens of Black feminist love-politics: Pedagogical practices amid pandemic online learning. *Journal for Multicultural Education, 16*(1), 90–101. https://10.1108/JME-08-2021-0160

Rodrigues, L. (2022). Decolonial feminism: María Lugones' influences and contributions. *Revista Estudos Feministas, Florianópolis, 30*(1), 1–14. https://doi.org/10.1590/1806-9584-2022v30n184278

Rogers, J.A. (2019). Invisible memories: Black feminist literature and its affective flights. In S. Ahern (Ed.), *Affect theory and literary critical practice: A feel for the text* (pp. 201–216). Springer.

Santos, B.S. (2007). Beyond abyssal thinking: From global lines to ecologies of knowledges. http://www.boaventuradesousasantos.pt/media/pdfs/Beyond_Abyssal_Thinking_Review_2007

Sawyer, J.E., & Rifino, M. (2020). Transforming educational alienation into collective agency in community colleges. In T.M. Ober, E. Che, J.E. Brodsky, C. Raffaele, & P.J. Brooks (Eds.), *How we teach now: The GSTA guide to transformative teaching* (pp. 223–237). The Society for the Teaching of Psychology.

Schmidt, H. (2019). Indigenizing and decolonizing the teaching of psychology: Reflections on the role of the non-indigenous ally. *American Journal of Community Psychology, 64*, 59–71. https://doi.org/10.1002/ajcp.12365

Seedat, M., & Suffla, S. (2017). Community psychology and its (discontents), archival legacies and decolonization. *South African Journal of Psychology, 47*, pp. 421–431.

Segalo, P. (2016). Decolonizing social psychology in South Africa. In *Decolonizing the university in Africa: Knowledge systems and disciplines* (pp. 165–177). Carolina Academic Press.

Segalo, P., & Simango, J. (2021). *Psychology carries a dark past: How the discipline can be Africanised.* The Conversation. https://theconversation.com/psychology-carries-a-dark-past-how-the-discipline-can-be-africanised-155165

Silva, J.M., Fernández, J.S., & Nguyen, A. (2022). "And now we resist": Three testimonios on the importance of decoloniality within psychology. *Journal of Social Issues, 78*(2), 388–412. https://doi.org/10.1111/josi.12449

Simango, J., & Segalo, P. (2020). Re-imagining psychology: An Africanist perspective. *Alternation, 27*(1), 67–84. https://doi.org/10.29086/2519-5476/2020/v27n1a5

Sonn, C.C., Arcidiacono, C., Dutta, U., Kiguwa, P., Kloos, B., & Torres, N.M. (2017). Beyond disciplinary boundaries: Speaking back to critical knowledges, liberation, and community. *South African Journal of Psychology, 47*(4), 448–458.

Sonn, C.C., & Stevens, G. (2021). *Decoloniality and epistemic justice in contemporary community psychology.* Springer.

Stetsenko, A. (2020). Transformative-activist and social justice approaches to the history of psychology. In *Oxford research encyclopedia, psychology.* https://10.1093/acrefore/9780190236557.013.466

Terre Blanche, M., Fourie, E., & Segalo, P. (2021). Teaching community psychology decolonially: A pedagogical journey. *Review of General Psychology, 25*(4), 369–384. https://doi.org/10.1177/1089268020974588

Thalmayer, A.G., Toscanelli, C., & Arnett, J. (2021). The neglected 95% revisited: Is American Psychology becoming less American. *American Psychologist, 76*(1), 116–129. https://doi.org/10.1037/amp0000622

Tyrell, F.A., Neville, H.A., Causadias, J.M., Cokley, K.O., & Adams-Wiggins, K.R. (2023). Reclaiming the past and transforming our future: Introduction to the special issue on foundational contributions of Black scholars in psychology. *American Psychologist, 78*(4), 367–375. https://doi.org/10.1037/amp0001170

Uluğ, Ö.M., & Acar, Y.G. (2022). A feminist companion to social psychology by Madeleine Pownall and Wendy Rogers [Book Review]. *Feminism & Psychology, 32*(4), 588–592.

Unger, K.R. (1998). *Resisting gender: Twenty-five years of feminist psychology.* SAGE Publications.

Vaughn-Johnson, K. & Rutherford, A. (2019). Teaching critical, multivocal histories of psychology: Uncovering diversity. *Integrating Multiculturalism and Intersectionality Into the Psychology Curriculum: Strategies for Instructors.* American Psychological Association.

Watkins, M., Ciofalo, N., & James, S. (2018). Engaging the struggle for decolonial approaches to teaching community psychology. *American Journal of Community Psychology, 62*(3–4), 319–329.

Yakushko, O., & Hook, D. (2017). Whatever happened to the human experience in undergraduate psychology? Comment on the special issue on undergraduate education in psychology (2016). *American Psychologist.* https://doi.org/10.1037/amp0000055

Young, J., Rodkey, E., & Rutherford, A. (2015). Sparking the historical imagination: Strategies for teaching conceptual and historical issues in psychology. *History & Philosophy of Psychology, 16*(1), 61–68.

Zembylas, M. (2022). Toward affective decolonization: Nurturing decolonizing solidarity in higher education. *Journal of Curriculum and Pedagogy.* 20. 1-20. 10.1080/15505170.2022.2034684.

Affective Injustice and Student Dis/Engagement

EDUARDO VIANNA, ARAMINTA POOLE, AND RAFAEL COSTA

I would walk into class feeling ok and, within minutes, I'd be flooded with feelings of overwhelming despair, inability, and confusion. Sometimes I would start crying after I asked a question and was still unclear with the response given. This is a constant thing for me: I cry all the time. Sometimes the crying didn't seem to have a specific trigger. I was used to these tears, but others were not, strong emotion is unacceptable in public and makes others uncomfortable. (Poole, 2017)

This quote was shared by Araminta when she was a participant in a peer-based learning community under the faculty guidance of Eduardo in collaboration with graduate students at LaGuardia Community College. Though crying and heightened emotionality are not commonly expressed in classrooms and other educational settings, other participants in the project, termed the Peer Activist Learning Community (PALC), often shared their experiences of a high degree of alienation and oppression in their college education. This is manifested in strong feelings of frustration, helplessness, and hopelessness toward college education and their future, coupled with anxiety about tests, assignments, and grades, as they struggle to complete their courses and maintain a good GPA. These feelings, referred to in the scientific literature as negative emotions (Fredrickson, 2001),[1] have significant implications for student engagement (Pekrun et. al., 2002). This chapter builds on both Araminta's and Eduardo's direct experiences as a former community college student and PALC participant and as faculty and PALC mentor, respectively. It was dialogically expanded in an iterative cycle of exchanges between the two of us and Rafael, a psychoanalyst and researcher-activist with indigenous people in Brazil, that evolved throughout the writing process until it culminated in its final version.[2] Our aim is to explore the role of affects in community college learning, especially as they relate to student engagement and agency.

According to the dominant cognitive perspective, learning is thought of primarily as a cognitive process, a matter of acquiring knowledge by processing information and forming concepts.[3] Until recently, with the exception of test anxiety, academic emotions had been largely neglected in educational psychology and related fields (Pekrun et al., 2002). However, as Araminta's quotes above painfully indicate, students' engagement with college can be intensely emotional. It was only in the last decade that researchers began systematically looking at the classroom as an emotional place (Pekrun, 2016), opening up ways to address students' feelings as situated in the dynamics of teaching-learning practices. Yet, students often feel that their emotions, especially 'negative' ones, are not only unwelcome in the classroom but are their own private feelings, stemming from inner processes in their minds and brains.

While the terms feeling, emotion, and affect have been variously defined in different disciplinary traditions, and are often used interchangeably, in this chapter we follow the terminology proposed by contemporary affect theory[4] (Seigworth & Gregg, 2010) according to which affect refers to "both our power to affect the world around us and our power to be affected by it, along with the relationship between these two powers" (Hardt, 2007, p. ix). In contradistinction to emotion, understood as how individuals interpret their private feelings, the term affect refers to relational, dynamic, open-ended, and socially situated processes. As philosopher Moira Gatens (2014) comments, the contagiousness of collective affects exposes the porous borders between self and other. This is critical to dispel individualist notions of affective self-containment that conceal this important aspect of our interdependence. Teresa Brennan (2004) contends that "the taken-for-grantedness of the emotionally contained subject is a residual bastion of eurocentrism in critical thinking" (p. 2). As she aptly notes, "if we accept with comparatively ready acquiescence that our thoughts are not entirely independent, we are, nonetheless, peculiarly resistant to the idea that our emotions are not altogether our own" (p. 2). Thus, we draw on this theoretical strand because it is conceptually useful to displace reductive, individualized notions of feelings and emotions as psychological dispositions, which dominate mainstream and popular psychological discourses. Moreover, our work draws on theoretical strands that posit affects as always embedded in social acts and practices in specific social and political contexts (Zembylas, 2013, 2018, 2021). For this reason we use the term affective dynamics throughout this chapter to convey the idea that affective phenomena, notwithstanding its subjective dimensions as private feelings or personal emotions, always originate in social interactions within community practices wherein participants simultaneously affect and are affected by one another—though often in asymmetrical ways, as we discuss below.

The affective dynamics we witnessed both in PALC and in classrooms seemed to manifest ambivalent engagement patterns—a mix of resistance and passivity positionings toward her view. We also do not posit a gap between the subject's affects and its cognition or appraisal of the affective situation, learning and college education, which become constitutive of students' learning conditions. As Araminta wrote in a blog post, later published in the journal of the college (Poole, 2019), "when you cry throughout a class, it doesn't leave much room for discussions or asking questions or trying to do anything but just fade away into the background." PALC participants reported similar negative feelings that interfere with class participation, strain communication with instructor and classmates, and ultimately constrain learning opportunities in the classroom. This is reflected in Araminta's struggle against the stereotype of an underperforming community college student, often taken by those representing the institution, and by students themselves, as an individual failing or mental health issue. As she shared in PALC: "[M]y failure to learn correctly manifested into a false certainty that I could not, that I was incapable of achieving such education. It fueled my brain's inadequacies. A problem solely in me. It was my inability to comprehend. I am a smart woman, I knew this, but I was 'life smart' not 'school smart.'"

For several decades now, those emotional responses to learning difficulties have been typically medicalized in educational settings, wherein they are treated as individual pathology while the role of social context is minimized (Venianaki et al., 2021). As Timimi and Timimi (2022) argue, "[t]his ideology, far from leading to enlightened progress that will prevent and/or ameliorate future mental health problems, inadvertently sets young people on a path towards alienation from, and suspicion of, their emotional lives and a lack of curiosity about, or tolerance of, suffering" (p. 12). They boldly assert that "[r]ather than preventing mental health problems, it is likely that this ideology, and the resulting practices it encourages, are creating them" (p. 13). Similarly, critical disability researcher Dušana Podlucká (2020) has described how institutional discourses and practices for students with disabilities in college locate disability solely within individual students, thus positioning them as the 'owner of the disability,' thus reinforcing a disabled identity (Podlucká & Vianna, 2021).

When she started attending classes in the community college, Araminta would usually despair and cry because she felt alone, lost, and harmed by a system that disregards her specificity, difficulties and facilities, as well as her life context. She and other PALC participants shared their frustration of being a student while working full-time and taking many courses taught in the banking model (Freire, 1970) wherein students are treated as isolated learners, handed top-down ready-made knowledge, assessed on individual assignments and tests, and rarely allowed to contribute to knowledge. As she wrote in a blog post:

> I feel like I'm a very passive student a lot of the time. I sit in lectures and take information but not create it. Of course, there are discussions in class but even then, you do not question the professor or disagree with a lesson. For the most part, it seems like you're not allowed to not agree. You just need to learn the material and then repeat it on the test. Just get it done, get that A, and leave. (Poole, 2019)

As the attentive reader will have already noticed, Araminta seems ambivalent about and vacillates in her stance toward the source and meaning of her emotions in learning. On the one hand, while critically examining her learning conditions, she can discern that her affects literally meant how she was being affected by intersecting social practices meant to isolate her; on the other hand, while drawing on her long history of having her learning struggles framed as psychopathology, she views herself as too emotional and attributes her learning difficulties to an intrinsic, biologically based deficit.

Based in a critical, relational, and situated view of affect (e.g., Boler, 1999; Zembylas, 2013), which was introduced to students in PALC, we resisted a medicalized interpretation of Araminta's (and other students') affective dynamics as a solely subjective experience. Following Araminta's lead, who dared to express or, as initially understood, not contain her feelings, pushed us to probe deeper. Thus, rather than dismiss or otherwise treat affect as symptoms to be eliminated, we sought to make affects epistemologically productive (Stodulka et al., 2018) by listening to them as a way of knowing about student struggles in the community college.

Theoretically, this chapter seeks to expand affect theory (Gregg & Seigworth, 2010) through the lens of the Transformative Activist Stance (TAS) developed by Anna Stetsenko (2017) to propose an account of affects as inherently agentive, indeed activist, and mutually constitutive of learning identities and contexts. Central to our argument, the notion of affective injustice (Whitney, 2018) sheds new light on the plight of community college students vis-à-vis their engagement in their courses. This inquiry represents a step forward in articulating a radically transformative pedagogy wherein affects can be embraced as a source of knowledge and agency in learning. Such an approach can have radical consequences for how we conceive of student engagement and the role of mental health approaches in relation to learning. In the next section we present a summary and the main findings of our work in PALC. We focus on how it provided Araminta and her peers the space and tools to critically examine and transform their learning conditions by connecting affects, agency, and engagement. Finally, we showcase how PALC embraced students' affects (Whitney, 2018) as instantiating activist positionings toward oppressive learning practices and how this affective uptake built solidarity, generating affects of excitement, joy, and a renewed energy to learn as an ineluctable facet of self and social transformation.

The Peer Activist Learning Community (PALC)

PALC was designed as a collaborative project to investigate how we can contribute to transforming alienating and oppressive practices in the community college by expanding student agency. Community colleges enroll about 41 percent of all undergraduates (Dougherty, 2023). Due to their open admissions policies and lower costs, they enroll the most diverse student body in terms of age, race and ethnicity, ability, and career aspirations (Whitt, 2011). Traditionally, community college students have encountered significant barriers to graduation, from need of remedial classes to financial and housing problems. Despite recent improvements, community colleges across the United States continue to struggle with disappointing graduation rates (Jacoby, 2022). Not surprisingly, the COVID-19 pandemic had a strong negative impact on retention rates. Retention rates declined the most in community colleges (National Student Clearinghouse Research Center, March 29, 2023). To meet the multifaceted needs of diverse students, community colleges offer a wide array of academic support programs and student services, such as tutoring, peer support, academic advising, and counseling. However, such services are usually inadequately coordinated due to the colleges' divided organizational structure, disciplinary priorities, and competing missions to educate students effectively (Whitt, 2011). Historically, community colleges have been sites of competing agendas, from providing vocational education and conferring terminal Associate's degrees to facilitating transfer to four-year colleges (Solorzano et al., 2005). Such competing goals also reflect the broader political divergence of educational agendas that have shaped how colleges and universities define the purpose of higher education. Based on his direct experience as a psychology professor, Eduardo witnessed firsthand how many students, caught in the midst of such competing agendas, struggle to take a coherent stance toward learning (Vianna et al., 2014).

The impetus for creating PALC was to contribute to transforming outdated educational practices in higher education, arguably a key obstacle to meaningful learning. Theoretically, PALC is inspired by advances in the Vygotskian project, particularly the Transformative Activist Stance-TAS (Stetsenko, 2008, 2017). The TAS defines learning and development as collaborative achievements that rely upon people enacting activist agendas grounded in a vision of how present community practices ought to be changed and, ultimately, what kind of future ought to be created. Grounded in the TAS, PALC aims at expanding student agency by coconstructing with them a critical-theoretical pedagogy (Vianna & Stetsenko, 2011, 2014) that focuses on the transformative role of collaboratively critiquing social practices and discourses using critical theories as analytical tools (Vianna & Stetsenko, 2017, 2019) to facilitate students' positioning (taking a stance) on social issues and practices by interrogating practices that reproduce inequalities to which they are subjected and may inadvertently contribute to (Vianna et al., 2014). Since its inception, PALC has been implemented as a voluntary, peer-based learning community. The initial cohort consisted of former students from his courses that Eduardo invited to join the group. Soon after, participants began inviting classmates and friends and PALC grew from word of mouth.

The overarching goal of PALC is to co-create meaningful educational practices by collaboratively investigating and transforming alienating and oppressive practices in the college and beyond. This involves fostering activist agendas that connect learning and identity development (Rifino et al., 2014; Vianna et al., 2014). In weekly Friday meetings, participants critically examine their college engagement vis-à-vis their learning goals and future aspirations. This entails (a) critically examining social practices and discourses that lead to inequality, poverty, racism, sexism, and other forms of discrimination, especially in education; (b) working out a positioning or stance on these issues, including on curricular and pedagogical issues; and (c) developing activist agendas aimed at contributing to social transformation. Participants collaborate to select readings and other sources of knowledge with which they can connect, contextualize, and transform their own knowledge, including their conceptions of teaching and learning practices. In other words, PALC members investigate their own struggles as community college students, which promotes synergistic links between their learning goals and their personal strivings as those relate to current affairs and the world at large. Over the years, PALC has been configured in particular cohorts, with distinct on-off phases, which represent different phases of the project. As students in each cohort graduate and transfer to four-year colleges, some remain involved in PALC, as was the case with Araminta. A couple of participants have continued their studies in graduate school and serve as mentors.

The TAS-based approach in PALC is in line with Freirean critical pedagogy, which seeks to break with the vertical patterns characteristic of banking education (Freire, 1970) and overcome the student-teacher contradiction. As Freire (1970) famously wrote, "[t]hrough dialogue, the teacher-of-the-students and the students-of-the-teacher cease to exist and a new term emerges: teacher-student with students-teachers. The teacher is no longer merely the one who teaches, but one who is himself taught in dialogue with the students, who in turn while being taught also teach. They become jointly responsible for a process in which all grow" (p. 80). Based in the TAS, PALC seeks to reposition students as experts of the social practices they engage in. According to Stetsenko (2017):

> [t]he oppressed have firsthand knowledge and, therefore, a deeper understanding of the true conflicts, contradictions, and injustices in our societies that are hidden from those who are privileged because the latter are complicit in the embedded hierarchies of power. It is the oppressed who struggle with injustices and face the most brutal contradictions in thus enacting the core struggles and dimensions of the world and, therefore, knowing it better. (p. 247)

Taking on the role of co-investigators of their own engagement with learning, the initial cohort in PALC found conspicuous gaps between academic learning and students' personal lives and professional aspirations (Rifino et al., 2014; Vianna et al., 2014). Most participants shared a general sense of disconnect, uncertainty, and contradictions in regard to their courses and overall college experience. Many seemed confused or unsure about future goals or projected careers, struggling to connect college learning to their aspirations and participation in community life, especially those who had received a mental health or learning disability diagnosis. All shared a constrained sense of agency in their courses with roots in previous school experiences, characterized by ambivalent engagement and a mix of feelings of frustration, anger, and resignation.

Affect Injustice: A Lens to Demedicalize Student Struggle

By the time Araminta wrote the blog posts whose excerpts we used above, she and Eduardo had known each other for almost two years. At the end of her last course with Eduardo, she joined PALC. As they both remember, she would cry in almost every meeting, so it was practically inevitable that we talked about that in the group. Araminta's striving to make sense of her 'emotional experiences,' was embraced by the PALC group, opening up a collective interrogation about the meaning of affective dynamics in learning that made us question some basic yet taken-for-granted assumptions. It made us wonder, for instance, why can't you cry in the classroom or in any public space for that matter? In a psychologist's office, it is very common for people to be brought to tears. In a psychotherapy session, affection is coaxed so that it can appear and be embraced. In that holding environment, in Winnicott's terminology (1963), affects can gain space and meaning. Interestingly, in PALC, the question 'why was she crying?' seemed to have become ever more elusive. Though Araminta could often explain what had set her off, she could not really say why she was brought to tears. Instead, she would joke about it, reassuring the group that it was just something that happened to her, not a big deal, and the group would move on with the current discussion.

Drawing on the critical literature on emotions in education (e.g., Boler, 1999; Zembylas, 2021) and the 'affective turn' (e.g., Ahmed, 2004; Brennan, 2004; McManus, 2011; Massumi, 1996; Ngai, 2005) together with TAS-expanded Vygotskian theory and critical pedagogy, we began peeling away the layers of affective dynamics underpinning Araminta's crying. Reading in PALC the critical theories mentioned above, especially Megan Boler's feminist scholarship on emotions in education, Araminta began questioning why certain types of emotions from certain students are constantly excluded from discourses about teaching-learning. One of the first insights that emerged was that emotions are not talked about as part and parcel of learning. As she wrote:

> [i]n the society that we all make up, the norm is that education and learning are non-emotive. But everybody always has emotions—we are human, and our emotions carry through everything we do. If I ignore my emotion, if I don't recognize it, I can't act in a good way. (Poole, 2019)

Araminta would cry in her classes, in and out of classrooms and PALC meetings, asking herself, "Why am I crying? There's no reason to cry." Those lines indicate Araminta's awareness of latent but powerful feeling rules, as Arlie Hochschild (1983) famously described, in her seminal work "The Managed Heart," the process of trying to induce or avoid certain emotional states.

Araminta's perception jives with affect theorists Adamson and Clark's (1999) point about the "deep-rooted tendency in our culture to deny the emotions any real significance in our understanding of the world" (p. 2). According to them, affective life is considered derivative, secondary, even unreal or imaginary, which is highly unfortunate, as affects can provide invaluable knowledge of the personal, social, and political. Thus, they urge us to pay attention to the affective sources and consequences of social injustice and inequalities of power, especially shame.

This brings us to issues of power in relation to affective dynamics in particular contexts. In her work on affective injustice, Whitney (2018) argues that dismissing someone's affect amounts to a refusal of its uptake, impeding the circulation of the affect within a given context. She (Whitney, 2018) discerns a political economy of affect whenever power asymmetries tilt the balance between affecting and being affected in a group or collective activity. Building on feminist (e.g., Marilyn Frye) and anti-colonial (e.g., Frantz Fanon) works, Whitney (2018) focuses on how anger expressed by individuals from oppressed groups can be denied any reference in an external and shared world, being thus turned into a mere affect, "an outburst of feeling without meaningful content" (p. 1). The upshot is that "affect operates unjustly between embodied individuals, systematically empowering members of one social group at the expense of others" (p. 5). Whitney (2018) calls attention to how the circulation of affective forces among people is not homogenous, as feminized and racialized social practices "discriminate between bodies whose emotions are seen as having intentional objects and bodies whose emotions are seen as 'mere' affect" (p. 6). This amounts to affective injustice as unwanted feelings are refused uptake and stay quarantined within the person (e.g., as shame), and end up producing a state of alienation, as if the subject had lost connection with her own power (Whitney, 2018). "When my anger is unjustly refused uptake, it is not appropriately moving to others; it does not *affect* them as it should" (p. 6, italics in the original). This way, the quarantined affects of marginalized persons is effectively disabled, refused where it is most needed and its refusal most unjust (p. 18). Looked at from this angle, Araminta's affective dynamics emerge within educational practices that refuse uptake and quarantine her affects, resulting in beleaguered feelings of frustration, being lost and defeated by the educational system. Reminiscing on her past experience for this chapter, Araminta had the following insight about how students come to adopt a medical discourse about their difficulties:

> The affect of constant dismissal assists in the ease to fall into the medicalization of learning difficulties. Hence the diagnosis seems to hit the nail on the head, it ends up confirming this feeling of worthlessness, these alienated and inadequate ideals about oneself, "I have a disease," "I have a problem in my brain," "I am the problem." In other words, it exempts the system of fault. Instead it places the blame on the student. It reinforces and does not allow for questioning the system, not addressing why so many struggle. To medicate and pacify is much simpler than actively working to improve and replace a complex structure that has been in place for decades. (Poole, 2019)

As a result of collaboratively investigating how they were affected as they struggled with their college education, PALC students came to see how the dismissal of emotions in learning contexts is itself constitutive of their affects and powerfully shapes student engagement efforts. As psychiatrist shame theorist Donald Nathanson (1996) points out, the very expression of affect is itself bound by shame, the permissible extent of expression of affect varying from one context to another. Being too emotional is bound by shame (p. 15), so those negative affects must be contained. Following Whitney's theorizing, we contend that, compounded by the stigma attached to minoritized students, who are the majority of community college students, this building up of frustration is not allowed to circulate in educational practices (Whitney, 2018). As such affects reach high levels of intensity, the accumulated *toxic waste* (Whitney, 2018) is bound to be expressed or come across as excessive emotionality, which is then interpreted as a symptom of psychopathology. Thus, instead of focusing on what students' affects can reveal about gaps and contradictions in teaching-learning and other institutional practices, the focus is routinely reversed, through medicalizing discourses and practices, to being about students' inherent internal states only. This not only interferes with class participation and course engagement but is also traumatizing to students who then begin to question, like Araminta, the purpose of trying to get a college education.

As she shared in a blog post:

> What's the point of studying if I don't feel valued, if I am so disconnected from teachers and colleagues who don't seem to accept how I feel. What's the point of it all? I study, I go to work, I barely pay my bills, will I ever graduate? And so the desire and enthusiasm to learn little by little wanes, until it breaks down in tears and shame. (Poole, 2019

As we can infer from her words, rather than merely disengaging from her courses due to a putative insufficient motivation, a notion that tacitly carries echoes of deficit views of students, the student seems thoroughly engaged in intense affective labor of sorting out her commitments and figuring out whether to keep trying or drop out. This also raises questions about the very notion of so-called "negative" affects for its connotations of deficit. As our discussion suggests, the complex of affective dynamics described by Araminta, including frustration, hopelessness, shame, anger, and despair, do not simply create barriers to student motivation and engagement. Such connotations of passivity, buttressed by medicalized discourses about 'negative' affects, obscure what those affects negate, which is precisely alienating, oppressive, and de facto dehumanizing learning conditions.

The Affective Turn in PALC

A few years ago, PALC students, including Araminta, collectively decided to investigate prevailing conceptions of learning in the college, including their own (Vianna et. al., 2019). This semester-long project, continuing the work of previous cohorts wherein participants investigated their own experiences as community college students, was built on participants sharing their struggles with courses while connecting learning with their future aspirations and participation in community practices. Collaboratively reading critical theories enabled PALC members to ever more broadly contextualize dominant conceptions of learning and development within the colonial matrix that reproduces class inequality, racism, and patriarchy. Connecting their personal difficulties in education with world historical struggles helped them to connect their conceptions and practices of learning with popular and academic discourses while identifying gaps and contradictions in them. This in turn led students to question and reframe the meaning of their frustration with students' constrained agency in most courses, their confusion about meeting the demands of their majors and their unease with career expectations. By sharing their personal sense of disconnect, uncertainty, and conflicts vis-à-vis their courses and overall college experience, they came to embrace so-called negative emotions not as merely individual subjective reactions but as part and parcel of their collective struggle for meaningful education. Gradually, their lack of engagement in courses, usually accompanied by feelings of resignation and resentment toward the faculty, began to evolve into sustained examination of the affective dynamics of their college engagement within a broader struggle against systemic inequality. This facilitated a broad transformation of positioning among PALC members, as we describe below.

The new project, taken on by Araminta's cohort, began by having students write peer-reviewed blog posts, which gave them the opportunity to examine their conceptions of learning. Equipped with theoretical concepts, PALC members began exploring the historicity of knowledge claims while building their learning agency as they investigated the myriad aspects of the intersection between curriculum and pedagogy in the college and beyond (often reaching back to high school and earlier). The culmination of their project was the presentation of their research findings and conclusions at a college conference. Among their findings, to which Araminta made substantive inputs, students realized that their conceptions of learning, shaped by popular and pseudo-scientific discourses through years of schooling, play a key role in the alienation, isolation, and individualism students face in education. As she explains in the following excerpt from a blog post she wrote, "when

I joined PALC in my second year at LaGuardia, my approach to learning was very narrow. I believed that some of us have 'it' and that some of us just don't. These beliefs, and my struggles to have 'it,' began when I was a little girl in elementary school, which is where I learned to be timid" (Poole, 2019).

Through this work, Araminta began to move away from a deficit view of herself (though still unfinished, as she insists) by tracing its origin to the traumas she has endured in her educational trajectory while turning the pain of her (and her peers') suffering, including the affective labor of trying to manage their feelings, into a source of knowledge about alienating and oppressive educational practices. As she wrote in PALC:

> I never thought of students as a part of education. That the knowledge is given to the student and if they can't manage to take the knowledge in, then it is framed in a way of "they can't learn". The position of the student was to sit and be quiet, take the material and move on to the next topic. (Poole, 2019)

In the following quote, Araminta explains some key aspects of their collaborative inquiry:

> Through PALC's inquiry of conceptions and practices of learning, a shift in preconceived beliefs about education and personal ability began. Prior to this inquiry, my understanding of how one learns was that people are told the information and their brain takes it in and files it away to be recalled later. The student is passive in the process, disconnected, and relies on the propensity of their brain. As we worked collaboratively, I realized that this way of thinking was problematic. Working together, I noticed my individual self was capable. I was slowly repositioning my stance on my ability. (Poole, 2019)

Repositioning themselves as experts on the conflicts, contradictions, and injustices in the educational system and society at large, was a key step toward turning students' affective dynamics into a source of knowledge about the intricate processes through which oppressive and alienating educational practices are reproduced– including by their own coopted agency, such as when they endorse deficit discourses to account for their learning struggles. In other words, in PALC they began to listen to their own affective dynamics as deeply felt intensities embodying knowledge about how the educational system affects students. At the same time, this was a process of affect uptake (Whitney, 2018), as students began listening to and embracing each other's feelings. Gradually, what had to be contained as unacceptable or undesirable in the classroom and in other institutional practices, which accumulated as quarantined affects, was mobilized and reclaimed not as mere subjective affects, but as instantiating an activist positioning of resistance and indignation toward a dehumanizing educational system. Thus, instead of attempting to eliminate unwanted, so-called negative affects, the work in PALC focused on acknowledging and honoring students' agentive positioning embodied in their affective dynamics. As Araminta realized later on in PALC:

> [b]ehind that crying is an emotion and a reason for that emotion. Instead of pretending that I don't have an emotion, if I say that it's okay that I have these feelings, I can become more aware [of what they mean] and can approach the emotion in a different way. (Poole, 2019)

Sometime around the semester following their inquiry project, PALC participants and Araminta noticed she was no longer crying so often. It seemed that, for her, PALC had turned into what Winnicott (1963) termed a holding environment, wherein students could listen to and learn from their affective dynamics without being fit into a previously established classification system of diagnosis or attempts at medicalization. Instead of denying their meaning, the work in PALC opened up a space to inquire about affective dynamics, embracing and making them active. Arguably, this affective turn was crucial for students to realize their potential and expand their agency. In Araminta's case it helped her to gradually de-identify herself from all the labels attached to her by the educational institution, to which, as she then realized, she herself had become attached, and which drained so much of her potential (Conde et. al., 2021). Listening to affects as embodiments of her struggle to resist alienating and oppressive educational practices helped Araminta realize that she had no intrinsic attention deficit, no problems in the brain. The resistance to learning in conformity with the banking model (Freire, 1970) and the signs of shame and tears on her face were rediscovered as a critical stance, the negation of dehumanizing education. The student and the teacher often do not know it yet, but this resistance is in itself already a sign of a transformative potential. Thus, quarantined affection can be unleashed as potential desire, the yearning for a welcoming and listening environment, where its transforming potential can be realized in agentive, activist learning.

In the following blog post, written toward the end of the project, Araminta wrote about this process of expanding her agency:

> In PALC we don't learn just to get it done. We are learning to improve our understanding and find meaningful ways to use and continue to learn. This aids in allowing students to be connected to their studies, lessening the shame of inadequacy and ineptitude and creating a sense of dignity and purpose, agency, not found in the typical classroom. Agency is a key part of learning. Agency was a term I was unfamiliar with and opened up my understanding of my place within the education system. As I worked with PALC and struggled to understand the meaning and importance of agency, my agency was growing. The

want to understand, to learn more, was stronger. I was beginning to see myself as an active part of the learning process. (Poole, 2019)

As she further described:

[b]y fighting against this passivity, continuing to take classes in what seemed a never ending struggle of inadequacy, I was taking a stance against the oppressive practices in education. I was finding my agency. Wanting and fighting to learn, not just for a test, but for greater knowledge provides dignity in a system that had always been demoralizing and shaming. With the work and knowledge I have done and continue to pursue through the collaborative learning space PALC has provided, I am proud to say I am still enrolled in school, and will complete my Bachelors. (Poole, 2019)

As we can read in Araminta's words, embracing the negation of oppressive institutional practices meant affirming her critical vision and activist commitment to social change, which gave rise to the joy of joining with others in an activist learning community. By developing a collective activist agenda grounded in their own individually unique contributions to transforming and taking their education in their hands, PALC participants turned negative feelings around. For instance, shame was turned into the pride of not giving in (or giving up) and fighting back. In sum, their affective dynamics were resignified and simultaneously overlaid with an emerging transformative activist stance, just as intensely felt, manifested as joy in their newfound 'collectividual' agency (Stetsenko, 2013).

Conclusion

In this chapter, we sought to critically examine the meaning of affective dynamics underpinning student engagement grounded in our experiences as a community college student and a professor (Araminta and Eduardo, respectively) who were also participants in a voluntary, peer-based co-curricular project led by Eduardo. We were joined by Rafael, whose insights, grounded in his practice of constantly listening to affects to unearth their history and meaning, were crucial to our evolving understanding of affective dynamics as agentive processes, in particular negative affects as embodying resistance. While calls for educational reform from a liberal education framework have placed student engagement efforts at the center of a plethora of pedagogical innovations in colleges, which we agree is key to meaningful learning and emancipatory educational practices, we contend that this notion needs to be further scrutinized for its tacit connotation of individual failing or deficit. Listening to Araminta, as she endeavored to make sense of her "emotional experiences," in light of our TAS-based critical-theoretical approach, opened up a collective inquiry that interrogated how affects "work, in concrete and particular ways, to mediate the relationship between the psychic and the social, and between the individual and the collective" (Ahmed, 2004, 119). Inverting the hierarchical logic of knowledge transmission, the student was repositioned as the one who teaches, as she is the one with deep knowledge of what it is like to go through an educational institution and find herself excluded, diagnosed, and medicalized. Though it almost goes without saying, while our analysis cannot be generalized to all students, it suggests that similarly powerful affective dynamics underpinning student engagement might be implicated in the struggles of many students as they confront inequities and injustices in their college education.

The collective inquiry in PALC, which continued through the writing of this chapter, encouraged us to think about the impact of denying students' affects any relevance by reducing them to individual psychopathology. Drawing on critical theories of emotions in learning (e.g., Boler, 1999; Zembylas, 2013, 2022) provided conceptual tools that framed Araminta's (and other students') affective dynamics in the classroom not as solely a subjective experience, thus redressing the affective injustice she was subject to for most of her educational journey. Rather, we sought to grasp affects not as self-contained in the individual. As affect theorist Teresa Brennan articulates (2004), affects "do not only arise within a particular person but also come from without. They come via an interaction with other people and an environment" (p. 3). Acknowledging the social, relational, dynamic, and situated nature of human affective dynamics disavows reductive, biomedical interpretations of so-called "negative" affects while questioning the role of educational institutions as sites that produce psychopathology among vulnerable students.

Inspired by the TAS (Stetsenko, 2008, 2013, 2017, 2018, 2023), our analysis also rejects mechanical views of the environment unidirectionally impinging on (affecting) students as though they were completely passive and devoid of agency. Thus, a central theme of this chapter was to provide a historicized, sociogenic account of the affective injustice community college students are vulnerable to without erasing the personal, agentive ways each one affects and is affected while wrestling against alienating and oppressive learning practices. By questioning students' internalization of deficit discourses about their learning difficulties, the work in PALC reveals how students' views matter, being constitutive of teaching-learning conditions.

Similarly, listening to and reconstituting the meaning of the very affective dynamics themselves is co-constitutive of learning conditions. Listening to and embracing affects, making them epistemologically productive (Stodulka et al., 2018), especially the affects of negation (to avoid reductive connotations of negative affects), give us a tool to frame issues of student engagement in terms of resistance to alienation and oppression, while moving away from deficit discourses about community college students. Rather than mere disengagement, with inescapable connotations of passivity, this point suggests the opposite, namely to approach affective dynamics as embodying and enacting agentive (activist) positionings toward learning (and other community practices). This calls for reorganizing teaching-learning practices in ways that position students as collaboratively trans/forming their learning conditions by providing space and tools for them to explore and thus co-author their affects, which centrally entails the motivation and desire to learn.

We hope our analysis contributes to recent expansions of critical pedagogy which posit that "education must not only enable people to recognize and explain injustice through critical analysis, but also help them develop critical affectivities through which they are moved to change it" (Amsler, 2011, p. 53, citing Burbules & Berk, 1999, p. 50). Thus, we call for connecting affective dynamics and agency within an ethico-political view of struggles for inclusive, emancipatory education.

Notes

1 While no single definition exists and more than 90 putative definitions have been proposed (Tyng et al., 2017), traditionally in the psychological literature, emotions are viewed as markers of well-being. Positive emotions, including joy, interest, contentment, and love characterize flourishing or optimal well-being, whereas the opposite is true for negative emotions, such as anxiety, sadness, anger and despair. The overall balance of positive and negative emotions has been found to predict judgments of subjective well-being (Fredrickson, 2001).
2 Regarding the authorship of this chapter, all authors contributed equally to its writing through several drafts to the point that it is not possible, for the most part, to discern who wrote what passages, save obviously for Araminta's direct quotes. The order of authorship reflects the fact that Eduardo, as the lead researcher in PALC, contributed most of the initial draft describing the work in PALC, whereas Araminta provided most of the empirical part of the chapter and Rafael contributed to the theoretical background and analysis.
3 This definition of learning cuts across a wide range of theories of cognitive psychology, from Piaget and Bandura but also to interpretations of Vygotsky's and related sociocultural theories, such as Bruner's.
4 According to Amsler (2011), while there is no consensus on the relationship between affect, feeling, and emotion, it is common in this literature to posit that "[a]ffects are 'pre-personal' and 'pre-conscious experiences that cannot be represented in language or generally even comprehended, "while "[f]eelings are our personal interpretations

of those affective experiences, and emotions are the social and socially recognized expression of these feelings" (p. 116). Critics such as Leys (2011) have argued that such conceptual separation between affect, emotions, and feelings carries a reductionist tendency that privileges the body over the mind in dualist terms. In consonance with her view, we also do not posit a gap between the subject's affects and its cognition or appraisal of the affective situation.

References

Adamson, J., & Clark, H.A. (1999). *Scenes of shame: Psychoanalysis, shame, and writing.* SUNY Press, Series in Psychoanalysis and Culture.
Ahmed, S. (2004). *Cultural politics of emotion.* Edinburgh University Press.
Amsler, S.S. (2011). From "therapeutic" to political education: The centrality of affective sensibility in critical pedagogy. *Critical Studies in Education, 52*(1), 47–63.
Boler, M. (1999). *Feeling power: emotions and education.* Routledge.
Brennan, T. (2004). *The transmission of affect.* Cornell University Press.
Conde, S.F., Vianna, E., & Pole, A. (2021). A cooptação neocolonial da agência por meio da patologização da pobreza, da diversidade e da desigualdade nos EUA como enfrentá-la com uma educação ativista transformadora. *Cadernos CIMEAC, 11*(1), 250–276.
Dougherty, K. (2023). *Choice is not always good: Reducing the role of informational inequality in producing and legitimating higher education inequality.* Columbia University, Teachers College, Community College Research Center. https://ccrc.tc.columbia.edu/media/k2/attachments/choice-is-not-always-good.pdf
Fredrickson, B.L. (2001). The role of positive emotions in positive psychology: The broadenand-build theory of positive emotions. *American psychologist, 56*(3), 218.
Freire, P. (1970). *Pedagogy of the oppressed.* Continuum.
Gatens, M. (2014). Affective transitions and Spinoza's art of joyful deliberation. In M.L. Angerer, B. Bösel, & M. Ott (Eds.), *Timing of affect: Epistemologies, aesthetics, politics* (pp. 17–33). Diaphanes.
Gregg, M., & Seigworth, G.J. (2010). *The affect theory reader.* Duke.
Hardt, M. (2007). Foreword: What affects are good for. In P. Clough & J. Halley (Eds.), *The affective turn: Theorizing the social* (pp. ix–xiii.). Duke University Press.
Hochschild, A.R. (1983). *The managed heart: Commercialization of human feeling.* University of California Press.
Jacoby, T. (2022). *Training tomorrow's workers: Next steps for New York community colleges.* Manhattan Institute for Policy Research.
Leys, R. (2011). The turn to affect: A critique. *Critical inquiry, 37*(3), 434–472.
Massumi, B. (1996). The autonomy of affect. In P. Patton (Ed.), *Deleuze: A critical reader* (pp. 217–239). Blackwell.
McManus, S. (2011). Hope, fear, and the politics of affective agency. *Theory & Event, 14*(4).

Nathanson, D. L. (Ed.). (1996). *Knowing feeling: Affect, script, and psychotherapy*. WW Norton & Company.

National Student Clearinghouse Research Center. (2023, March 29). *Stay informed with the latest enrollment information*. https://nscresearchcenter.org/stay-informed/

Ngai, S. (2005). *Ugly feelings*. Harvard University Press.

Pekrun, R., Goetz, T., Titz, W., & Perry, R.P. (2002). Academic emotions in students' self-regulated learning and achievement: A program of qualitative and quantitative research. *Educational psychologist, 37*(2), 91–105.

Pekrun, R. (2016). Academic emotions. In K. R. Wentzel & D. B. Miele (Eds.), *Handbook of motivation at school*. (pp. 120-144). Routledge.

Podlucká, D. (2020). Transformative anti-ableist pedagogy for social justice. *Outlines. Critical Practice Studies, 21*(1), 69–97.

Podlucká, D., & Vianna, E. (2021). The ethics of affects in transformative activist qualitative research: Struggle and solidarity in collaborative inquiry. In V.L. Trevisan de Souza & L. Tateo (Eds.), *Qualitative research and social intervention: transformative methodologies for collective contexts* (pp. 35–61). Springer.

Poole, A. (2019). Developing agency. *In Transit, 9*. http://ctl.laguardia.edu/journal/v9/default.htm.

Rifino, M., Matsuura, K., & Medina, F. (2014). The peer activist learning community: A peer perspective. In Andy Blunden (Ed.), *Collaborative projects: An interdisciplinary study* (pp. 322–326). Brill Academic Publishers.

Seigworth, G.J., & Gregg, M. (2010). An inventory of shimmers. In M. Gregg & G. Seigworth (Eds.), *The affect theory reader* (pp. 1–25). Duke.

Sólorzano, D.G., Villalpando, O., & Oseguera, L. (2005). Educational inequities and Latina/o undergraduate students in the United States: A critical race analysis of their educational progress. *Journal of Hispanic Higher Education, 4*(3), 272–294.

Stetsenko, A. (2008). From relational ontology to transformative activist stance: Expanding Vygotsky's (CHAT) project. *Cultural Studies of Science Education, 3*(2), 471–491.

Stetsenko, A. (2013). Theorizing personhood for the world in transition and change: Reflections from a transformative activist stance. In J. Martin & M.H. Bickhard (Eds.), *The Psychology of personhood* (pp. 181–202). Cambridge University.

Stetsenko, A. (2017). *The transformative mind: Expanding Vygotsky's perspective on development and education*. Cambridge University Press

Stetsenko, A. (2018). Research and activist projects of resistance: The ethical-political foundations for a transformative ethico-onto-epistemology. *Learning, Culture and Social Interaction, 26*, Article 100222.

Stetsenko, A. (2023). The Tasks of Reality and Reality As the Task: Connecting cultural-historical activity theory with the radical scholarship of resistance. In N. Hopwood & A. Sannino (Eds.), *Agency and Transformation: Motives, Mediation, and Motion* (pp. 56-83). Cambridge University Press.

Stodulka, T., Selim, N., & Mattes, D. (2018). Affective scholarship: Doing anthropology with epistemic affects. *Ethos, 46*(4), 519–536.

Timimi, S., & Timimi, Z. (2022). The dangers of mental health promotion in schools. *Journal of Philosophy of Education, 56*(1), 12–21.

Tyng, C.M., Amin, H.U., Saad, M.N., & Malik, A.S. (2017). The influences of emotion on learning and memory. *Frontiers in Psychology, 8*, 1454.

Venianaki, A., Timplalexi, E., & Dafermos, M. (2021). The medicalisation of learning difficulties through the prism of Bronfenbrenner's bioecological approach: the case of the remote and mountainous areas of Chania Prefecture. *Outlines. Critical Practice Studies, 22*(1), 138–180.

Vianna, E., Hougaard, N., & Stetsenko, A. (2014). The dialectics of collective and individual transformation: Transformative activist research in a collaborative learning community project. In *Collaborative projects: An interdisciplinary study* (pp. 59–88). Koninklijke Brill.

Vianna, E., Rifino, M., & Medina, F. (2019). Transforming conceptions and practices of learning: A collaborative inquiry with and for community college students. *In Transit, 9*. http://ctl.laguardia.edu/journal/v9/default.htm

Vianna, E., & Stetsenko, A. (2011). Connecting learning and identity development through a transformative activist stance: Application in adolescent development in a child welfare program. *Human Development, 54*, 313–338.

Vianna, E., & Stetsenko, A. (2014). Research with a transformative activist agenda: Creating the future through education for social change. *Learning In and Across Contexts: Reimagining Education, 113*, 575–602.

Vianna, E., & Stetsenko, A. (2017). Expanding student agency in the introductory psychology course: Transformative activist stance and critical-theoretical pedagogy. In R. Obeid, A. Schwartz, C. Shane Simpson, & P. Brooks, (Eds.), *How we teach now: The GSTA guide to student-centered teaching*. Society for the Teaching of Psychology.

Vianna, E., & Stetsenko, A. (2019). Turning resistance into passion for knowledge with the tools of agency: Teaching-learning about theories of evolution for social justice among foster youth. *Perspectiva, 37*(3), 864–886.

Whitney, S. (2018). Affective intentionality and affective Injustice: Merleau-Ponty and Fanon on the Body Schema as a theory of affect. *The Southern Journal of Philosophy, 56*(4), 488–515.

Whitt, E.J. (2011). Academic and student affairs partnerships. In J.H. Schuh, S.R. Jones, S.R. Harper & Associates (Eds.), *Student services: A handbook for the profession* (pp. 482–496). Jossey-Bass.

Winnicott, D.W. (1963). *The maturational processes and the facilitating environment*. International Universities Press.

Zembylas, M. (2013). Revisiting the Gramscian legacy on counter-hegemony, the subaltern and affectivity: Toward an emotional pedagogy of activism in higher education. *Critical Studies in Teaching and Learning, 1*(1), 1–21.

Zembylas, M. (2018). Reinventing critical pedagogy as decolonizing pedagogy: The education of empathy. *Review of Education, Pedagogy, and Cultural Studies*, *40*(5), 404–421. https://doi.org/10.1080/10714413.2019.1570794

Zembylas, M. (2021). The affective dimension of everyday resistance: Implications for critical pedagogy in engaging with neoliberalism's educational impact. *Critical Studies in Education*, *62*(2), 211–226.

Zembylas, M. (2022). The affective turn in educational theory. In *Oxford research encyclopedia of education*. https://oxfordre.com/education/view/10.1093/acrefore/9780190264093.001.0001/acrefore-9780190264093-e-1272

Centering Humanness in Project Development and Learning Goals

KAYSI HOLMAN AND STEFANIE SERTICH

The LaGuardia Mellon Humanities Scholars (LaGuardia Scholars) program was an extracurricular program, started in Fall 2016 as part of the CUNY Humanities Alliance, a grant-funded program generously supported by the Andrew W. Mellon Foundation. The original idea in developing the grant proposal was to support a pipeline program that would encourage students to go from community colleges to four-year colleges and on to graduate school. The CUNY Humanities Alliance, as a partnership between LaGuardia Community College (LaGuardia) and the Graduate Center (GC) of the City University of New York (CUNY), was also exploring a model of formal connection between the two institutions where graduate fellow instructors would be placed with faculty mentors and teach in the community college. The LaGuardia Scholars program was built as an extracurricular program to support LaGuardia students in building academic and career pathways in, and enrich their engagement with, the humanities. We began with a small cohort of only eight scholars the first year, and had 20–30 in following cohorts. The initial plan was for faculty and graduate instructors to identify promising humanities students from their classes to enter the program, where they would gain further opportunities for engagement in the humanities, additional mentorship, and encouragement to transfer to four-year colleges and ultimately pursue graduate school. It became so much more. The LaGuardia Scholars program became a transformational experience for those engaged in it, and there are two important reasons why (neither of which are restricted to those privileged enough to have a generous budget).

First, we created the program with what we call human-driven pedagogy where we recognize and center the full humanity of the people in the room–including us and the scholars. This meant coming together *with* the scholars to create a space that acknowledges and welcomes everything they are and everything they bring to the table: their home, their work, their interests, their educational aspirations, their career goals, their bodies, their minds, their gender, race, ethnicities, nationalities, languages, sexual orientation, mental and physical abilities, politics, religion, economic status, and curiosity. For an extracurricular program based at one of the country's most diverse colleges, where close to 100 native languages are represented, and more than half the students live in New York City with household incomes less than $25,000 a year (Office of Institutional Research & Assessment, 2021), human-driven pedagogy seemed simply necessary.

Second, the work of the program was done mainly through students designing and creating a year-long project that meaningfully connected their interests as a person, their academic journey and skills, and their life aspirations. Theoretically, our program goals were to increase awareness of the humanities, connecting identity and aspirations, build pathways to academic success, practice interpersonal communication and presentation skills, and engage in mentorship/leadership. In practice, that meant we followed a four-stage process of project development: (1) projects began with a human-driven ideation process; (2) each scholar received feedback from their peers and faculty mentors throughout the year, and were influenced by enrichment activities outside the classroom; (3) students were encouraged to refine and change their project; and (4) the program culminated each year in a public showcase, again designed and created by the scholars, that highlighted their work and allowed the community to experience and interact with their work.

The impact that this program had on the scholars astounded us! While in the LaGuardia Scholars, or immediately afterward, many scholars changed majors, changed their future educational plans, and/or changed their long-term career aspirations. As always, we'll let the scholars speak for themselves on how the program impacted them (typos and misspellings included):

- "I learned what I wanted to do with my life. I changed my major and career path. [I]t helped me to decide who I wanted to be."
- "[T]he program made me realize what I want to do with my education. They reminded me that I am going to school because I want to make a difference or even enhance my life. [I]t made me gain confidence and made me decisive for choosing my current major instead of continuing a major that I did not want."
- "My experience with the Humanities Scholars program was very awarding and one that I will cherish forever. At first I was nervous but

it got me to open up to my peers and mentors. In addition my mentors were there to guide me and help me along the way."
- "I enjoyed being able to design my own project and have the freedom to direct how I would present it. All of our mentors were patient and offered valuable advise. Having food at the meetings was great because I would often have food for the rest of the week, which helped to alleviate stress. It was great meeting other scholars who were passionate about their projects. I have nothing, but good things to say. Being able to choose our own enrichment activities was also quite the treat."
- "[P]articipating in enrichment activities has impacted [m]y career goals because allowed me to explore the great outlook of humanities isn't found in a particular job but rather humanities has a great horizon in any job you go too . In addition its allowing me to pursue a medical career and have a outlook in the humanities side of it."
- "[T]he humanities is a subject that is relevant in all aspects of our lives. It is an important foundation to build in order to make change or improve our society and world."
- "I learned that the humanities is related to every part of our lives and that is a creative field. Academia without the humanities would do us injustice."
- "It made me really think about how I want my career (music) to impact the world, and allowed me to put alot of thought into ways to facilitate that beyond my career choice of teaching music."

These are just snippets, a taste from those who filled out a basic survey at the end of their year in the program. Hour for hour, the Humanities Scholars program is *less* hours than a 3-credit-hour course. How often do we, as teachers, get course feedback like that?!

Seeing this feedback from scholars in the first couple of years, we were floored! We felt like we had stumbled on some secret recipe for student engagement, empowerment, transformation, and agency. We kept staring at each other and asking: How can we take something that's a voluntary program and have it involve and impact as many college students as possible? The obvious answer is to find a way to embed the components that make it successful into classrooms.

This is when we look to you. This is our challenge for you: use human-driven pedagogy, and a project process like ours, and see what happens! It can't hurt to try, and it could make a remarkable difference, to you and your students.

Much of what our program does is already happening in classrooms. We met for two hours every other week while school was in session for an academic year. The time scholars spent on their project outside of meetings was flexible, but not even close to what someone would spend on one course's homework. Most courses have a project, be it an essay, research paper, presentation, etc. Most courses provide feedback and opportunities to revise that work. And yet most courses are not heralded as transformative experiences by the students in them. Almost all higher education courses have requirements/limitations: content and skills set by our institutions and departments, textbooks or canons that must be followed, building blocks needed for continued study in our field, etc. Even when we are limited by those requirements, there are still opportunities in our pedagogy and activities that are more inclusive of our students' experiences (Moore, 2012).

We believe that by using a human-driven pedagogy that acknowledges and respects students as humans first, and by facilitating four particular stages of project development, courses can be remarkable and life-changing experiences.

We think that with these elements, with small modifications to work you are already doing—that does not make teaching harder or more complicated—faculty, or college students on their own accord, could change a simple course into a transformative experience. This chapter will include a detailed description of the four main stages of project development that we use: (1) human-driven ideation, (2) refinement, enrichment, and guidance, (3) permission to change, and (4) public production. And, it will also include curriculum segments that folks can modify and use to change their class experience. The beauty of this method is that it doesn't have to happen in *every* class (though it would be fantastic if it did!). We believe it should happen, at some time, for everyone enrolled in college.

Developing our Pedagogical Approach

Discussions of pedagogy so often become term-laden and vague. Two practitioners who say they employ "critical pedagogy" in their classrooms may have very different definitions and understandings of what that means and how it is operationalized in the classroom. When two people are using the same terms to describe very different operationalizations, it makes working together more difficult and detailed in the planning stages. We were lucky. It is exceptionally rare to find another pedagogue so completely different in skill sets and experience, who happens to have the same pedagogical philosophy.

Our differences are numerous; as are our similarities. Kaysi Holman, who was the Director of Programs and Administration of CUNY Humanities Alliance, has spent 20 years working with nonprofits and educational organizations dedicated to social justice, equity, and access to higher education. Stefanie Sertich, the Director of the Theatre Program at LaGuardia, has spent 20 years as a faculty member and director of countless theater productions. Kaysi is an administrator, who manages projects to exacting timetables and navigates complex groups of students, faculty, and administrators toward individual and shared goals; Stefanie is an artist, who manages theater productions to exacting performance schedules and navigates groups of artists, students, faculty, and administrators toward the institutional, program and individual goals. Ultimately, all our experience meant that the LaGuardia Scholars program was designed by a theater artist and a social justice administrator, who had deep philosophical and pedagogical alignment.

During our first planning meeting for the project, we began by discussing the projects we had both been engaged with and our vision for how to move forward with the LaGuardia Scholars program. Kaysi brought a detailed calendar timeline, project-based pedagogical methods, and a list of educational and career planning activities. Stefanie brought inspiring videos about student-developed performances, community-building exercises, and presentation-of-self movement-based activities. We both came to the table with little ego and big trust, which allowed us to delve into our work together without a preset agenda or territoriality. This deeper conversation about our previous experiences with implementing critical pedagogy and sparking student engagement was essential to our solidarity as partners and our collaboration. Inexplicably, through this basic show-and-tell, it became obvious that we shared many pedagogical values.

We both, first and foremost, acknowledge our students as humans. We fully recognize that they have jobs, families, responsibilities, challenges, and interests that go far beyond the campus or their work with us. We respect and love that they can bring ideas, experiences, critiques, and imagination that are beyond us. We understand that students are most engaged when they're working on a practical project that they're actually passionate about—not just for a grade or to make their teachers or families happy (Almulla, 2020; Buchanan et al., 2016; Maida 2011). We see them as embodied people, who get tired, feel hunger, experience emotions, get sick, and need movement (Bird & Sinclair, 2019; Nguyen & Larson, 2015; Thompson, 2017). We know that students can and should lead the direction of the class, or in our case, the program (Ahn & Class, 2011). All these pedagogical frameworks have names: critical pedagogy (Freire, 2000; hooks, 1994), reality pedagogy

(Emdin, 2016), student-centered pedagogy (Ahn & Class, 2011; Jones, 2007), project-based pedagogy (Buchanan, 2016; Maida, 2011), embodied pedagogy (Bird & Sinclair, 2019; Nguyen & Larson, 2015; Thompson, 2017). For us, the crux of the matter is that participants in our program are not merely students; they are humans—people with fully developed intellects, who are fully functioning in the world.

Most teachers espouse that students are not passive learners or empty receptacles to be filled; however, when we refer to our students, we so commonly invoke the notion that they are lacking or seeking knowledge that we have to provide to them (this is true even when we are teaching a subject we are not precisely an expert in and it is our first time teaching it). Within academia, there is an objectifying and essentializing of the role of students wherein we assume that (1) their primary role in life is that of a student (not as workers, mothers, fathers, siblings, or parts of cultural or social groups); (2) while students choose their major, the departments determine what and how students ought to learn within that subject matter (though the canon has expanded to the point where no one scholar could truly learn everything within a discipline); and (3) instructors are the ultimate authority in evaluating how much or how well a student has learned the material they were supposed to gather from a class (though most instructors have spent at least a decade steeped in academia, which privileges eurocentric, white, masculine, and English-only forms of knowledge) (Matsuda, 2006).

When you center humanness, it's strange and stiff to talk about what you have to "teach" someone. "... Here, no one teaches another, nor is anyone self-taught. People teach each other, mediated by the world, by the cognizable objects which in banking education are 'owned' by the teacher" (Freire, 2000, p. 80). We are all familiar with the "I learn so much from my students" trope. What is so often meant by that statement is that while faculty are teaching their students the academic currency of proper grammar, essay structure, and research methodology, the students are "teaching" the faculty about contemporary memes and pop culture. It so very rarely means what it should: that the people in a classroom fundamentally shift the way each person thinks about the world, that students teach faculty theory and experience and ideological precepts that shift and forward faculty's scholarship.

Though individually and together, the co-authors believe we have a tremendous amount of information to share with other people, we believe the same is true of our students. We see ourselves as facilitators of a rich process of discussion, reflection, and action, that engages everyone in the room as a whole person, and is driven by the people in the room (where we are $^2/_{15}$ or $^2/_{30}$ of the equation). For example, when we decided on small- and large-group humanities enrichment activities,[1] we asked the students to look into options, and come prepared to pitch enrichment activities to each other. We pitched some activities as well, but again, we were $2/15$ or $2/30$ of the discussion. Then, we decided together what enrichment activities we wanted to embark on as a group. This approach places students in the role of decision- and knowledge-makers, grounded in their incredibly personal and ambitious engagement with the humanities.

A crucial part of our collaboration with each other, and in developing this project, is our shared commitment to allow the students' interests, scholarly goals, and career ambitions to drive the program and the activities that we do. This is more than just focusing on what their majors are, or what media they're consuming, or their eventual careers. We address them as full humans, whose interests (what they love to do), scholarly goals (their classes, majors, educational plans and aspirations,), career goals (however defined or undefined) and person (their culturally specific, gendered, racialized, embodied experience) are all valued, accepted, and aligned (when possible). This takes an essential trust in our students that they ultimately know what is best for themselves, that they know what they need to learn and how they need to develop. Students always ultimately choose their own course of action, regardless of what structures we put in place, what supports we offer, or what discipline we try to enforce. Each individual must decide whether sleep or homework is more necessary, whether going to a job or going to class is more important in the immediate and the long-term. Transparency and imperfection become staples throughout the year as guideposts for both us and the students on a continuous basis. By being transparent and demonstrating vulnerability, we earn the students' trust. They see us modeling imperfection and growth in our dynamic with each other and with them. This creates trust and comfort within the larger group, allowing the students to demonstrate their own vulnerability as they choose.

Trusting students to determine the direction of a program (or a course) does not mean that the program (or course) is without a curriculum or goals.

Our Program Goals

Another thing the two of us have in common is that we are both extremely experienced project managers, and planning this project was no different than any other. The short description from the grant proposal, along with LaGuardia's core curriculum, and our own experience with students, gave us plenty of foundational materials to build program goals. We were both excited about all the possibilities, and began simply enough by asking ourselves: What did it mean for the program to be "successful"? What did we want folks in the program to have accomplished by the end of the year? What skills and resources would folks need in order to complete their projects and create a showcase at the end of the year? This is much like defining the learning goals in course-planning, and outlining the activities and lesson plans based on those learning goals. The initial answer was a simple set of five goals, each with a driving question underneath it, and many sub-components:

1. Increasing Awareness of the Humanities
What do you risk[2] to learn about others on a human level?
- Increase empathy and understanding of the world through learning cultural context and historical perspective
- Better understand human behavior in ourselves and others
- Consider the global perspective of social issues that may be present in our own communities (home, LGCC, NYC, US, World) and how we connect to them personally
- Gain an understanding of what the humanities are and their lifelong value
- Learn teamwork through shared goals and projects
- Become acquainted with Humanities Enrichment resources in the community

2. Connecting Identity and Aspirations
What do you risk to put your aspirations first? Where do your family, friends, and social constructs come in as obstacles?
- Build social and emotional awareness, including listening skills, openness, reflection of past knowledge, etc.
- Connect students' interests to their academic life
- Recognize the strength of the cultural resources (family and community background) that we bring with us
- Learn to live with uncomfortableness: *Things will go wrong. How do you handle it?*
- Connect to a positive mindset and the ripple effects of such

3. Building Pathways to Academic Success
What are you willing to risk/sacrifice to be successful?
- Take responsibility for ourselves as learners and understand the requirements of life in college
- Actively engage in the community of LaGuardia Community College
- Persevere when facing obstacles

- Build a vision of future humanities academic and career pathways
- Gain access to opportunities in the humanities
- Engage in professionalization activities (resume, cover letter, portfolio, practice interviews)
- Perform community service
- Improve digital literacy skills

4. Practicing Interpersonal Communication and Presentation-of-Self Skills

What are you willing to risk to put yourself out there?
- Practice oral communication (eye contact, tone of voice, pacing, diction, etc.)[3]
- Learn about physical presence
- Gain confidence / get over the jitters
- Learn how to communicate with others that are different than you
- Experience public scholarship, both online and in person

5. Engaging in Mentorship/Leadership

What are you willing to risk when you lead?
- Practice listening and empathy skills
- Learn about resources
- Engage in a leadership role
- Help plan and produce events

The first and third goals were motivated by the description of the program in the grant application. The second and fourth goals stemmed from core competencies at LaGuardia. The fifth was mostly our play space. Overall, we agreed that these were foundational skills for people who face structural, systemic obstacles to their success. We hoped for all of us to leave with a better understanding of ourselves, other people, the systems and structures, and some practices to maneuver through, over, or around obstacles that we faced.

While each of these goals speaks to information or skills we hoped students would develop during the program, notice that these are all things that we, as instructors, can benefit from and learn from. Keeping with our principals of human-driven pedagogy, instructors are also considered as humans in the room. We both believe that skills and knowledge are a practice, and that everyone is always growing and learning, whether they recognize it or not. Growth and learning are not always linear and are rarely predictable, but we hoped to use these goals to narrow the focus of our program.

Once we had this open guideline, we then had to operationalize these goals into activities, and finally put them all on the schedule. As you can probably guess, some of the goals above suggest the corresponding activity (e.g., practice oral communication); however, others are less straightforward (e.g., increase empathy and understanding of the world through learning cultural context and historical perspective). So, how did we begin to transform these more general goals into practical details? Strangely enough, the answer lies in our pedagogical theoretical framework.

Implementing Human-Driven Pedagogy in our Program Curriculum

The first thing we agreed on was that scholars were busy people, whose first priority would never be this program (or frankly, any class). When people are not worried about how to pay their rent, or buy food, or get metro cards, they are worried about their families, their jobs, their classes, and their friends. In order to even get folks interested in a program like this, we understood we would have to provide some remuneration, either financial support or course credit for participating. For us, providing a stipend was the easier method, and so the scholars were each given a $1,000 stipend for the year, tickets to attend enrichment activities in the city, and metro cards to get to and from our activities. We also ensured that there was always food. Every meeting, every outing, we anticipated hunger. And, make no mistake, students are hungry (Nazmi et al., 2019; U.S. GAO, 2019). In our third year, one scholar always came, at 6 p.m., having been in classes since 9 a.m., and had never eaten before we saw him. For him, there was either no time or no money. Other scholars casually discussed often choosing between buying the metrocard to come to college or buy lunch that day. Because of this, every one of our sessions had time at the beginning for everyone to settle in and eat food.

Creating a human-driven space also means believing folks when life happens, and they could not make it to meetings, whether they have a specific reason or life was so much that they just couldn't that day. It is not productive—for the instructor, student, or the group—to have someone present just because they feel they have to. We wanted them to be there, to be present and engaged in a way that is helpful to them and the group. The only way to do that is to ensure that it is a guilt-free, inspiring, and engaging atmosphere. With the isolation and alienation currently present in much of higher education, particularly for students of color and first-generation students (Loo & Rolison, 1986; Suarez et al., 1997; Suen, 1983), reminders of responsibilities, guilt trips about missing sessions, and strict accountability practices simply become tools of disempowerment that remove scholars' innate motivations to engage in the work they aspire to do. If you have trouble imagining a guilt-free environment that is motivating, we would challenge you to close your eyes and imagine waking up in the morning with eight completely free hours ahead of you. You feel well-rested and energetic. What project would you be genuinely excited to work on for part of that time? (Really, close your eyes, take a few deep breaths and do the exercise ... we'll wait.) Now, open your eyes and think about all the ways you've been forced through the years to internalize guilt around productivity. Have you ever felt too busy to take a sick day, even though you needed one? Or had to go to work when you had been up all night with your baby? Or felt guilt and shame and stress to finish a paper, chapter, or manuscript by an arbitrary deadline when you really could have used another week or even two to finish it? When we don't fully understand students and the circumstances of their lives outside the classroom, and practice compassion toward them as humans, we prioritize passing on this internalized guilt in the name of productivity, sometimes railroading over student's innate aspirations and motivations. So, we had absolutely no attendance policy or requirement, though we checked in with students individually if they missed two meetings in a row, without judgment or scolding, just to see how they were (and not in a veiled way to imply that we expected to see them back in our sessions soon).

It was also essential to us that these values, of taking life into account, didn't just end with our facilitation planning. During project planning sessions, we asked scholars to explicitly incorporate times when they would be focused on other things—work, exams, birthdays, family, holidays—before planning their work with us. We also integrated our lives into our discussion of educational and career goals. Our first cohort helped us realize just how much their families influenced the majors they were in, and the career paths they had been exposed to. How much money was enough money for them? More is always better, but when you get more specific than that, the answer depends a lot on their family responsibilities and life expectations. How did they need to work every day to be as happy and productive as possible? Did they prefer working alone, in a silent place? Or did they need to be surrounded by people as excited as they were? Variance in personality has to inform a person's career choice, otherwise, they will be miserable daily. These are fairly basic concepts in project and career planning, which were both added to our dialogue because they are skills that we as facilitators practice often, that are somehow often missed when working with students.

Along with being human, we recognized that students have bodies. We all too often, in academia, treat ourselves and others as disembodied heads, ready to contain and disseminate information (Nguyen & Larson, 2015). The body is considered incidental, rather than integral, to our work. Not in embodied educational practice (Bird & Sinclair, 2019; Nguyen & Larson, 2015; Thompson, 2017). We are lucky that Stefanie is a certified yoga instructor and in some cohorts we had dance instructors or other movement practitioners in our cohort, but not all our embodied activities required their expertise. On the first day, we play a common name game (which we, in turn, learned from the Theatre of the Oppressed) where everyone moves away from the tables, and pairs introduce themselves to each other. Then, they take their first partners' name, and find a new partner, introducing themself as their first partner's name. And, on this goes, stealing names from people, re-introducing themselves until about half the group have gotten their own names back, at which point, they leave the introduction mill. Not only does this help students listen to and pronounce all the names in the group, it's a great segue into discussing identity, and how good it feels to get your name back or how aimless it feels when we don't (this emotional affect happens every time and is more powerful than you might expect). We also play theater games about presentation-of-self and conveying different types and levels of energy using our body, which helps with public speaking and discussions with each other on difficult subjects (for those in the know, we use Woosh! every year). We engage in empathy exercises where you take on the words, mannerisms, and expressions of someone you're speaking with, which helps with cross-cultural understanding and community-building (this is called verbatim theater, if anyone wants to try it). We have stretch breaks or breathing exercises every single meeting. Even taking three deep breaths as a group (which takes maybe two minutes of time) creates a more grounded, relaxed, and amenable group dynamic.

Treating students as human also means being flexible in our agendas for each session. One session, we had planned 15-minutes to do a quick poll and discuss what resources scholars needed to support them in transferring to a four-year college, so that we could take that information to invite folks to a future session to discuss it with them. So many of the scholars had already experienced such difficult transfer issues that we needed around an hour for everyone to share and trouble-shoot situations with each other before we could move on as a group. As the facilitators, we could have exerted authority, and forced the group to move on to another subject, but shutting down their conversation in this way would have made them feel unheard in the moment, and more resistant to discussing concerns with the transfer office staff in future sessions. So, as facilitators, we noted for the group that the agenda was actively shifting, asked if that was alright with everyone, and let them have the space to expand their discussion as they needed that session.

This should, by now, go without saying, but human-driven pedagogy also means addressing positionality and privilege, as well as some hard sociopolitical realities that people face daily. And, that has to be done with care. We have to make space for heavy discussions, and sit with our own discomfort sometimes. In these conversations, it's crucial to not assume that you have the most experience or best understanding of equity and oppression in the room. Even if some aspect of equity in higher education is part of your research and scholarship, you haven't lived all the various positionalities represented in the room. Your students are brilliant at understanding oppression, privilege, and equity. One of the most eloquent explanations of inequality in higher education we have ever heard came from one of our scholars, and went into the introduction of this book: "The 3.9 GPA that I have, as an international student, who is forbidden from having a job, should not be compared to the 3.4 GPA that another student got while working two jobs and supporting their family."

Our human-driven pedagogy involves several elements above that all interact with each other. So, what does all that translate to, in real terms, every time we meet? We've included as an addendum our shorthand agendas for the entire year, as well as an annotated version of our first meeting so you can get an idea of the flow and thoughtfulness with which we craft our work with the students. Our agendas for each two-hour session roughly include an initial 10- to 15-minute section where we do updates and allow everyone to settle in together, followed by a 45-minute interactive section where the scholars are working to develop their own ideas (through prompts or with mentors), working in small groups for peer feedback, presenting to each other in the full group and getting peer feedback, or some other form of interactive activity. Then, we do a short break that focuses on the scholars as a whole person, including grounding exercises, vocal warm-ups, community-building activities, presentation-of-self activities, etc. Finally, we do another interactive session, again centered around, and ideally, driven by the students.

Through these biweekly meetings and the humanities enrichment activities, the Humanities Scholars are exposed to modes of critical and creative thinking, various historical and cultural perspectives, and aesthetic appreciation. Meanwhile, we guide scholars through designing and creating a year-long project that is meaningful for them as an individual and the community at large. The program culminates each year in a showcase, again designed and created by the scholars, that highlights their work and allows the community to experience their work. We're very careful not to say "presentation," "performance," "exhibition," or any other words that indicate the format and materiality of the showcase, and each year, the students surprise us with their creativity and ingenuity!

Four Stages of Project Development

Students complete oodles of projects during the course of undergraduate study. Most courses include a paper, research, presentation, debate, performance, production, creative project, etc. Those are often treated as simply things they have to do to get a good grade. Let's be honest, we know as teachers, these are rarely enjoyable, and rarely meaningful once the class is over. It's just another hoop to jump through. We believe that there are a couple of main components to project development that many student projects lack, which turns them into rote effort, rather than a self-motivating, inspiring, achievement to be proud of. These are namely: student ideation, refinement and guidance, permission to change, and public production. When we put all this together, something sort of miraculous happened: we found our students were inspired, motivated, and proud of themselves in a way that we have rarely seen in higher education teaching.

Stage 1: Student Ideation

It was essential to us, in human-driven pedagogy, that the projects they worked on were natural extensions of their interests and aspirations, and could function as stepping stones for their future portfolios or transfer applications. This wasn't just allowing students to pick their own topic or format for their project. There was a lot we could have dictated about the projects. We could have said they were "research" projects, that the final format would be a "presentation," or any other formulation you can imagine for the type of project and the final expression of it. We intentionally veered away from that because we wanted the program to be open to and conducive to people in a variety of majors and life paths. If you have a film student trying to create a portfolio of short works, an actress trying to develop her singing skills, and a childhood development student interested in curriculum building, why would you have all those students do the same type of project? How could we possibly find one mode of expression that would allow them all to develop the skills they needed?

On the other hand, we wanted something that connected all of the projects, to give meaning and cohesion to the group. We wanted to do more than simply throw them to the wind and say "choose a project, any topic, any medium, any expression, and let us know what that is." This is a mistake made by many professors for class papers and projects. There's nothing to tie the project to, too many possibilities to choose. Only the most self-directed students wouldn't struggle with that lack of guidance and structure. We decided to have a theme for the year, a loose one-word theme that could be interpreted and connected to in many different ways. For the four years of the program, these themes were "risk," "hope," "know," and "value."

Stefanie had an exercise (learned at a conference) to develop project ideas grounded in the person's aspirations and identity. So, we modified it, first to prime students in the theme for the year, and then to further define their project ideas. This is how it appeared on our agendas:

Discussion of this year's theme: Risk (approximately 30 min)

- As a group, we'll brainstorm and list out words associated with "risk"
- Break into small groups to identify more words, and identify one person in the group to act as note-taker and reporter
- Come back together, and note-takers report back to everyone
- Everyone, individually, think about questions and ideas this raises for you
- Pair up, share and discuss one question that you have with your partner. The partner who is talking will talk for 2 minutes without interruptions (this will feel like a long time). Partners who are listening, try to simply listen without interrupting or giving any verbal feedback.
- Discuss with each other, and finalize each of your individual questions and write it on a sticky note and post on a wall for everyone to see
- Read through all the questions (either gallery walk, or facilitator can read them)

By giving scholars literally one word, and a little bit of structure to continue the conversation, they came up with the most brilliant, deep, rigorous, meaningful questions that were 100 percent theirs—from one word!

The next step is the most important. We used some methodologies here to encourage stream-of-conscious writing and reflection, as well as instinct-driven decision-making and analytical thinking. The trick with this activity is that students need to keep writing for the time, and the facilitator has to keep it moving. You can even abbreviate the times if you need to for the sake of your agenda. This is our, now not-so-secret, recipe for student project ideation:

Student-Generated Aspirational Projects

- Write 3 words you bill yourself as / your passions (1 min)
- Write 3 words to describe the things you do (1 min)

- Write three short anecdotes about where your interests (art, skills, vocations) and your activism (any acts you have done) line up and if any projects have been born from that intersection (5 min)
- Now make a list of all the things you are passionate about. Don't edit yourself. Keep your pen moving. Doodle if you have to but don't let your pen come off the page (3 min)
- Make a list of three projects that you want to create, this can include artistic projects, social justice projects, academic projects or a way to expand your craft. Let yourself dream big (5 min)
- Choose one project and write it again on a new place on your paper (1 min)
  - Why do you want to bring this to the world? (2 min)
  - What scares you about making this project? (2 min)
  - What amazing thing could happen if you did this project? (2 min)
  - Who do you need to make this project happen? (2 min)
- Share your ideas with the group

That's it! Step 1 is done. It takes about two hours altogether to do both activities, particularly if each person shares their project ideas with the group (which we recommend for both community-building and further refinement). Note of caution here, don't be concerned if this creates *enormous* goals that could never be accomplished in one semester or year!! Folks in our group have started with the aspirations to write a book, start a daycare center, conduct research experiments, create a historically accurate video game, make documentaries, start a literary magazine, and much much more! The project development process doesn't end here. This is the beginning.

If you're a student reading this, please note that you can do these activities on your own whenever a professor tells you to choose your own topic for a paper or project. We believe it will help connect your choice of project to your other interests and aspirations!

Stage 2: Refinement and Guidance

Doesn't refinement and guidance happen in every course project? Even for a paper, a student might share their paper topic with other students in class and get feedback, and then they submit it to the professor for feedback and approval. Then, they submit drafts of at least portions of their paper that the professor reviews and provides comments on. That *is* a form of guidance, but it's not what we're talking about here.

Our process begins by being explicit that there *will* be a refinement process. To facilitate this process, we have students present various lengths of elevator pitches to describe their project, with slightly different questions/prompts each time. "Present your project idea and why it's important to bring it into existence (1 minute)" is a very different prompt from "present your project with respect to what material form it takes, who the intended audience is, and what impact you want it to have on them (2–3 minutes)." This iteration necessitates refinement of particular aspects of the project, helps the student become clearer and more focused about their ambitions, and also gives them *so much* practice presenting their project in front of other people. They do these elevator pitches, in large groups and small groups, at least every other session with us. During most of these sessions, we also ask folks listening to be actively involved, often by writing particular feedback on notecards that are then given directly to the presenter. To begin, a lot of these listening activities serve as mirroring exercises, such as "what is the core value behind this project idea?" or "what is one keyword that stood out to you during the presentation?" or "what feeling did the presentation evoke for you?" These mirroring experiences allow the presenter to see what is coming across to the audience in their presentation. As sessions continue, these feedback moments get more intensive, with peers and faculty mentors who have expertise in either the topic or creative medium discussing each project, at least in small groups.

During this refinement process, we always have one or two students who stick roughly to the exact same idea. These students tend to need mentors that will challenge them to go deeper and be more nuanced in their approach to the project. There are also one or two students who get a bit stuck in never-ending revolving ideas, having difficulty deciding which one to stick to in developing the project. These students tend to need someone to encourage them to make one idea stick and begin the work.

Finally, most of our time in refinement and guidance is spent setting realistic goals in the time we have. A scholar may not be able to write, compose, and produce a whole hip hop musical in one year, but they may be able to write the script, co-compose some of the songs, and do a live reading of at least one act. Even if they can't *complete* their dream goal in the time you have, they can work toward it and accomplish a piece of it in the time. The point is that none of these student processes are wrong, and all of them should be encouraged and met with support. Doing this in community with each other is so powerful because not only does each scholar actively refine and revise their ideas, but they also get to witness the refinement and participate in each others' processes. Making the process transparent also normalizes that it is a process; that no one has a perfectly refined project concept and plan during the ideation phase.

Stage 3: Permission to Change

This component goes hand-in-hand with refinement and guidance. Every time the project changes—the idea shifts, the goals become smaller and more realistic, unseen obstacles come up, they move two steps forward only to move one backwards—there has to be explicit, direct permission to change. We can't emphasize this part enough!! In our experience, almost all students we engage with have such anxiety and guilt around project changes. In undergraduate class projects, unchangeability is often implicit in the structure of the project progression: students choose a topic, then a thesis statement in that topic, then make an outline based on that thesis, etc. Each step builds on each other with little room to change topics three times because they had a change of heart or a new idea came to them a week after the first class session about the project. Comparatively, in project management, outside of academia or even in hierarchically higher positions within academia, these project changes are completely normal and *expected* to happen as projects evolve (Ibbs et al., 2001).

Instead of waiting for one or two brave souls to approach us sheepishly and ask permission to change something about their projects, we openly talk about change being expected throughout the process. We proactively bring it up in almost every session. Open, direct communication and excitement about *their* process—and the million roadblocks scholars encounter—is the way to *interrupt* any internalized guilt or hesitance that has been created by repeated engagement in restrictive or rigid project processes that prohibit or strongly discourage change. To facilitate this, and a group understanding of where everyone is in their process, we actually engage in a classic project planning session early in the program, and we regularly have students update the group in terms of what they've done so far and what still needs to be done or where their focus is next for the project. The biggest thing that helps is simply us saying "if your project has changed, or you've encountered problems, that's okay! We expect things to change through the year. That's a normal part of any project." Without this affirmation, students hide the obstacles, try to push through and cover over any "faults" in their original design, without embracing the opportunities that those problems present.

This is one of the few times that we, as facilitators, actually invoke our authority as "professors" to reassure students. While we have no continuing authority over scholars, as they are not being graded by us, and already receive stipends for participation, there is presumed and perceived authority because of our positions within the institution and program. In almost all moments throughout the program, we eschew that power and continually resituate scholars as the decision- and knowledge-makers. In this particular instance, we've found that flexing our authority to tell them that we *expect* change works to counter their internalized guilt and anxiety about project changes.

It's also crucial to note that not everyone moves through projects the same way. One student may need 4–5 sessions to think through the conceptual orientation of a project, and know the materiality easily, while another is completely vague about the materiality, but knows the topic in detail. This is *their* journey, not ours to dictate or prescribe. People's brains work very differently, and the project process is different for each of us, and yet this is still an expectation in higher education that we process everything in exactly the same manner. For example, we often expect that 30 students can follow the exact same process to write a paper. In our experience, that expectation of homogeneity has already been internalized by our students.

This internalized expectation that project plans can be scripted in advance and should be implemented flawlessly based on some external standard is particularly evident when very big aspirational project goals are limited by realistic timelines. One of our students, who wanted to build a videogame in a year, comes to mind. He came to one of us about 7 months into working on the project, and felt like he needed to drop out of the program and not showcase his work because he hadn't been able to complete the video game. Kaysi's response was to simply ask him to tell her where he was in his process, what he had done so far. Because she was curious and open, instead of frustrated and disappointed, she found out that he had literally spent hundreds of hours doing 3D modeling that was physically and historically accurate!!! Yet, he was ashamed that he had not achieved enough! There just aren't words to describe the feelings of that moment. Astonished, impressed, dumbfounded, and heartbroken for him are as close as we could get. That also wasn't the only conversation that we had like that. Another one of our students had wanted to do a music fair to introduce other folks to different genres of music. He also came to one of us several months in, wanting to drop out of the program. Apparently, he taught music to kids at a school of rock, and his supervisor had left suddenly and he had to take over many of those responsibilities, while working another job to pay the bills and going to school full time. Again, instead of assuming that he had failed the project task, we considered this other "work" that was originally outside the scope of his project ideas. He was, after all, an aspiring music teacher, and he was already actively engaged in that work. Kaysi asked about his work at the school of rock, and it turns out that he developed his own curriculum and trained his students to do live performances. We asked if he would consider presenting his curriculum, or leading his students in a performance for the showcase instead of his original project plan? He ultimately decided to make a short film showing his teaching practice at the school of rock, and his students rocking out in their practice space! Both of these brilliant, motivated, productive humans came to us ashamed, guilty, and feeling like they had failed. In any other program or class, they might have. Instead, we got to showcase how magnificent their work was, even though it was outside anything we had imagined at the beginning of the semester.

Stage 4: Public Production

The final component is pretty simple: have some element of scholars' work that is public. This was not a requirement of our funder, but was a component of our projects that was important to us. Having an in-class presentation or a public blog post is not the same as having to prepare for, rehearse, and come face-to-face with an unknown "public" and scholars thinking through how they can engage that public in a meaningful exchange about their project. This can be as simple as doing some of their writing in a public context on a website (which is especially effective if you can coordinate some folks to write comments and responses to the posts). It can be in-person by inviting another class of students to experience your students' work. For us, this was quite involved. We had an annual showcase, with a day for tech and rehearsal before the showcase, and everyone from faculty to deans to families of students joined us for the showcase. Given Stefanie's experience with theater production, and her team of crew that helped set up staging, lighting, and props, and even staffed the event, we were able to showcase student works in an incredible and professional way that went way beyond the level of standard "student presentations." It was amazing to see scholars' parents, grandparents, children, and friends mixing with Deans and faculty, all of whom were so excited and proud to see the scholars' work!

To set up this public presentation, we hyped up the opportunity of the showcase early in the program, providing an implicit expectation that everyone would present their projects publicly. As the year progressed, some students inevitably would have life interfere and they would be so busy that their project would never come to full fruition. Some of those students would present their project as a work-in-progress. Others would forgo presenting altogether. Students who chose not to present publicly were never met with disappointment, anger, or being dropped from the program. There was no loss of respect or credentialing. There was no repercussion, other than the natural consequence of a missed opportunity. Those who did choose to present their work publicly, gained incredibly from the experience of presenting to the public—the confidence, the willingness to take risks. You could see the change in one night. They started the evening full of anxiety, nervous about showing their work and whether it was "good" enough, despite all of our rehearsals and support. The first presentations were stilted and full of jitters. By the time they presented it a third time.

This public production raises the bar. It changes the project from simply a dialogue within a closed group, or with one person—the professor—to a public showing for themselves. During the process of preparing for this, or beginning public production, some students naturally have to face fears and worries about sharing their aspirations and their work openly. It's a tough moment, for all of us. For the scholars, we build in numerous practice sessions where they present to each other, in small and large groups, varying aspects of their presentation, from simply introducing themselves and their project idea, to giving elevator speeches, to later giving mini-presentations. We also integrate grounding practices and presentation-of-self activities into our curriculum, so scholars can build skills to help regulate nerves and other emotions that come up with public presentation. To have scholars present publicly, as the facilitators of this program, you also have to face your own fears. To make things public as a professor, you have to be vulnerable in a way. You have to release your control. That's an important step in doing human-driven pedagogy and trying actively to not be an authority figure. And, at the end of it, we found our students to be so much bolder and more confident about sharing their brilliance with the world.

Conclusion

Recognizing students as humans first comes so naturally for both of us as facilitators, and we often use the same words that other people do to describe project processes (e.g., project refinement). And yet, the results or student experience from our program was not similar to students' experience in classrooms. It felt, to us, like a little bit of magic. It took us years to conceptualize and articulate this difference and answer the following questions: How is our program different from other leadership programs? How is it different from college courses? Why does our simple two-hours-every-other-week program have students raving at the end about the impact of it on their lives? Is it because it is a voluntary program? Is it because of the students we attract? Those factors may have some impact on the program's outcomes, but we also think it is how the program is shaped, mostly how we interact with students that creates its impact. And yet, the way we interact is so simple: we treat them as people. We understand when they have a stressful life moment, when they encounter a problem, when they are too tired to continue, or too energetic for chairs. We meet them, openly, where we are and where they are. We have goals and they do too, and we work together to accomplish what we can in the time we have together. We pull in all our experience and expertise—as a political advocate, a theater director, a project manager, a yoga instructor—and we recognize and incorporate their experience and expertise—as poets, musicians, filmmakers, coders, actors, teachers, and linguists.

Facilitating a program like this was not as simple. We had to jump administrative hurdles to remunerate the scholars, navigate everyone's busy and shifting semester schedules, ensure we had a room on campus for meetings, connect with faculty and other mentors for the scholars, and secure a lot of help across the campus to put on a showcase that grand each year. Connecting with other faculty who are invested in similar publicly engaged work with their students, and college administrators with the power to unlock calendars, were an essential part of our success. We also had the extreme privilege of being able to remunerate scholars with a stipend, provide food and metrocards for them, and take them to amazing events throughout the city because of our funding. Even without these privileges, though, we could have done much of the same work. We could have worked to secure course credit for the time spent with us, provided time to eat (and encouraged scholars to bring food or coordinated with local food banks), and found free events and happenings in the city.

What was needed to take a standard extracurricular program and make it into a transformational experience were those four steps of project development, and human-driven pedagogy. Projects must come from scholars' aspirations and motivations; they need support to refine their ambitious ideas; they need encouragement and curiosity in crucial moments where life happens and the project has to change; and it has to be not just for us, as facilitators or teachers, but for themselves and for their community. All of these components, provided within a banking model of education or any form of top-down, hierarchical instruction, would only inspire more anxiety and powerlessness among students. Utilizing a framework of human-driven pedagogy, that recognizes and welcomes everything that they bring to the table, and acknowledging that other human needs come first, were necessary to the overall success of our program.

We struggled to describe our process because it is so simple, and yet it is so dramatically different from much of higher education instruction. This model could be used in first-year seminars, many project-based classes, or extracurricular programs like ours. The point is that we have to do better, as teachers, than the standard hierarchical educational model that has been passed on to us. We don't take someone else's syllabus and teach it for the next 30 years. Why would we do the same with teaching methods? Let's do better, together. Consider the ideas and pieces of programming that we've developed. Take what's useful, and let us know how it goes!

Notes

1 Humanities enrichment activities were opportunities to engage with the humanities outside of the classroom, out in the city. This could include a trip to a museum or art gallery, a night at the theater or an opera, a historical food tour, or even a poetry night or book launch. Again, we were very fortunate to have grant funding to take students on outings that would have been otherwise financially unattainable, for the students and for our program. However, in the course of brainstorming for these activities, we came across quite a few activities that were free or very inexpensive that we absolutely could have afforded.
2 "Risk" was the theme word for our first year of the program, and motivated the framing of these questions. Stefanie had used the word in a class assignment previously, and the conversation had gone well. In future years, we asked similar questions using different theme words, such as "hope" or "know." The final theme word, "value," was selected by the LaGuardia Scholars themselves.
3 We do this in a non-hierarchical way. The point is not to modify the natural speech patterns of people, but to help each other convey ourselves more purposefully and meaningfully. We are *not* prescriptive about "correcting" students in their intonation, dialect, grammatical practice, or cultural linguistic norms.

References

Ahn, R., & Class, M. (2011). Student-centered pedagogy: Co-construction of knowledge through student-generated midterm exams. *International Journal of Teaching and Learning in Higher Education*, 23(2), 269–281. http://www.isetl.org/ijtlhe/ ISSN 1812-9129.

Almulla, M.A. (2020, July 5). *The effectiveness of the project-based learning (PBL) approach as a way to engage students in learning.* Sage Open. https://doi.org/10.1177/2158244020938702

Bird, J., & Sinclair, C. (2019, August 1). Principles of embodied pedagogy: The role of the drama educator in transforming student understanding through a collaborative and embodied aesthetic practice. *Applied Theatre Research*, 7(1), 21–36. https://doi.org/10.1386/atr_00003_1

Brown, A. (2017). *Emergent strategy.* AK Press.

Buchanan, S.M.C., Harlan, M.A., Bruce, C., & Edwards, S. (2016). Inquiry based learning models, information literacy, and student engagement: A literature review. *School Libraries Worldwide*, 22(2), 23–39.

Dugan, J.P., & Komives, S.R. (2007). *Developing leadership capacity in college students: Findings from a national study.* https://citeseerx.ist.psu.edu/viewdoc/download?doi=10.1.1.462.9299&rep=rep1&type=pdf

Emdin, C. (2016). *For white folks who teach in the hood—and the rest of yall too: Reality pedagogy and urban education.* Beacon Press.

Freire, P. (2000). *Pedagogy of the oppressed* (30th Anniv. ed.). (M.B. Ramos, Trans.). Continuum. (Original work published 1968)

hooks, bell. (1994). *Teaching to transgress: Education as the practice of freedom.* Routledge.

Ibbs, C.W., Wong, C.K., & Kwak, Y.H. (2001, July 1). Project change management system. *Journal of Management in Engineering, 17*(3). https://doi.org/10.1061/(ASCE)0742-597X(2001)17:3(159)

Jones, L. (2007). *The student-centered classroom.* Cambridge University Press.

Loo, C.M., & Rolison, G. (1986). Alienation of ethnic minority students at a predominantly white university. *The Journal of Higher Education, 57*(1), 58–77. https://doi.org/10.1080/00221546.1986.11778749

Maida, C.A. (2011, January 1). *Project-based learning: A critical pedagogy for the twenty-first century.* Policy Futures in Education. https://doi.org/10.2304/pfie.2011.9.6.759

Moore, A. (2012). *Teaching and learning.* Routledge.

Nasmi, A., Martinez, S., Byrd, A., Robinson, D., Bianco, S., Maguire, J., Crutchfield, R.M., Condron, K., & Ritchie, L. (2019). A systematic review of food insecurity among US students in higher education. *Journal of Hunger & Environmental Nutrition, 14*(5), 725–740. https://doi.org/10.1080/19320248.2018.1484316

Nguyen, D.J., & Larson, J.B. (2015). Don't forget about the body: Exploring the curricular possibilities of embodied pedagogy. *Innovative Higher Education, 40,* 331–344. https://doi.org/10.1007/s10755-015-9319-6

Office of Institutional Assessment & Research. (2021). *LaGuardia Community College, The City University of New York 2021 institutional profile.* https://www.laguardia.edu/uploadedfiles/main_site/content/ir/docs/institutional-profile-2021.pdf

Suarez, S.A., Fowers, B.J., Garwood, C.S., & Szapocznik, J. (1997). Biculturalism, differentness, loneliness, and alienation in Hispanic college students. *Hispanic Journal of Behavioral Sciences, 19*(4), 489–505. https://doi.org/10.1177/07399863970194007

Suen, H.K. (1983). Alienation and attrition of Black college students on a predominantly White campus. *Journal of College Student Personnel, 24*(2), 117–121.

Thompson, B. (2017). *Teaching with tenderness: Toward an embodied practice.* University of Illinois Press.

U.S. Government Accountability Office. (2019, January 9). *Food insecurity: Better information could help eligible college students access federal food assistance benefits.* https://www.gao.gov/products/gao-19-95

Addendum 3
LaGuardia Mellon Humanities Scholars
Curriculum/Agenda Outline

- WORKSHOP 1
    - Introductions: each person gives the story of their first name
    - Overview of the Program, including introduction to enrichment activities & final presentation requirements
    - Break: Name Game
    - Unpacking Humanities activity
    - Discussion of Theme: Know
- WORKSHOP 2—Some mentors present, but not assigned yet
    - Enrichment activities brainstorming/selecting
    - Energy Break with Woosh
    - Big Think: Defining Individual Projects
        - Talk through the what you can accomplish, what scares you, and why does the world need you, who can help
        - *Abstract core value or lesson from your project*
- WORKSHOP 3
    - Project Presentations:
        - *What's the idea?*
        - *Why did you want to make it happen? What amazing thing could happen if you did this project?*
        - *Who do you want to impact and how do you want to impact them?*
        - *What is realistic to do in a year?*
        - *What feedback would you like from the group?*
    - Listeners:
        - *Yellow: What are the core value(s) that this project addresses?*
        - *Green: What is one question you have about the project?*
    - Project Planning basics – how to step-by-step write a plan for your final project, starting at the final project itself, and working backwards by weeks to fill in details and deadlines.
    - Introduction to ePortfolio program site
- WORKSHOP 4
    - Meet the Mentors!
    - Presentation skills:
        - *Articulation and diction*
        - *Warming up body and speech*
        - *Getting prepared*
    - Project pitches again in front of mentors
    - Break out in small groups with Mentors
- WORKSHOP 5—With FI Fellows
    - Introductions

- o Break out into small groups based on 4+ Social Justice topics
- o Report Back
- WORKSHOP 6—Enrichment Activity
- WORKSHOP 7
  - o Transfer Q&A
    - *Transfer process, and how to find particular school's processes*
    - *Finding out what credits transfer*
    - *Transfer Scholarships or financial aid*
  - o Career Center Introduction
  - o ePortfolio student pages
- WORKSHOP 8 – Mentors
  - o Update from each Scholar on where their project is at
    - *Materiality*
    - *Emotion*
    - *Keyword*
    - *Question*
  - o Breakout with Mentors
- WORKSHOP 9
  - o Upload Bios, Project Descriptions, and Photos to ePortfolio
  - o Physical presence (and fostering positive mindsets)
  - o Being a successful student
- WORKSHOP 10 – Career Day at the GC with FI Fellow
  - o Career planning basics – what you love doing, what you're good at, what you can make money at
  - o Mini Resume workshop
- WORKSHOP 11 – Mentors!
  - o Update from each Scholar on where their project is at
  - o Breakout with Mentors
- WORKSHOP 12
  - o Finalize Bios, Project Descriptions, and Photos on ePortfolio site
  - o Planning for the showcase – How are we organizing all of this? Are there tracks? Are things happening simultaneously?
- WORKSHOP 13—Mentors!
  - o Update from each Scholar on where their project is at
  - o Breakout with Mentors
- WORKSHOP 14—FI Fellows?
  - o Enrichment activity all together OR
  - o Scholars get feedback from FI Fellows on their projects
- WORKSHOP 15—Mentors!
  - o Audience experience and interactivity of the showcase
- SHOWCASE Rehearsal in the evening with Mentors
- SHOWCASE Tech in the evening
- SHOWCASE!

Addendum 4
Annotated First Workshop for the LaGuardia
Mellon Humanities Scholars

Kaysi & Stefanie's comments: As students enter, we shake hands with, welcome, and introduce ourselves to each scholar. Establishing this relationship is important from the very beginning. We also encourage them to get dinner from the buffet table and select a seat at a round table. Food is necessary for long meetings with community college students. Inviting the students to get food on their own and select their seat welcomes them to the space, and their active role in it.

6:00 **Welcome and Financials**
Stefanie and Kaysi welcome the fellows, and make sure all of the financial paperwork is filled out. Each person also has a name placard that they can write/draw on and put in front of them.

Kaysi & Stefanie's comments: Paperwork is boring, but necessary. If we don't do it during the first session, it often doesn't get done or turned in by students outside of the session. So, we make space and time for it, and allow for another activity (not to mention eating dinner) for students that have already completed it. Many students leave classrooms without knowing each other's names, and simply providing blank pieces of paper for students to write their names on can help with that. Providing lots of colorful markers also allows our Scholars to begin expressing their creativity and personality.

6:20 **Names, Introductions, Community Agreements**
Everyone goes around in a circle, and tells the group their name and why you were named that.

Kaysi & Stefanie's comments: Our program is reliant on students taking the lead and being comfortable talking. Most sessions, the students are actively engaged in discussion within the first 15 minutes of the session. It's easiest to get people talking about things that they know well. Getting them to discuss how their name was given to them is also a storytelling exercise that allows them to start engaging in narratives about themselves and where they come from.

Our program helps students think and consider their own authenticity. Allowing the students to reflect about their name and share origin or a story about themselves, may begin the process of self inquiry which develops authenticity.

Then, Stefanie and Kaysi introduce the idea of community agreements, and ask Scholars to contribute and discuss community agreements that they'd like to use to support open discussions in the group.

Kaysi & Stefanie's comments: Community agreements are important in establishing trust in each other and comfort with discussions. We allow the students to lead and suggest these instead of offering our own. This underscores our fundamental understanding that this community and space is theirs.

Establishing trust is essential to the success of our program. Creating community agreements begins the process of building a group dynamic and intimacy. It helps create a space that is communal, comfortable for individuals to share their aspirations and ideas, and feels "safe" for each student as a person. However, "safe space" must be clarified and established by the students, not us. It is imperative the students take initiative in this area so they can share with everyone what they consider as agreements in their new community, and define the terms through which we all interact with each other.

6:40 Unpacking "The Humanities"

Kaysi & Stefanie's comments: First, we show a blank poster board with a roughly-drawn circle on it, and ask the students the simple question: "What is this?" Everytime a student gives us an answer, we say "yes, and what else?" Then, after 5–6 answers have been given, we ask, "What would a mathematician say this is?" and wait for a couple responses. Then, we ask "What would an artist say this is?" and wait for a couple responses, and finally we ask "What would a child say this is?" and wait for a couple responses. By the end, students are usually excited to talk. So, we point out that they were able to come up with such varied descriptors from something as simple as a roughly drawn circle on a paper. And, then we enter into the exercise to define "The Humanities". The exercise has them excited to talk to the group and each other, and excited to share all of their ideas, no matter how different theirs are from those of other people. It has allowed us to completely avoid the blank "I don't really want to speak up because I might be wrong" deer-in-headlights silence that often comes when a group of people is given a cold ask to share their opinions on a topic.

Pair up with someone you don't know. You will have two minute each to tell the other person how you define the Humanities and why it's important to your life. The person who is listening will write down keywords about the humanities on sticky notes. We will then go around the circle and you'll be responsible for introducing your partner and their ideas to the rest of the group.

Kaysi & Stefanie's comments: This is a great way for the scholars to get to know each other a bit better, and to actively engage in listening to each other's' ideas.

We begin our first day with the concept of the humanities and later our theme for the year. This acts as a sort of "priming" for the students, signaling to them that these concepts are important. After this, we rarely have to turn the conversation back to the humanities or the theme—the scholars do that themselves. By discussing these concepts early in the program and grounding the discussion in the scholars' own experiences with them, the scholars take ownership of the concepts and carry them through the program.

The topic of unpacking the humanities may seem like a daunting and time consuming task. However, the way the exercise is scaffolded allows the students to share their ideas with one another, then with the group. The students also start to begin to build trust with one another by adding why the Humanities is important to them, personally.

7:00 **Overview of the Program**
- Biweekly workshops
- Enrichment activities
- Year-long project and final audience experience
- Advisor/Mentor

Kaysi & Stefanie's comments: This is our only section of "talking-at" that we do, nearly the entire year. Rather than framing it as their responsibilities in the program, or our expectations of them, we talk to them about the opportunities presented in the program that they can take advantage of—all the things we are committed to supporting them with. We also forewarn them that the next time we meet, we'll be working with them to develop ideas for their year-long projects that will forward their scholarly and career interests and goals, and that we'll all come with ideas for enrichment activities to pitch to each other—museums, plays, workshops, outings, cultural experiences—that engage with themes or methods they want to engage in for their projects.

An exciting part of this program is choosing and experiencing the enrichment activities. Being able to choose what the students want to experience is a form of empowerment. A unique aspect of this program is the amount of resources available for enrichment activities. This is uncommon for community college students to have this amount of resources available to them.

7:15 **Stretch/Movement Break**

Kaysi & Stefanie's comments: We always build in a stretch or movement break, based in theatre or yoga practices. For the first day, we play a "Name game" where each person shakes hands and introduces themself to another person. Then, you take the name of the person you just shook hands with, and introduce yourself to another person. And, again, you take the name of the person you just shook hands with ... and on it goes. You can stop when you get your own name back.

The game teaches students to be better listeners through this game. It also opens the conversation of identity. What does it feel like to get your name back? What does it feel like to not? This is an opportunity to discuss identity and the importance of being validated.

7:20 **Discussion of This Year's Theme: Risk**
- As a group, we list out "tricky" words associate with "risk," such as "change," "fear," "education," "career," "boundaries," etc.
- Break into small groups to identify more words, and identify one person in the group to act as note-taker (5 min)
- Come back together, and Note-takers report back to everyone
- Everyone, individually, think about questions and ideas this raises for you (2 min)
- Pair up and share and discuss one question that you have with your partner. Partners, try to simply listen without interrupting. (2 min each)
- Discuss with each other, and finalize that question and write it on a sticky note and post on a wall for everyone to see (5 min)
- Read through all the questions (either gallery walk, or instructor can read them)

Kaysi & Stefanie's comments: Leading students through the process of discussing the main concept, and exploring related concepts, helps them to form their own questions related to the humanities, their experiences, and hope. This also allows the students to start to think about big societal questions and how they relate to them. This is crucial. The students shape the questions that drive our work for the year. We don't. We give them one word (well, technically six words, as we give them a handful of associated "tricky" words). They do all the rest of the work, and the groups' direction for the year is based on the overarching questions that they provide to each other and to us.

This also begins the conversation that students' previous knowledge and experiences are valid. In fact, we are demonstrating that not only are their experiences and questions valid, but crucial to the work that we do together over the course of the year. In this discussion, many topics, issues, and personal struggles are raised that we could never have dictated or even predicted. That's the beauty of working with diverse students. We return to this conversation again and again throughout the year.

7:50 **Take Home**
- Brainstorm and research enrichment activities: think about what types of enrichment activities you would like to do this year, research a couple, and be ready to "pitch" them to the group.
- Register on CUNYHumanitiesAlliance.org
- For next time: Bring your calendar, so that we can start planning out our enrichment activities

Kaysi & Stefanie's comments: The first year, we selected most of the enrichment activities and pitched them to the Scholars. For our second year, we had scholars pitch their own enrichment activities to the group, which has lead to more involvement and activity overall. There's a great camaraderie that is established as Scholars find and pitch enrichment activities that are related to and will help their peers on their projects.

Socially Engaged Administration and the Potential for Graduate Education

KATINA ROGERS

Engaged Administration: Pedagogy, Public Engagement, and Preparing Future Faculty

In today's capitalist landscape, public universities are under tremendous pressure to prove their worth on an ongoing basis—to students, parents, legislators, the public, grantmakers, and the list goes on. Particularly now, since the COVID-19 pandemic has ravaged colleges and universities and laid bare the inequities that students face, it is clear that public institutions are vitally important but also deeply underfunded. This underfunding has many repercussions. The increasing reliance on adjunct faculty members means governance and service roles are on the shoulders of a small number of tenure-track faculty members, leaving them spread thin. In this context, administrators play an increasingly important role to design, execute, and report on academic and ancillary programs, and to advocate for support. Though "administration" often gets a negative reputation in college and university settings as overly bureaucratic or as an instrument of neoliberal capitalism, thoughtful and responsive administration is the backbone of an effective program.

In this chapter, I argue that socially engaged administration is a key to developing more equitable systems and structures in higher education. In particular, administrative work—including program planning, budget management, hiring, evaluation, and more—can make use of effective teaching strategies to focus on student needs and voices in order to foster an environment of collaboration and community. This work is an essential component of resistance against the prestige economy, which dominates higher education at all levels and institution types. Successful administrative work makes a case for the value of higher education both within the institution and publicly, making it an important bridge position for advocacy and public engagement.

In addition, exposing graduate students to the workings of administration is a valuable component of professional development. No matter their future careers, graduate students need to know how programs are developed, how budgets are created and managed, and how and why to conduct thoughtful evaluation. This exposure and engagement can enable students to more deeply connect their scholarship to matters of policy, curriculum, and higher education reform.

Administrators play a key role in setting and advancing institutional goals at every level of higher education, from departments and centers to the institution as a whole. However, as in many educational hierarchies, most senior administrators are white (Bischel et al., 2018)—so there is often a disconnect between those creating and running programs and the students the programs intend to serve. As a white woman in a mid-range administrative position, if I create programs that echo only my personal experience, they are likely to reinforce inequity. Inviting student voices is an important step, but the work does not stop there. Greater inclusion and broader representation in senior administration is essential to shaping equitable policies. I encourage administrators (especially white administrators) to examine and work against unconscious biases in hiring and in program development within our offices, and to consider how those biases affect environments of research and teaching.

In an environment that prioritizes cost efficiency and other neoliberal or market-oriented logics, administrators have an opportunity to advance a philosophy of care and abundance, not only as an idea but as a concrete practice. To do this requires a sense of why the work matters—not only to them, but to other constituents as well. This clarity can help them to articulate their message in powerful ways. If we as a community of teachers, learners, and knowledge workers are going to convince the public that higher education is for all of us—that it is a *public* good—I would argue that administrators have an opportunity and responsibility to take up that cause. This opportunity is one reason that it is so important to hire administrators with a broad range of backgrounds and experiences.

This effort is a focus of my own work and that of my colleagues at the Graduate Center, CUNY, where I worked from 2014 until 2021 as an administrator in the Futures Initiative and CUNY Humanities Alliance programs. As a program focused on connecting graduate education and community college teaching, the CUNY Humanities Alliance takes engaged pedagogy seriously—not only in the classroom but throughout its entire structure. Its success requires a robust and thoughtful network of administrators working behind the scenes. Administrators are often in a position to make the case for the value of a program—the social impact of research, the surprising results of an experimental teaching method, the individual stories that illustrate an initiative's impact. Making the case in this way helps bring the work of teaching and learning far beyond the classroom, and provides a lens into the work happening all across colleges and universities in a way that resonates with different publics. Such work can be an intellectually engaging and satisfying career pathway for humanities scholars. From writing and public presentations to mentorship and problem solving, administrative roles encompass a wide range of work that draws on skills and expertise from graduate training.

Indeed, there is a growing body of research that attends to the possibilities and challenges of administrative work in advancing an equity-driven agenda in higher education. Two of the key scholars on this subject are Adrianna Kezar and Julie R. Posselt (2019), whose edited volume *Higher Education Administration for Social Justice and Equity* offers a multifaceted consideration of the opportunities to support social justice by working within institutional structures of finance, governance, collective bargaining, and more. Scholars such as Linda Tuhiwai Smith, Eve Tuck, and K. Wayne Yang (2018) have also made clear that these structures themselves are sites of colonial and capitalist values, with physical colleges and universities constructed on stolen indigenous land (often using the labor of enslaved people), and therefore the work of creating equitable spaces of learning may not be fully possible within the existing systems. Educational reform can be incremental or radical, working from within or building something new. Both modes require careful thought, a deep understanding of the higher education landscape as well as broader cultural and historical contexts, a strategic mindset, and efficacy. In this chapter, I argue for the scholarly merit of administrative work and provide more information to emerging scholars considering it as a career path.

My own work has been primarily within and adjacent to university structures. I will begin the chapter by briefly discussing my own academic background and career trajectory. Then, I will describe some of the nuts-and-bolts of what it looks like to conceptualize and run a program, and from there will address why it matters. Far from mere paper-pushing, this is intellectual and pedagogical work. The best-run programs rely on administrators who understand the scholarly community—its needs, strengths, and challenges. The work requires significant landscape research, writing, and ongoing analysis of the project's success. Administrators must also be able to synthesize all this and advocate for the program's goals—in this case, the value of the humanities, the importance of engaged pedagogy in community college classrooms, and graduate education as a public good.

I see this kind of scholarly administrative work as being part of a broader picture of graduate education reform—one that focuses on the value of teaching and learning in the classroom, but in relation to many different publics and with a wide range of goals. Socially engaged administrative work requires not only excellent research and writing skills but also resilience, flexibility, collaboration, persuasiveness, creativity, and reliability. Not many graduate programs currently offer systematic training in those areas; such training would provide a significant benefit to individuals, programs, and institutions alike. As an added benefit, equipping graduate students for administrative careers offers skills and perspectives that are deeply useful in all careers, whether in the classroom, as a researcher, or in virtually any other context. Moreover, academic institutions and programs need a much wider range of voices working in administrative capacities and shaping programs. Thinking more broadly about what constitutes scholarly success and how programs can best prepare their students has the potential to encourage more students to consider this type of pathway. I see this type of training as one element of a larger effort to develop creative, sustainable programs that support students, faculty, and staff in an embodied way while also establishing a powerful network of vocal advocates for higher education as a public good.

My Role and Pathway

My own career pathway can serve as a case study in the kinds of engagement that can be a part of program administration, and in the many ways that a pedagogical approach is useful and powerful beyond the classroom.

First, I would note that my professional context changed significantly in the time between writing the first drafts of this chapter and its eventual publication—a time that also coincided with the COVID-19 pandemic. In September 2021, after working at the Graduate Center for seven years, I left my position in order to start an independent educational consultancy. While it was a very hard decision to leave CUNY, an institution I care about deeply and where I have loved working, my hope was to carry the lessons I learned there to institutions nationwide.

Before taking this step as an independent scholar and consultant, I was deeply embedded in midlevel administrative and leadership work at the Graduate Center. As codirector of the Futures Initiative, a small but influential interdisciplinary initiative based at the Graduate Center and extending throughout the CUNY system, I managed programming, recruitment, events, budgets, and more. The CUNY Humanities Alliance was a joint project between the Futures Initiative and other entities at the Graduate Center, such as the Teaching and Learning Center. As one of several project areas under my purview, my main role—especially in the first phase of the CUNY

Humanities Alliance grant—was at a structural level rather than in the day-to-day workings.

In the earliest stages of conceptualizing the program, I collaborated on the program's design and helped write the grant proposal to secure support from the Andrew W. Mellon Foundation. My role evolved as the program matured—from grant writing, to program planning, to reporting and broader advocacy. A role like mine is highly intellectually engaging; I drew on my doctoral training every day in both direct and indirect ways. Because much of my work happened behind the scenes, I'd like to use this chapter to pull back the curtain a bit in order to show what I do and why it matters. But first, I would like to share how I got here, in case my story sparks ideas or possibilities for others who may be interested in this work, or for anyone advising graduate students on future pathways.[1]

My academic and professional route has taken me from a PhD in comparative literature, through education-focused positions at foundations and professional societies, to my position in public higher education at CUNY. I constantly draw on skills I learned as a doctoral student—particularly close reading, textual analysis, understanding critical theory, language skills, and research and writing skills more broadly. That said, the ways I have used these skills have evolved over time and across different professional contexts, and sometimes in surprising ways. There was no clear pathway that I set for myself at the outset of my professional journey; rather, I have made decisions about my own career path based on a complex set of needs, desires, circumstances, and experience, as everyone does. At each decision point in my career, I found it difficult to predict where I might be a few years later, and where a particular decision might lead. The work I have been able to do along this path has offered unexpected opportunities to think systematically about higher education, and to be a part of conversations and projects that have real impact beyond my own discipline.

At the Futures Initiative, my colleagues and I worked toward institutional change in higher education through a dual focus on equity and innovation. As the program's codirector, I found myself applying so many skills, methods, and insights that I gained during my graduate studies—as well as many that I have learned experientially. I worked on our program's strategy, mission, and programming; wrote and implemented grants; guided and mentored our team of graduate fellows; managed our program's budgets; and more, all while continuing to research and write.

A major focus of my work is on developing sustainable and sustaining programs that model what higher education and graduate education can be at their best. My academic background helps me to understand the constraints, motivations, and stakes of the various constituents in any of our programming, and also gives me a greater degree of credibility with faculty and senior administrators. Creating these types of programs requires both an eye for detail and a sense of the broader landscape and stakes, and I have found that working at the level of systems and structures is deeply satisfying at both an intellectual and pragmatic level. I am outside of departmental structures and have the freedom and fluidity to work with faculty, students, and staff across a wide range of program areas and campuses. My research has taken new directions, expanding from an area of deep content knowledge (the twentieth- and twenty-first-century fiction that I focused on in my graduate work) to a broader examination of the architecture of higher education. In my role at CUNY, I was often able to immediately put this research into practice, bringing the two into close alignment and breathing life into the theoretical work that I do.

One challenge in creating holistic and sustaining programs is that higher education operates on an economy of prestige. In this economy, the so-called life of the mind takes center stage, leaving little room for attention to physical and emotional well-being. A humanizing orientation—one that prioritizes people over prestige—is essential to creating supportive and sustainable structures. This shift in orientation is central to my argument and proposed models for graduate education in *Putting the Humanities PhD to Work* (Rogers, 2020), and it is at the heart of the Futures Initiative. For instance, as a program, we focus partly on innovation, as do many digital humanities and digitally oriented centers and institutes. For the Futures Initiative, though, innovation alone is insufficient; to be meaningful, new technologies or methodologies must be used in service of equity in higher education, a positioning that upends the question of prestige and the usual gloss of educational technology to instead center equity and the public good. We strive to create an organizational structure that embodies this goal as well.

Working with students, faculty, and administrators here has opened my eyes to a wide range of stories and experiences, centering on the power of education and the importance of access to it. Understanding education as a public good in the context of a huge public university system in the heart of a thriving city that is also home to massive income inequality means that engaging with a broader community is critical to what we do. I am constantly learning, and I have the distinct joy of knowing that our work matters.

What This Work Looks Like: Conceptual Beginnings

In today's university, administrative work requires a great deal of flexibility and rapid context switching, with many program directors representing their institutions at high levels in national conversations while also chasing paperwork, running meetings, and providing emotional support and mentorship. What this work looks like on a day-to-day basis changes over the lifespan of a project or program, with each phase bringing new challenges and opportunities for growth and reflection.

From abstract design and strategy to detailed budget and personnel planning, the early stages in the development of a new program (say, a grant-funded program or recently developed center) are crucial. The conceptual stage is usually highly collaborative, and leaders with visionary ideas really shine—anything is possible, and the more creative ideas that are brought up for discussion, the more likely it is that the collaborators will find an approach that is unique, high impact, and feasible. (There will likely be many ideas that are two out of three, but that usually isn't enough for a successful project.) This stage involves thinking through the goals of the individuals and the institution, the strengths of the people involved, opportunities (which sometimes look like gaps in existing programming), available resources, and sustainability. Slowly, the group refines the big-picture thinking into a plan that can be executed, evaluated, shared, and perhaps expanded.

The earliest iteration of CUNY Humanities Alliance was built on the imagination of many, including colleagues at the Futures Initiative, the Graduate Center, and the Andrew W. Mellon Foundation. It was also built on what we had seen and learned from students, faculty, and staff across CUNY. For the development of the CUNY Humanities Alliance, this conceptual phase involved many internal meetings and discussions, outreach and conversations with prospective partners at other CUNY institutions, high-level conversations with program officers at the Mellon Foundation and with CUNY senior leadership, and a lot of sketching ideas and possible program designs as we imagined new possibilities. Without the administrative roles of the co-directors of the Futures Initiative, programs like the CUNY Humanities Alliance would not be possible.

While much of this part of the process is expansive and imaginative, sometimes I feel like my job involves a lot of saying "no"; as the person with her hands in the budget and the most direct involvement with personnel and projects within the Futures Initiative, I typically have a clear sense of what our group can manage and what exceeds our bandwidth. But I have learned that sometimes, it is important for me to take risks on projects that are exciting even if I do not feel 100 percent confident in the outcome. Those projects are often the most rewarding, though they do sometimes involve what looks like failure along the way.

At the end of the conceptual phase, if we are writing a grant, we will refine ideas into a clear and compelling narrative and write a budget. For the narrative, having a sharp sense of objectives and potential impact is essential, as is clear writing. This complements the budget, one of the most politically and strategically important documents; it is where the details live, and where the priorities of a program are most clearly spelled out. Even learning to read and understand a budget is powerful, and can give you valuable insight into an institution (or company, or program). This is another area where a pedagogical approach can be valuable: after realizing the limited exposure that most graduate students have to processes like these, I began running lunchtime workshops for graduate fellows in our program on topics like reading and analyzing budgets, applying for grants, and more. While each specific process may look different—funding agencies all have their own protocols, budgetary expectations, and modes of evaluation, for instance—understanding a set of guiding principles can go a long way toward demystifying the process.

As a program progresses, the balance shifts to include more outward-looking communication—finding the right ways to publicize the program and increase its impact, advocating for resources, and more. As part of my work with the CUNY Humanities Alliance, I have done a lot of public speaking and have helped facilitate student and staff participation in conferences and events. This is an essential step. While there are certainly spaces that need to be private, in most cases a university program that is invisible beyond its participants cannot be considered a success. In higher education, institutions are always looking for successful models to emulate and best practices to adopt. When a foundation invests in a program, as the Mellon Foundation has with the CUNY Humanities Alliance, it is with the hope that other institutions nationwide will learn from the successes and challenges of such a program. With that in mind, administrators must have plans in place for evaluation—how they will know whether the program was successful—as well as communications.

Throughout each of these steps, internal communication and management remains essential, as skillful administrators empower others to do their best work, provide guidance and mentorship, and recalibrate the program as needed based on outcomes and feedback. There is a constant back-and-forth with others in and around the program to ensure that specific projects are on track, budgets are being appropriately used and documented, milestones are being met, and that everyone is generally doing ok.

What This Work Looks Like: Ongoing Leadership

Part of a role like mine is largely what might be expected of a project manager or program director. At the Futures Initiative, I worked with my team—many of whom were graduate students themselves—to conceptualize our program's ongoing strategy and programming, building an annual calendar each year that takes into consideration the various deadlines and timeframes of our institution. This collaborative, team-based process created the best outcomes for the team, but also the most opportunity for professional development for the graduate students. I delegated responsibilities for each of our project areas in a way that established equitable workloads and gave each team member a portfolio of meaningful work that they could point to when applying for future positions. This required balancing the program's immediate needs with the mentoring responsibilities to the individual. I oversaw communications and outreach, helped to design reports and program evaluations, and conducted weekly meetings as a group and in one-on-ones with each team member. I sent a lot of emails. I got a lot of emails.

As a small program within a much larger organization, we at the Futures Initiative ended up managing a lot of informal processes that complement the official procedures. I conducted regular performance evaluations and helped to monitor the progress of our team members, and ensured that these processes were in sync with CUNY procedures. For team members who did not fall into the usual HR program evaluation process, I still conducted evaluations so that everyone had a structured opportunity to give and receive feedback. Our team ran competitive processes each year for fellowships, grants, and course proposals, and evaluating each application was a major part of our year's work. We also collaborated with many other programs at the Graduate Center and across CUNY, and I did a great deal of outreach to share the kinds of work that our program engaged in. I gave invited talks, ran workshops, and spoke on conference panels to share the kinds of outcomes our program achieves, and I wrote chapters (like this one) to articulate why our work matters and how it fits within the broader landscape.

Beyond that, there was a significant portion of my work that was likely invisible to anyone except my team. Some of this would likely be categorized as "service" in a faculty position—mentorship, advising, and guiding the graduate students and postdoctoral fellows on our team, for instance. Given the intensity of graduate school, this involves a great deal of care work, helping each member of our team to manage their competing obligations and reach their goals. Our team worked hard. Our weekly meetings included a sometimes-daunting agenda of upcoming events and responsibilities. And yet, they became a source of sustenance for all of us: the three staff members, one postdoctoral fellow, and seven graduate students who made up the core Futures Initiative program team.

What This Work Looks Like: Care Work of Administration

The care work involved in running a program in a sustainable way can sometimes take a toll, particularly as it is often invisible. But it is also one of the most deeply rewarding elements of the work. It is also deeply pedagogical in nature, providing constant opportunities to teach skills that are often undervalued but essential for navigating the academy or running a program. Even though my teaching did not typically take place in the classroom, I constantly helped my team members to scope projects, figure out landscape research, determine the most useful methodologies, and articulate their findings. I helped them to navigate the hidden curriculum of the academy and celebrate their victories.

For many students on our Futures Initiative team, these elements of support and the resulting joy of the community were a welcome counterbalance to the toll of graduate school, which—in its current manifestation—causes many students to experience significant emotional, psychological, and physical challenges that have nothing to do with their studies. I heard these burdens and anxieties in my one-on-one meetings with students. For each moment of inspiration as a student works toward their degree or a scholar advances in their career, there may be dozens of demoralization, too often building to severe anxiety and depression (Andrzejewski 2023). Inadequate funding leaves many students and scholars to rely on food stamps and forego health insurance. Anxiety and depression produce physical manifestations, negatively affecting health and making it all the more challenging for people to persist in their chosen pathways (Bonifacio 2022). The first years of professorship are little better, with pressures increasing while support from mentors and peers vanishes (Wilson 2012).

For scholars who are women, People of Color, have disabilities, identify as LGBTQ+, or identify with other groups underrepresented in the academy, the burden on mental and physical health can be even steeper, leading many to opt out for a wide range of personal and professional reasons (Jones 2019). The ability to push through unsupportive environments is not what a PhD is designed to measure, but these obstacles—wholly unrelated to a student's intelligence, creativity, work ethic, commitment, or research skills—often become the breaking point that prevent someone from reaching their goal.

Suffering should not be a prerequisite to entering "the profession," and yet it is commonly accepted as the way things are, leaving difficult navigation work to students. As Melissa Phruksachart (2017) asked in an article exploring how to support future faculty of color, "in light of these non-life-sustaining conditions, what would it take, and what would it look like, for minoritized subjects like women and queers of color to flourish in the academy?" (p. 117). For Phruksachart (2017), mentorship and the development of intentional community were key to weathering the depleting environment of graduate school and its unequal power dynamics. Changing the structures that erode mental health is difficult, but worthwhile; doing so creates the possibility of sustaining scholars and enabling them to do their best work.[2]

By grounding their programmatic decisions in research and best practices, and by focusing on the values they or their institution genuinely hope to advance, scholar-administrators have the opportunity to create space for students and faculty to work differently. They can bring great ideas into the messy and constrained realities of institutions. At the Futures Initiative and the CUNY Humanities Alliance, we worked within a complex system and sometimes could not carry out all the plans we dreamed up. But the reality is that no system is free from obstacles, and we are able to do meaningful work nonetheless. When we encountered roadblocks, we tried to make them transparent to the graduate students working in our programs so that they would have a chance to understand the negotiations, compromises, fluidity, and unexpected opportunities that give rise to various decisions. This in turn helped shed light on the hidden curriculum of graduate education, helping to level the playing field for students who may be the first in their families to attend college or graduate school.

While the Futures Initiative and the CUNY Humanities Alliance may be unique in many respects, they are built on elements that could be applied to any higher education context—whether in a department, a workplace, or an extracurricular group. These translatable elements include trust, material support, and a shared mission. In annual surveys requesting feedback, Futures Initiative graduate fellows routinely cited collaboration and trust as two of the most important components of the program. Some of the ways we worked toward solidifying these pillars of our program included rotating leadership duties, such as meeting facilitation, collaborative agenda setting, intentionally bringing other parts of our life and research into the discussion, and creating structures for feedback and reflection as a matter of routine. These tools could be adapted and used by any program. (We also made tea for one another and shared baked goods, which I highly recommend.)

Why This Is Scholarly Work

All of this is undoubtedly work. But is it scholarly? I argue that it is, and in fact I believe that I am engaging as deeply and critically with my doctoral training than I might in a faculty career. This is because my role is not only focused on one area of expertise, but rather on the broader architecture of higher education and how many different elements fit together. That kind of big-picture architectural thinking requires a deep understanding of the academic community, as well as the many other communities and audiences that are adjacent to or influenced by the work happening in colleges and universities.

This is also an argument that Lisa Brundage, Karen Gregory, and Emily Sherwood (2018) advance: "We instead advocate for our work to be recognized as coequal with scholarship production ... not really 'alt' at all" (p. 308). For these scholar-administrators, as for me, the challenge of defining our work exists alongside the reality that the work itself is intellectually engaging and has the potential for significant impact that goes beyond our local programs.

I am almost constantly involved in some type of landscape research—keeping an eye on what is happening in various research and programmatic spaces, what trends are shifting, what funding opportunities are available, what new projects are getting started. Often this research has a purely internal purpose, to ensure that our program is doing work that remains meaningful and timely and to get a sense of potential collaborators or funders. Other times, the research has a different destination. Perhaps it becomes part of a grant proposal, a blog post, or an op-ed. I am writing more now than ever in my life, across many different registers—from formal scholarly monographs to institutional announcements to casual blog posts (and thousands of tweets). My writing has become clearer and more direct through my administrative work.

Administrative work has also pushed me to set clear goals, and to determine ways to assess a program's success (as well as opportunities for improvement—and there are always ways a program can be improved). And it has encouraged me to learn how to better articulate the rationale for the work that we do—why the humanities matter, and why higher education matters. That advocacy is perhaps the underlying goal of all that we do—we don't want these programs to simply stop here, but to radiate outward and support a broader argument for the importance of education as a public good.

Graduate Education Reform More Broadly

I see administrative work as having scholarly as well as activist potential. Not only is there a strong advocacy component as I described above, but also there are constant opportunities to have an impact on individual student lives, structural elements of programs and institutions, and perspectives of fellow administrators and faculty. An agenda of higher education reform must include engaged administrators, since those roles are spaces where so many decisions are made (and since budgets are such powerful documents, as I mentioned earlier). One thing that drew me to this work was the possibility of having an impact at a broader structural level. That, to me, is a really exciting possibility.

The possibility for structural change that supports social justice is also where the tie to public scholarship comes in. While so much administrative work is invisible, it shapes the structures that define so much of what emerges from colleges and universities. Administrators smooth the road, or they create barriers. They determine priorities and allocate resources. Before a project becomes visible outside the university, someone must make space for it within the institution. And because administrators are also working up the chain to convince others (funders, more senior administrators, etc.) to support their goals, they also focus a great deal of energy on advocating for what they believe is important. This advocacy is important for long-term development as well as for day-to-day student experience. Administrative structures can create a sense of distance or one of trust; an environment of competition or one of generosity. Socially engaged administration can make it possible to build a university that creates space for empowerment and growth—one where students and faculty thrive. The end goal is not the program, but the effect that the program has on real people.

Developing sustainable and inclusive programs that deeply support students and faculty requires administrators who understand the importance of supportive and inclusive environments, and who understand the structural power imbalances that perpetuate inequality. But hiring people is not enough: just as students and faculty need to be well supported in order to thrive, the same is true for administrators. The work can be emotionally draining, with many people turning to administrators for support of various types. As informal mentors, students sometimes turn to people in roles like mine for guidance on matters they may not be ready to discuss with their advisor—things like future career goals, family planning and other life choices, anxiety and other mental health challenges, and concerns about their dissertation or department. For People of Color in these roles, the pressures are often much greater, with a steady stream of microaggressions and bias undermining their work (Matthew 2016).

As I argue in *Putting the Humanities PhD to Work* (2020), I believe that reform can and should take place at multiple levels simultaneously, with students, faculty, and administrators all creating opportunities for change through decisions large and small. I contend that recognizing the expansive social value of the knowledge, skills, and approaches that recent graduates have gained during the course of their studies means understanding the wide range of institutions and contexts where they can make a significant impact. Faculty and administrators have an opportunity to adjust graduate program structures to better equip students to take on a wide range of roles where they can apply their deep humanities training. Even without knowing exactly what pathway a graduate might take, since career opportunities are constantly evolving, the curiosity and love of learning that spark a desire to pursue a graduate degree is something to celebrate. To make this a reality, administrators must work to develop sustainable programs that support students and staff.

One question I grapple with is whether the kinds of spaces offered by programs like the Futures Initiative and the CUNY Humanities Alliance can be incorporated into academic departments. I am not sure whether they can, at least in the current configuration of higher education. The non-evaluative nature of extracurricular programs makes them fundamentally different from the hypercompetitive pressure of departments. Certainly, some elements of our program's work can be incorporated—such as collaborative and project-oriented goals, shared time and space, and rotating leadership—but it is hard to know whether those actions will bear the same fruit when embedded in the inherently competitive structure of a graduate academic department.

While unraveling the prestige economy of graduate education may not be an achievable goal, it nonetheless underscores the vital need of holding space where students can think, act, and work differently. Where support and sustenance work are offered alongside research questions. Where material realities are not brushed aside as a distraction from the so-called life of the mind. Where joys and sorrows can be present, and can have a bearing on intellectual questions. Where challenges and critiques can be made safely, with care, as a way to collectively grow stronger. My hope is that programs like these can help students feel more secure pursuing research that matters to them and to their communities, and in turn that work can help the public to see the value of higher education and graduate education in a more concrete and compelling way. Creating these spaces is administrative work. And this is what brings me hope: that my work as a scholar-administrator, though often invisible, might make it possible for others to shine.

Notes

1. I describe this pathway in more detail in *Putting the Humanities PhD to Work: Thriving in and beyond the Classroom* (2020). Some parts of this chapter are adapted from the manuscript.
2. I share more about this in "Cultivating a Joyful Workplace through Trust, Support, and a Shared Mission," *Making Graduate Education Work: Imagining a Thriving Future for the Humanities*, forthcoming from the Modern Language Association, co-edited by Stacy Hartman and Yevgenya Strakovsky.

References

Andrzejewski, A. (2023, July 5). Academics don't talk about our mental illnesses. We should. *The Chronicle of Higher Education*, sec. Opinion.

Bichsel, J., Pritchard, A., Li, J., & McChesney, J. (2018). *Administrators in higher education annual report: Key findings, trends, and comprehensive tables for 2017–18 academic year*. CUPA-HR.

Bonifacio, A. (2022, October 25). My career as a professor is soaring. I've never been so depressed and anxious. *Slate*.

Brundage, L., Gregory, K., & Sherwood, E. (2018). Working nine to five: What a way to make an academic living. In *Bodies of information: Intersectional feminist digital humanities* (pp. 305–319). University of Minnesota Press.

Jones, L. (2019, July 25). Endless exodus: Faculty of color leave the academy in search of fulfillment. *Diverse: Issues in Higher Education*.

Kezar, A., & Posselt, J. (Eds.). (2019). *Higher education administration for social justice and equity*. Routledge.

Matthew, P.A. (2016). *Written/unwritten: Diversity and the hidden truths of tenure*. UNC Press Books.

Phruksachart, M. (2017). On mentoring future faculty of color. *Feminist Teacher, 27*(2–3). 117–132. https://doi.org/10.5406/femteacher.27.2-3.0117

Rogers, K. (2020). *Putting the humanities PhD to work: Theory, practice, and models for thriving beyond the academy*. Duke University Press.

Smith, T.L., Tuck, E., & Yang, K.W. (2018). *Indigenous and decolonizing studies in education: Mapping the long view*. Routledge.

Wilson, R. (2012, June 3). Why are associate professors so unhappy? *The Chronicle of Higher Education*, sec. News.

Notes on Contributors

Rafael Costa is a practicing psychoanalyst and activist researcher with indigenous groups in the Amazon, Brazil. He has a Master's degree and a bachelor's degree in psychology from Federal Fluminense University (UFF) and Pontifical Catholic University (PUC), respectively. He has carried out ethnographic research with indigenous healing practices and is the director of the Guardians of the Forest Institute (IGF), a nonprofit organization focused on cultural, educational, ecological and indigenous rights initiatives in partnership with indigenous leaders from Huni Kuin and Yawanawa villages. He is also a founding member of a therapist training network in Rio de Janeiro, where he offers seminars and supervises analysts in training. Drawing on insights from affect theory, psychoanalysis, Brazilian perspectival anthropology and, recently, the transformative activist stance, his research interests focus on the intersection of indigenous cultural practices of Amazonian peoples of the Pano linguistic branch group and decolonial approaches to mental health and human development.

Leigh Garrison-Fletcher is a Professor in the Education and Language Acquisition Department at LaGuardia Community College, CUNY. She teaches introductory linguistics, sociolinguistics, and first-year education courses. She was a faculty mentor in the CUNY Humanities Alliance from 2017 to 2020. Her research focuses on the education of multilingual students in the U.S., with special emphasis on inclusive pedagogies and linguistic social justice. She developed and has co-led a faculty development seminar at LaGuardia on Language Across the Curriculum for the past six years, putting this research into practice.

Davide Giuseppe Colasanto has a PhD in Modern European History at the Graduate Center, CUNY, where he graduated in 2022 with the dissertation "Virility and Defeat: Masculinities in Italy between Fascism and the Sexual Revolution." His research interests are the history of sexuality, post-fascism, and violence during the twentieth century. He has published articles on the relation between sexuality and European identity, and on Allied soldiers' emotions during World War II. A practitioner of student-centered pedagogy, he is a former Humanities Alliance Fellow and he has taught critical thinking courses at LaGuardia Community College and European History courses at Queens College, CUNY. He is currently living in Apulia, Italy where he manages a regenerative agriculture farm.

Kaysi Holman is an intentional community builder dedicated to equity and social justice. She was a community organizer, political advocate, and nonprofit leader, before returning to academia. After working at Duke University and HASTAC (Humanities Arts Science & Technology Alliance & Colaboratory) for several years, she served as the Director of CUNY Humanities Alliance from 2016 to 2021. During the pandemic, she returned to nonprofits to lead Diversity, Equity, Inclusion and Belonging and professional development initiatives as the Director of People & Culture for 10,000 Degrees, a nonprofit dedicated to educational equity. She holds a J.D. from Arizona State University Sandra Day O'Connor College of Law and a B.S. in Cognitive Psychology from Vanderbilt University.

Sujung Kim is an interdisciplinary scholar and Project Director at the Center for Advanced Study in Education at the Graduate Center, CUNY. She is committed to the empowerment of students from diverse identities, ethnicities, classes, and nationalities who are culturally, socio-economically, and politically marginalized, to become critical agents for social justice in higher education. Her research interests are located at the intersection of class, race, power, and subjectivity. Toward these goals, her teaching and research focuses on the social, cultural, and political foundations of higher education, with special attention to community colleges, internationalization, STEM education, and doctoral education reform in the humanities and humanistic social sciences. She undertook an ethnographic research and program evaluation study with CUNY Humanities Alliance from 2018 to 2021.

Araminta Poole is a current student in the City University of New York (CUNY). She completed her associate's degree at LaGuardia Community College (CUNY) and transferred to Hunter College (CUNY) to complete her bachelor's degree in social psychology. While attending LAGCC, Araminta acted as a peer mentor and co-researcher in the Peer Activist Learning Community (PALC), which was featured in the New York Times. She wrote and published the article, Developing Agency, for the LaGuardia journal, In-Transit. Araminta presented the work and research of PALC in several local, regional, and national conferences, including at the 2022 annual conference of the Association for the Study of Higher Education ASHE.

Mike Rifino is a PhD candidate in Developmental Psychology at the Graduate Center, CUNY. Drawing on Black feminist and queer emotion/affect theories, he examines the sociopolitical contexts that promote shame, loneliness, and alienation and its implications for learning in community colleges. He also studies the decolonial turn in curriculum and pedagogy with a focus on undergraduate psychology education. His recent publication "Loneliness through the lens of Black feminist love-politics" was published in the *Journal of Multicultural Education*. Mike Rifino's dissertation was awarded the 2021 Graduate Student award by the Cultural-Historical Research SIG of the American Educational Research Association (AERA).

Katina L. Rogers is the author of *Putting the Humanities PhD to Work: Thriving in and beyond the Classroom* (Duke University Press, 2020) and the founder of Inkcap Consulting. With over a decade of experience as a researcher, administrator, and educator, Dr. Rogers works with colleges and universities to design and implement creative, sustainable, and equitable structures for graduate education. Her work has been featured in the *New York Times, LA Review of Books, The Chronicle of Higher Education*, and *Inside Higher Ed*, as well as a wide range of podcasts and public speaking engagements. Her career has included work at The Graduate Center, CUNY, the Modern Language Association, the Scholarly Communication Institute, and the Alfred P. Sloan Foundation. She holds a PhD in Comparative Literature from the University of Colorado at Boulder.

Micheal A. Rumore is a Marion L. Brittain Postdoctoral Fellow at the Georgia Institute of Technology. His research explores the intersections of Indian Ocean studies and African diaspora studies. In the classroom, his teaching is informed by engagements with critical pedagogy and multimodal rhetorics. Other nerdy, barely academically adjacent interests include distorted guitars and fighting games. His writing can also be found in venues such as *History of the Present, Social Text Online, Studies in the Fantastic*, and *Guernica*.

Oliver Sage is a PhD candidate in French Literature at the Graduate Center, CUNY. Their research is focused on cyclical violence and the refusal of narrative closure within the works of modern and contemporary authors experiencing intersecting forms of marginalization. They also write and present on gender transgression, race, disability, and radical solidarity in literature, pedagogy, and culture, among numerous other obsessions. Outside of their academic pursuits, their special interests include fiber and textile arts, birds of the northeastern United States, and communal interspecies survival.

Stefanie Sertich is a director, choreographer, Professor of Theatre at LaGuardia Community College, CUNY and National Coordinator for the ASPIRE Arts Leadership Program through the Kennedy Center's American College Theatre Festival (KCACTF). She served as codirector of the LaGuardia Mellon Humanities Scholars program in the CUNY Humanities Alliance from 2016 to 2020. Her research focuses on devised theater for social change and the process of building communities through the art of theater.

Eduardo Vianna is a Professor in the City University of New York (CUNY) in the following programs: the psychology program at LaGuardia Community College and the developmental psychology and urban education PhD programs at the Graduate Center. He received his PhD in developmental psychology at the CUNY-Graduate Center after completing his medical studies, including a specialization in child psychiatry in Rio de Janeiro, Brazil. Following recent advances in Vygotskian theory, especially the Transformative Activist Stance, he has carried out research in various settings that serve underprivileged populations. His current research on applying critical-theoretical pedagogy to build a peer-based co-curricular program in a community college was featured in the *New York Times*. Among his awards, Dr. Vianna received the 2010 Early Career Award in Cultural-Historical Research SIG of the American Educational Research Association and currently serves as chief editor of Outlines Critical Practice Studies. He is currently Co-PI in the five-year NSF grant titled "Building Capacity: A Faculty Development Program to Increase Students' Quantitative Reasoning Skills" (NSF DUE #18325078; $1,800,000.00).

www.ingramcontent.com/pod-product-compliance
Ingram Content Group UK Ltd.
Pitfield, Milton Keynes, MK11 3LW, UK
UKHW022122230426
12048UKWH00011BA/658